Research for Architectural . . . .

This book provides a clear guide for practitioners looking to establish or already conducting research projects in a practice context and graduate students looking to support their studies and role within practice.

The book is divided into three key sections. The first section, across Chapters Two and Three, discusses why research is relevant to practice, how it benefits both practice and their clients, the breadth of topics, and tackles the key challenges facing research in practice and discusses how to overcome them, including how to fund research in practice. Section two, across Chapters Four to Seven, focuses on the mechanics of a research project, providing a step-by-step guide to reviewing literature and publications, data collection and research methods, ethics, writing up and publishing.

In the final section, Chapter Eight presents profiles of twelve architecture practices ranging in size, structure, location, research interest and approach, followed by illustrated profiles of their design influenced research work. The practices featured here are Counterspace Studio, ZCD Architects, Baca Architects, Tonkin Liu, Pomeroy Studio, Architecture Research Office, Architype, Gehl Architects, Hayball, PLP Architects, White Arkitekter and Perkins&Will.

With practice based examples throughout, beautifully illustrated and written in a clear and accessible style, this is an essential guide to conducting research that is relevant for architectural practices of all size, location and expertise.

Katharine A. Martindale, PhD, is a researcher, writer, lecturer and urbanist with academic qualifications in architecture, urban design, geography and planning policy and twenty years professional experience in research led roles in academic institutions, private consultancies, think tanks and government offices in the UK, US, Canada and Australia.

Research for
Architectural Practice

Katharine A. Martindale

LONDON AND NEW YORK

First published 2022
by Routledge
2 Park Square, Milton Park, Abingdon, Oxon OX14 4RN

and by Routledge
605 Third Avenue, New York, NY 10158

Routledge is an imprint of the Taylor & Francis Group, an informa business

British Library Cataloguing-in-Publication Data
A catalogue record for this book is available from the British Library

Library of Congress Cataloging-in-Publication Data
Names: Martindale, Katharine (Katharine A.), author.
Title: Research for architectural practice / Katharine Martindale.
Description: Abingdon, Oxon; New York: Routledge, [2021] |
Includes bibliographical references and index.
Identifiers: LCCN 2021002557 (print) |
LCCN 2021002558 (ebook) | ISBN 9780367470111 (hardback) |
ISBN 9780367470135 (paperback)
Subjects: LCSH: Architectural practice. |
Architecture—Research—Methodology.
Classification: LCC NA1995 .M37 2021 (print) | LCC NA1995 (ebook) |
DDC 724/.7—dc23
LC record available at https://lccn.loc.gov/2021002557
LC ebook record available at https://lccn.loc.gov/2021002558

ISBN: 978-0-367-47011-1 (hbk)
ISBN: 978-0-367-47013-5 (pbk)
ISBN: 978-1-003-03283-0 (ebk)

Typeset in Scala Sans
by codeMantra

Research:

The creative work undertaken on a systematic basis in order to increase the stock of knowledge, including knowledge of man, culture and society, and the use of this stock of knowledge to devise new applications.

The Frascati Manual
OECD Publications, 2002

Contents

Contents

Acknowledgements

Chris Bryant of Alma_nac, Melonie Bayl Smith of Bayl Architecture, Peter Clegg and Joe Jack Williams of Fielden Clegg Bradley Studios, and Darryl Chen of Hawkins\Brown for their early reviews of the proposal. Thank you to Ben Morgan of BowerBird, Fiona MacDonald of Matt + Fiona, and Neil MacOmish of Scott Brownrigg for sharing their expertise, and to Edward Denison of the Bartlett School of Architecture, Eva Cabezuelo of C-re-a.i.d, Maximiliano Arrocet of Amanda Levete Architects and Nicola Rutt of Hawkins\Brown for providing images of their work, and Cait Warther, Hufton+Crow, Greg Storrar, Alex Peacock, George Brown, Frank Oudeman, Dennis Gilbert, Darren Carter, Jack Hobhouse, Richard Ash, Henry Lam, Dianna Snape, Emily Bartlett, Jonas Jörneberg, Anders Bobert, Guy Nordenson, and Catherine Seavitt for granting permission to use their images.

Huge thanks go to Stephen Cassell, Adam Yarinsky and Kim Yao of Architecture Research Office, Mark Lumley of Architype, Richard Coutts of Baca Architects, Sumayya Vally of Counterspace, Birgitte Bundesen Svarre of Gehl, Fiona Young of Hayball Architects, David Green, Ryan Ramsey, Carl Knutson and John Haymaker of Perkins&Will, Ron Bakker, Andrei Martin, and Marta Gonzalez-Ruiz of PLP Architects, Jason Pomeroy of Pomeroy Studio, Anna Lui and Mike Tonkin of Tonkin Liu, Anna-Johanna Klasander and Camilla Lystrand of White Arkitekter, Dinah Bornat of ZCD Architects, and their teams for giving their time to participate in the interviews and sharing their process, the design and research projects, and for providing images of their work.

Several sections of this book, in particular Chapter Eight, were conducted and completed as the global Coronavirus pandemic initiated national shutdowns, uncertainty, and new working practices affecting architects in every country. That, under such difficult circumstances, all the practices included in this book continued to provide their support, both through interviews and supplying images and publications, made working with them for this publication a personal as much as a professional privilege. My gratitude extends also to the team at Routledge for their patience and support during this process.

Chapter One

Introduction

The role of research is becoming increasingly important to practising architects. Many new practices starting out, including all those featured in Chapter Eight, include research as part of their practice, and most large architecture studios have established research teams over the last 30 years. However, there exist several misperceptions about the role and relevance of research for architects and their practices. Research can be seen as an academic pursuit that has little impact or relevance to the practical practice of architecture or clients, as traditionally, research has not been part of the architect's remit. This is in part due to the perception that the pragmatic, scientific approach of research is incompatible with the creative process. However, with the evolution of practice through fields such as parametric design and issues of environmental performance and sustainability, alongside the resolve to demonstrate expertise, this is changing.

The aim of this book is to demonstrate that research is not only relevant to practice but essential, and that the academic process of research can be adapted and made relevant to practice. For those who already see the benefits of research, in part because of growing interest from clients, this book addresses the knowledge gap in research training reported by practices interested in research but unclear where to start, the process, and how to fund, and tailor research to their practice and their clients. This book offers a practical guide to developing, funding, and conducting research independently and in collaboration, both for graduate students and practitioners.

This book's seven core chapters fall into three categories. First, the motivations for and scope of practice-based research and its financing. Second, taking the research process from proposal to publishing, and then finally, international case studies from established research-driven practices.

Chapter Two discusses the motivations and benefits of conducting research in practice, the barriers, and how to overcome them. The second part of the chapter discusses the breadth of current research reviewed by sector, ranging from workplace and materials testing, to aged care design and education buildings, and then cross-sector approaches such as post occupancy evaluation and Modern Methods of Construction. As funding research work is the most frequently cited challenge for practice, Chapter Three reviews research and development tax schemes, client commissioned work and academic collaborations, and concludes with details of funding sources available to practitioners.

The second section, Chapters Four to Seven, focusses on the mechanics and processes of a research project. Chapter Four discusses how to develop proposals for a research project and make them relevant to practice, funding bodies and the wider industry. Chapter Five sets out the literature review, referencing and citations, before moving on to discuss the range of data sources and their reliability, different collection methodologies and analytical approaches, before concluding with a guide to writing up.

Chapter Six discusses a range of ethical issues that practice may encounter, including an overview of research ethics and how this works when collaborating with an academic partner, the issues to be considered when children and vulnerable adults participate in the process, issues of data capture, storage and management, and addressing plagiarism and copyright issues. With the research completed, Chapter Seven reviews the benefits of knowledge capture and management in practice, and the varied options for publishing research, from books and academic journals, to exhibitions and industry events, and social media.

In the final section, Chapter Eight discusses how research is approached and conducted in twelve practices located in Australia, Denmark, Singapore, South Africa, Sweden, the United Kingdom, and the United States. The case studies range in size from micro to global and demonstrate different fields of expertise and interest, and approach to process, funding, and publications, and each is accompanied by a profile of their research. This chapter offers an insight into the structures, processes, and challenges that each face and how they address them with the ambition that those reading this chapter can take inspiration from these and identify a path forward for their own research.

Chapter Two

Making the case for research in practice

2.1 Introduction

Establishing a new area of work within practice faces challenges, concerns, and questions. As they relate to research, this chapter aims to address these; first among them, 'why do architects in practice conduct research?' There are several, regularly cited motivations for conducting research in practice that span developing and demonstrating expertise, making space for new thinking, supporting passion projects, innovating, raising the practice profile, and attracting new clients, colleagues, and collaborators. The concerns and challenges addressed in the following section discuss funding, training, senior level support, university research partnerships, issues of confidentiality, and the persistent stereotype that research is the preserve of large practice. The range of practice based research embraces a great diversity of topics reflecting the architectural interests of a practice. Collated through interviews, publications, presentations and practice websites, and are arranged here by sector topic and then cross-sector approach.

2.2 Why do architects in practice conduct research?

Among those practices interviewed specifically for this book, along with other architects engaged in discussions regarding research and the benefits to their practice over several years, there has been universal support for research and its continuing benefit to their practice. The motivations and benefits, discussed below, varied between practices but many were shared perspectives and were not dictated by size, research focus or geographic location. There were six recurrent responses with the drive to develop and demonstrate practice expertise and to encourage innovation, the most frequently cited. This was followed by fulfilling client commissions, taking time to focus on passion projects, fostering and introducing new thinking, raising the practice profile, and the unexpected increase in response to recruitment opportunities.

2.2.1 To expand and demonstrate practice expertise

The opportunity to develop expertise in a field was most frequently cited by practitioners as their motivation for engaging in research, and this was evident across all sectors. As Irene Gallou, Head of the Specialist Modelling Group at Foster + Partners notes, "in the short term it is gaining knowledge and expertise and developing interesting partnerships in other fields of expertise" (Martindale, 2017, p. 22). In the longer term, becoming known as a specialist in a field, and being able to demonstrate that expertise beyond architecture, was viewed as essential to their approach to design, the evolution of the practice, and when attracting new clients. The opportunity to build on, or expand, the skill set offered to clients on existing projects as an added benefit to their research, is an approach adopted by White Arktekter (see Section 8.5.3). Richard Partington, founder and director of Studio Partington, stated that their research enables them "to advise clients on best practice and building performance and in this way can offer a different service" (Martindale, 2017, p. 42).

When accompanied by a publishing and marketing strategy, past research strengthens a practice's ability to win future research and design commissions, as well as establishing collaborative partnerships, particularly in academia. For ZCD Director Dinah Bornat, their research, published on an open-access basis on the practice website, has established the practice as experts in engaging with young people and children in the design of urban spaces. This has, in turn, led to invitations to speak and write, new design work, further research commissions, and additional collaborations and supporters, including their local mayor. In interview, Bornat noted that publishing their research work "was a more effective method of winning work than entering competitions" and that it has allowed the practice to charge higher fees for their work.

2.2.2 To innovate

Innovation is frequently linked to research in job titles, websites, and the professional literature, and often the initial perception of innovative research in practice is that it is the exclusive domain of high tech material development, new software, or robotic design. However, practice understanding of innovation and the route to it through research is much broader. At the core of the determination to innovate is the need to answer a question that is not available elsewhere, a quest for new knowledge, a better solution or to improve an operation or process. This point was highlighted by Jason Pomeroy, Founder of Pomeroy Studio, who remarked in interview that the innovation in their zero energy future developments built on existing "knowledge of passive environmental design principles, balancing lessons learned from past cultural practices with new technologies and techniques" developed by the practice.

Innovation was considered to be significant by all of the practices interviewed for this book. With the competitive advantage innovation can offer, or at least promise, of universal concern was the aim to drive innovation in design. For Tonkin Liu directors Mike Tonkin and Anna Liu, this was the main function of research within their practice, while for Ron Bakker of PLP Architecture it is of far greater significance; "innovation is the biggest driver in the global economy". For Fiona Young, Director of Hayball's Sydney studio, research is considered essential as it "significantly de-risks a project from the initial design phases through to project delivery, enabling us to innovate." For Hayball, this innovation extends beyond the ambition to increase the environmental sustainability of their school buildings to support new pedagogical thinking for the spaces they design.

2.2.3 To fulfil passion projects

Not all of the research conducted in practice is directly related to design projects, the subject of a commission, or an investment in the direction of the practice to develop a new field of expertise. For some, encouraging individual staff members to develop small projects, supported by providing paid time away from usual activities and research expenses, is widely viewed as a staff perk that introduces new thinking to design projects and fosters new working collaborations across the practice and with external partners. In some cases, these have later developed into further commissions in both research and design, or research streams within the studio.

Several large practices, including Perkins&Will, White Arkitekter and Fielden Clegg Bradley Studios, have established programmes to which staff can submit small research proposals. Arup's scheme, part of Arup University, offers a ring-fenced fund totalling £5 million per annum which covers the scheme that aims to establish collaborations with external organisations. Successful applicants are afforded a short period of time to focus on the project, usually a week or two, expenses, mentorship and guidance on research methods and writing. This structure and scope is replicated at other practices.

In almost all cases, it is the larger practices that operate such schemes but smaller studios also support staff looking to explore ideas and develop research projects. A principal at Amanda Levete Architects, Max Arrocet's passion for football and previous experience on the design team for the Estadio Santiago Bernabeu in Madrid, combined with an awareness of the shortage of available land for public sports facilities in high-density urban areas, led to the development of Pitch/Pitch (AL_A, 2020). Research work for Pitch/Pitch included a needs assessment and scoping study, materials development for the structural elements, and an accompanying digital management and booking system. The resulting design is a demountable and reusable system of sports pitches that can stack vertically and fit into a standard 40 ft shipping container for transportation and secure storage, intended both for temporary occupation in meanwhile space, as well as for longer term tenure (Figure 2.1).

2.2.4 To introduce new thinking

The benefits of conducting research related to design projects and speculative or passion projects were widely acknowledged among the interviewee group. Anna-Johanna Klasander Director of Research and Development at White Arkitekter considers it an effective method to "get some oxygen into the office". The acknowledged advantages focused on the introduction of new thinking to the practice through new methodologies, effected by exposure to new ideas through collaborations, new or adjacent fields of literature, data and approaches that could be applied to design work. It was suggested that in some circumstances, research projects had the potential to discover something new that might take a project in a different direction. This 'out of the box' thinking was more likely to be identified in research projects not linked to practice design projects but rather those following an independent thread either as passion

Figure 2.1: The Pitch/Pitch proposal for stackable football pitches. © AL_A

projects, new fields of architectural focus, or speculative ideas. In some cases, these were later developed as larger or ongoing research projects.

2.2.5 To raise the practice profile

As both Dinah Bornat and Max Arrocet can attest, the publication and any subsequent media coverage of research work can distinguish a practice from the typical stories of architectural work. If the research project is dramatic enough, demonstrating radical thinking, this potential is amplified. PLP Architecture has employed this to great effect with two research proposals. Their proposition for a 130 m tall timber tower with Cambridge University (Ramage, Foster, Smith, Flanagan, & Bakker, 2017) and their integrated travel initiative IUMO (PLP Architecture, 2020), both speculative and collaborative projects, have initiated engagements with clients, policymakers and the media (Braidwood, 2016; Mairs, 2016; Perry, 2016). Founding Partner Ron Bakker, confirmed that "even if the research itself doesn't turn into a project in its original form, elements of that can become research commissions and even when that doesn't happen, it becomes an interesting starting point for a conversation with a client". Their collaboration with Cambridge is ongoing and the timber tower has developed into commissioned architectural projects in Europe (see Section 8.5.2).

2.2.6 To deliver commissioned research

Although they do occur, direct commissions from clients are less common than most practices would like. For most, conducting research is the demonstration of their expertise that leads to architectural commissions. For Baca Architects, Pomeroy Studio and Architype, research is an integral aspect of the design project, while White Arkitekter have developed research projects for many of their architectural projects with clients following initial conversations, and Counterspace Studio launched the practice with research commissions from other architectural studios.

Historic England commissioned Allies and Morrison Urban Practitioners to conduct a London-wide analysis of the character of Greater London and its development over 1,000 years, to inform their 'Keep it London' campaign and later submission to the London Plan Review. The team reviewed historic maps, historic and current land use, street structure, transport infrastructure, existing densities and heritage designations to develop a new map using Geographical Information System (GIS) software. The final report, *Locating London's Local Character and Density*, recommended a rethink of the central, urban and suburban approach to characterising the city to view places at a more individual basis that would retain the character of each area while allowing for future growth (Allies and Morrison, 2016; Manning, Rifkin, Noble, Garofalakis, & Elsea, 2018).

2.2.7 To attract talent

Although more of a consequence rather than a motivation, several of the practices interviewed for this book discussed the number of job applicants who were attracted to the practice because they were known as a research engaged or led practice. This was particularly noticeable in graduating architects who sought out opportunities to work on research projects alongside design work. While several practices discussed the rise in unsolicited applications hoping for research related roles, Richard Coutts, Director of Baca Architects, reported that one vacancy notice was withdrawn after 24 hours as they'd already received over 200 applications. While three practices mentioned that they'd linked their research activities to a greater number of better qualified graduating architects to choose from, including Director of Research at Perkins&Will, John Haymaker, who remarked that after delivering presentations or lectures at schools of architecture he always left with 'a box full of resumés'.

2.3 Overcoming the barriers to conducting research in practice

There are as many reasons practice offer for not conducting research as there are motivations to initiated and continue with it. Below are the seven most frequently cited challenges and approaches to overcome them. First among them is securing research funding, followed by common problems encountered when working with academia, the lack of research training and CPD, knowledge capture and management, and a lack of support at a senior level. This section concludes by discussing concerns regarding research findings, notably post occupancy evaluation, publishing, gaining a client's approval to publish, and the apprehension that this will lead to a loss of competitive advantage.

2.3.1 Finding funding

Identifying a source of funding, whether externally or in-house, is repeatedly reported as the single greatest barrier to conducting research in practice. The costs associated with research can include new software, technical equipment and travel expenses although covering staff costs is the greatest concern, as it typically accounts for the greatest proportion of project costs.

There are several sources of funding for research available to practice and fall into four main categories. The first is external funding acquired through grants, commissions or competitions specifically for the purpose of conducting research. Accessing these funds is challenging for almost everyone and the value of many of the grants available is quite small. However, the aphorism 'money attracts money' couldn't be more relevant in this circumstance. Obtaining seed-funding demonstrates a level of trust and therefore reduces risk, attracting match funding from other sources and supporting more substantial grants. For their publication, *Neighbourhood Design* (Bornat & Shaw, 2019), Dinah Bornat of ZCD Architects stated that the practice had been able to attract funds from additional sources based on earlier successful funding applications, and the confidence afforded by an academic co-author and key funding partner at the start of the project.

The second funding option is incorporating research into the design process. This is possible at various stages but is most effective if incorporated at the start of the design process with discussions with the client at the briefing stage, as White Arkitekter successfully demonstrate. This would translate as Stage 0,

Strategic Definition and Stage 1, Preparation and Brief, on the RIBA Plan of Work. Although the 2013 Plan mentions research and development in Stages 2 and 3 and that it should respond "to the Initial Project Brief or in response to the Concept Design as it is developed" (RIBA, 2013), the speed at which design work occurs can sometimes mean that it advances at a greater pace than the research with findings delivered too late to be of much use. Unhelpfully, this reference of research and development has been omitted from the 2020 update (RIBA, 2020), replaced by post occupancy studies at Stage 7, when it should be defined at Stages 0 and 1 along with other research work, and conducted in Stage 7. It should form a continuous cycle rather than just be bolted on at the end.

The third source of funding for research in practice relies on the designation of in-house funds. Almost all practices that have established research agendas, regardless of their size, focus, or design approach, have conducted their early research projects without external financing. Persuading any grant agency or client to fund a free-standing research project is challenging without being able to demonstrate some previous experience. Several of the practices in Chapter Eight have included research components to architectural projects and published their work, building from there. Practice was split on whether the research component was considered to be billable and this was often a reflection of the client and the relationship with them, meaning that research time was covered by the practice. While most practices have continued with some level of internal funding, larger practices with established research programmes, specifically designating a portion of their profits, often allocating 10%, to funding research activities. However, internal investment is an aspect of a practice's ethos and identity that a client can respond to positively.

Finally, the fourth option which funds, rather than being a source of funding per se, is the research and development (R&D) tax break offered by most countries to small- and medium-sized businesses. Eligibility criteria and the approach adopted by the relevant government agencies varies between countries, but those who reported that they had made claims had been successful and would make further applications in the future. If the research is conducted with the required rigour and within the guidelines set out by the relevant R&D scheme, this remains one of the most consistent sources for funding for research in practice. Currently, however, not all projects that might be relevant to practice are covered so requires investigations at the outset that might help better align the project with R&D requirements.

Chapter Three provides further details on sources of research grants to which other practices, including those profiled in Chapter Eight, have successfully applied as well as a more detailed discussion of R&D tax schemes.

2.3.2 Working with academia

The approach to working with academics, the benefits and challenges, both perceived and experienced, varies greatly. Besides the opportunity to become involved with the education of subsequent generations of architects, for practitioners the advantages of academic engagement includes the research work conducted by students on or for practice design projects, establishing long-term working relationships, and recruitment. Mike Lumley conveyed the benefits to Architype; "university collaborations have increased the rigour with which we approach our research and thinking about design projects" (Martindale, 2016).

The drawbacks include funding, costs, scheduling, focus, and output. The first financial barrier is finding an academic to work with and afford their rates. Senior academics can bill out at substantial rates and, depending on the project or overheads, practice regularly remarks on the higher than anticipated rates that, in many cases, kills the collaboration. The second financial challenge is research grant funding. Despite media reports that universities are awash with high-value research grants, this is rarely the case, particularly in architecture. Academic research funding, discussed further in Chapter Three, is difficult to acquire even for established and senior academics, with success rates depressingly low, particularly in subjects related to the built environment. Where these are successful, practice needs to be involved with the grant before the application is submitted. As all grant applications require detailed financial costings, joining a research project that has already been granted funding is unlikely to cover practice costs.

The second challenge is the pace at which academic research can run. Projects in practice are conducted faster and delivered sooner than most university research, which can be slowed by protocols and committee requirements. This can result in an architectural project that has been completed while the research project is just beginning. The lead time for an academic project can be one to two years, particularly where academic research council funding is sought, before a project commences. Although it is unlikely that all collaborations require this length of preparation, all academic collaborations require advance planning. Finally, the third challenge comes in the form of difference in purpose and output for research as Mike Tonkin noted in interview, "the aim of research in academia is to publish, while the purpose of research in practice is to build." This could make joint projects incompatible particularly where issues of client confidentiality are at the fore. However, as the case studies in Chapter Eight attest, academic collaborations can be effective, run in parallel, and deliver mutually beneficial outcomes.

There are several routes to engaging universities in a research capacity. The first, and most common, is through ongoing teaching engagements which lead to research collaborations either through academics working with practitioners on projects or supporting students in their studies including and, occasionally, PhD sponsorship. In most cases, the entry point for these options has been through alumni associations, with practitioners returning to the schools they graduated from. Where geography or other circumstances prevent this, schools will post advertisements on academic job websites and usually have an outreach, liaison, or research funding office that is well placed to discuss such options.

A further option for UK practitioners, Knowledge Transfer Partnerships (KTP), is a government mechanism that connects universities, research organisations, and graduates with businesses to conduct research. The nominated researcher, or associate, works within the business while being employed by the academic partner or research organisation. Although some of the costs of the scheme are funded by a grant for the one- to three-year duration, the business partner is expected to contribute between £35,000 and £55,000 per year depending on the size of the business and the project conducted and includes the cost of the associate's academic supervisor (UK Government, 2020). The KTP scheme has been the starting point for several architecture practices including Architype, but ZCD director Dinah Bornat raised the concern that for many small and micro practices this is unaffordable.

2.3.3 Overcoming a lack of research training

There is no lack of interest from recently graduated architects in participating in research and research-led design work in practice. One interviewee, a practice partner, suggested that this may be attributed to the hope that the graduate's role would expand beyond detailing staircases and doorways rather than a genuine enthusiasm to engage in research. Although it is likely that there is no single motivation and that several coexist, all of the practices interviewed noted that they received significantly more graduate applications for research-related roles than for non-research roles. However, almost all criticised the standard of research education in graduate architecture courses as being insufficient and in some cases acknowledging similar weaknesses in their own education. The implications for both relate to the lack of rigour with which practice based research is conducted compared to that of research institutes and universities.

To compound this, externally delivered Continuing Professional Development (CPD) in research training remains limited. Several practices overcame this, and a lack of academic education, with in-house training, often informed by their own publications. Baca Architects' publication *Aquatecture* (Barker & Coutts, 2016) is deemed essential reading for all new employees. With a dedicated researcher leader, larger practices were efficient at delivering their own training to those who applied to the funding schemes discussed above but the size of some studios determined that it was challenging to induct all staff. While small practices did not have a research-only leader, those best placed to deliver such training and drive the research agenda in practice, were often directors or senior members of the practice and likely to be short of time.

2.3.4 Size matters, or, is research is only for large practice?

One of the most commonly held misperceptions regarding the research in practice is that a studio needs to be a large organisation, at the top end of the AJ100 for example, with clearly identified and ring-fenced funding and a specialist team, to be able to conduct and deliver research projects. As Chapter Eight demonstrates, this is not the case. All of the small practices discussed later are recently established studios, and all were established with a determination to actively engage in research, and delivered work as strong as their larger counterparts.

While there are benefits to operating a research team at a larger practice including the possibility of specialist, research staff and internal funding options, for example, being a larger firm doesn't necessarily translate as having a large research team or wielding greater influence over design outcomes. Both are an issue of scale and with that comes complexity particularly with respect to communication and dissemination, at least internally, of research findings. On the matter of staffing, rather than large, stand-alone teams, most larger practices have very small research dedicated teams of fewer than five people, with most projects and part-time researchers embedded within design teams across the practice, an approach adopted both by PLP Architecture and Perkins&Will.

2.3.5 Support for research at a senior level

All architectural practices, regardless of size, age or focus, require a research champion at the highest level. Without this, successfully delivering a research agenda and output is unlikely. Research has not always been part of architectural education and so forms a departure from traditional working practices for some long-established studios. For several large practices, their research program is a later introduction. Delivering this level of change in approach, introducing a new research team or department, can only usually be delivered by staff with the seniority and authority to make such changes. The research program at Perkins&Will, a practice established in 1935, came 70 years later following the acquisition of Busby and Associates, whose existing research agenda was led by Principal Peter Busby.

   While for many small practices, including all of those interviewed for this publication, a determination to embed research in the design process was part of the driver for establishing their own company and can prove an advantage. Helena Rivera, founder of A Small Studio remarked that "by conducting research, we diversify the type of work we do and actively seek out the projects that interest us. This gives us control over the work the studio is doing" (Martindale, 2017, p. 9). In addition, larger practices, whose partners rarely held a PhD, were more likely to take on PhD graduates to run their research departments and teams. Research in small practice is more likely to be led by a senior partner or director as part of their role and supported by more junior colleagues with a similar role split.

2.3.6 Post occupancy evaluation and the fear of being sued

Post Occupancy Evaluation (POE), evaluating a building and its use usually within the first 12 months after its completion and subsequent occupation, has broad support among international industry bodies including the Royal Institute of British Architects (RIBA), American Institute of Architects (AIA) and Australian Institute of Architects. However, the uptake in practice has been much lower than these institutions, and most architects, would like. When discussing the infrequency of POE research, the common response voiced by architects is a fear of being sued for failing to deliver a building to the specification presented at the design stage.

One architect noted that when they do discuss POE services with a client, the offer is extended only to those clients with whom they have a very good relationship, know well, and therefore have the confidence that they will not be sued. There are no statistics available that would support or refute this concern which, given the sensitivity of the issue and potential commercial impact, is not surprising. In 2015, the RIBA sought to address this issue through an agreement with an established insurance company already working in the creative sector and with many architecture practices, but practices reported that the company did not provide the cover for claims that might arise from POE findings.

Despite this, there are many practices that are determined to conduct post occupancy studies. In terms of human assessment, POE is an established part of the workplace design process and is becoming more common in other sectors including education and healthcare but is much less prevalent in housing. Both Baca Architects and Architype have adopted research and design strategies for their practice that rely on building performance assessment aspects of POE data. A growing awareness of the environmental impacts of buildings highlighted by movements such as Architects Declare may shift opinion on this for both architects and clients, making POE a necessity. See Chapter Five for further information on POE methodologies.

2.3.7 Publishing, non-disclosure agreements and the loss of competitive advantage

Publishing research findings is an issue of ongoing concern for architects in a manner which does not seem to present the same concerns to other built environment specialisms or, clearly, academia. The most frequently cited concerns arise from the notion that by publishing, a practice risks diminishing its unique expertise, losing its intellectual property and, consequently, clients. Second to this is the specific request from clients that research work be conducted without publication of any form or even mention on a practice website, and so many contracts include confidentiality agreements which block dissemination of the research. This poses two key problems. First, is that without some evidence of original research work makes it difficult to practice demonstrate the knowledge gained, winning further research work or funding. The second can arise out of collaborations with academic partners who rely on the use of data and research outcomes to publish. However, this isn't always an impediment to a research partnership as academics continue to work on confidential projects.

Many architectural researchers, including case study interviewees, have found that far from being problematic, publishing has elevated the practice profile and won them clients who were attracted by the research-driven design approach. However, the restrictions of confidentiality agreements pose a serious problem for most. In overcoming this, one option is to generalise the findings drawn from several projects, identifying trends if sufficient cases and contracts allow. Another option would be to tailor the contracts that accommodate the later use and anonymisation of data. Both Baca Architects and Pomeroy Studio offer a different approach, where research conducted by both practices remains the property of the practice as does the option to publish. For both, this is as much about sharing their research and knowledge with the wider industry as it is demonstrating their expertise and attracting future clients, and for both practice principals, this has led to international speaking opportunities and media work.

2.4 The scope of practice based research

The breadth of research in architecture practice is often assumed to be limited to the development of new, high-tech materials or post occupancy evaluation, but it is far broader than that. Research conducted reflects a practice's area of architectural expertise or ambition to work in a particular design sector. The work from practitioners in this publication includes research on primary years education, educational buildings, flooding, community engagement, environmental sustainability, master planning, Modern Methods of Construction, post occupancy evaluation, healthcare design, housing, and development of new materials. Beyond these case studies, research in practice includes a wide range of topics that have influence and informed design work and practice. This section of the chapter discusses key areas of research by sector, followed by cross-sector, process-driven research.

There are three sectors that attract the attention of researchers but are less common across the architecture industry given the infrequency of work in those fields seeking a better integration of research into design and includes museums (Gensler, 2017; Hughes, 2016), healthcare facilities (Naccarella, Redley, Sheahan, & Morgan, 2017) and new modes of mobility (Braidwood, 2016), and so are not included here but the last two do appear in Chapter Eight. Practice research in urban mobility and socio-spatial integration includes the engineering of mechanical systems and structure, transport and mobility options for an ageing population, smart transport, and transport orientated development with practices including Bjarke Ingels Group, UNStudio and Foster + Partners among several practices working on Hyperloop schemes.

2.4.1 Research across design sectors

Workplace

Workplace is one of the most prolific and well-researched sectors within architectural practices globally, and aspects of this occupancy analysis-based investigation are conducted by almost all practices working in this field. Topics include the benefits of proximity and density in workplaces for interaction and collaborative working, ergonomics of workplace design, creative workspaces and industrial parks, innovation districts, group culture and ethos in practice, links between the office and mental health, stress and wellness, and the environmental performance of workspaces, including air quality and acoustic attenuation.

US-based multidisciplinary practice Gensler has a long and well-established research programme in workplace (Gensler, 2020). The practice published their first workplace survey in 2005 and three years later announced that their "US and UK Workplace Surveys [found] a direct connection between workplace design and business performance" (Gensler, 2017, p. 240). The annual Gensler Workplace Performance Index, trademarked the same year, had logged more than 100,000 respondents over its first seven years (Gensler, 2012). As the practice has accumulated data, the trends identified have evolved with the 2020 report focussing on the issues raised by open plan and unassigned seating, and the impact of nature on the workplace.

London practice Hawkins\Brown, working in collaboration with commercial real estate company Jones Lang LaSalle, has expanded on this with 'Industrial Rehab', an analysis of 30 large scale industrial conversion projects. The re-purposing of large industrial buildings to provide social, commercial and

Figure 2.2: Illustrative proposal for the retrofit of the former press hall, part of the proposed redevelopment of the Printworks site in Canada Water, London, by Hawkins\Brown. © Hawkins\Brown

community spaces, food and retail spaces, and academic research facilities (Hawkins\Brown, 2018). Included in the publication are two of their own projects, a proposal for the redevelopment of an almost 10,000 m² former newspaper print works in Canada Water in London's Docklands into workplace with greening of the expansive landscape (Figure 2.2) and The Gantry at Here East, the conversion of the former media centre at the London Olympic Village site in East London (Figures 2.3 and 2.4).

Housing

Although housing is an extensively researched area in academia and think tanks, it receives comparatively less attention from practising architects. This is not for lack of interest. Where housing research is conducted, the field is broad and includes density issues including suburban intensification and MATT housing, high-rise, high-density housing and implications for high-density urbanism, architectural configurations, wellbeing and health in the home, and Universal Design. Delivering affordable housing dominates practice research with a broad

Figure 2.3: Some of the 21 artist studios at The Gantry at Here East, designed to fit the stripped back steel grid. © Hawkins\Brown

ambition to influence the policy agenda around housing in specific sectors including social housing, slum dwellings, refugee and informal settlements, new models of housing, multigenerational housing, housing design standards, and speculative propositions.

One such speculative project is Peter Barber Architect's proposal, the '100 Mile City'. The "street based, linear city a hundred miles long, 200 metres wide and 4 storeys high" would encircle London and be accompanied by a monorail system, shops, schools and small factories (Peter Barber Architects, 2019). The drawings, model, writing and short film formed part of Peter Barber's exhibition at the Design Museum in London in 2018–2019 that documented his championing of social housing.

Figure 2.4: The cladding for each of the studios at The Gantry at Here East was inspired by a different period in the social history of the site, including nineteenth-century scientist Raphael Meldola and his passion for blue, and Bronco toilet paper. © Hawkins\Brown

Finding agreement on that theme is Dutch practice Sputnik, whose project 'Good Affordable Housing' reviewed 15 government subsidised housing associations from across The Netherlands, a country in which housing associations own 2.7 million houses. The self-initiated project was prompted by the introduction of a new policy in 2013 that reduced the subsidy for social housing and levied a landlord tax against the housing associations where the gap between the social housing and private rental and sales markets increased sufficiently to become unaffordable. This, the study suggested, would "lead to the demand for smaller, more compact houses" and so proposed a range of compact housing typologies for different groups (Sputnik Architects, 2020). Data was gathered from almost 1,500 tenants to determine housing need, and who later tested the designs in full-scale models built at TU Delft Faculty of Architecture, providing feedback used to finalise the design.

Aged care

With an ageing population worldwide, this is a diverse and established research agenda with projects examining specialist care facilities, adaptations in urban areas including street furniture and surfaces, universal design, multi-generational living, long-term housing need including bungalows and sheltered accommodation, mobility and different modes of personal and public transport, care homes and dementia care, Universal Design, adapting existing dwellings, health and wellbeing, and designing out loneliness and isolation. Often research in this field extends beyond individual buildings and their interiors to include the wider implications for the built environment.

With "20 million households the over 55 bracket, and the number of people aged 85+ is set to double over the next 20 years" (Park, Ziegler, & Wigglesworth, 2016, p. 1), this is a developing topic. Dwell, a three-year collaborative project between Sarah Wigglesworth Architects and the University of Sheffield explored the housing needs of this group, the gap in the market, and the design options required of new housing. Through engagement with older residents in the design and evaluation processes for houses and neighbourhoods, they developed a series of prototypes "designed to improve mobility and well-being for current and future generations of older people" (University of Sheffield, 2016). The project is ongoing and managed by the practice.

Education

Research in the education sector spans the complete age range from kinder-garten to university and includes the design of schools, libraries, universities and specialist research facilities, blended and collaborative learning spaces, the potential to improve learning and socialising and encourage play, landscape design, and planting, designing for students with special needs such as autism and physical disabilities, social interaction between students and staff, modular school design, and the environmental impact and maintenance of the buildings. This topic is a core part of the research focus of several of the practices featured in Chapter Eight including Hayball, Architype and Architecture Research Office.

For their project *What if academics interacted as much as students?*, Australian practice Hassell reviewed the working practices of academics and the spaces they required. "Academics need to do deep, focused, individual work without disruption" but the "average person does 10 different work activities in a given day, many of which aren't suited for a private office" (Sheahan, 2016). With increasing emphasis placed on collaborative research working and teaching methods, their architectural response, profiling the Melbourne University School of Engineering, Creative Industries Precinct at the Queensland University of Technology, Brisbane and the Global Change Institute, The University of Queensland, Brisbane, and proposed a series of spaces to support different working activities and facilitated collaborative engagement with colleagues.

Listed and heritage buildings and landscapes and their conservation

The research of significant historic buildings, structures and their urban and rural landscapes, social and cultural significance, evolving understanding of their significance, and the narratives surrounding them, are established research topics for schools of architecture. Research in this category falls into four main groups; ancient and heritage-listed buildings, monuments and sites, materials for maintenance, conservation, and the maintenance and conservation of contemporary buildings.

For their 'Cathedral Cities in Peril' Foster + Partners, in collaboration with English Heritage and Terence O'Rourke, compared Delft, Lund, Tübingen and Bayonne in an assessment of the development pressures of England's smaller cathedral cities and historic towns and the risk to their character and aesthetic quality (Foster + Partners, 2015) for a traditional consideration of architectural heritage. However, the care and management of twentieth-century buildings such as the Sydney Opera House (Ballesty et al., 2007), MAT housing (Calabuig, Gomez, & Ramos, 2013), and brutalist architectural icons (Croft & Macdonald, 2019), is becoming increasingly important.

This is exemplified by a project led by the Asmara Heritage Project in collaboration with the Bartlett School of Architecture at University College London and winner of the 2016 RIBA President's Medal for Research. The award-winning project was a summary of the 1,300-page Nomination Dossier submitted to UNESCO in 2017 presenting a survey of the old city of Asmara that documented the urban landscape and all of the 1930s modernist architecture (Figure 2.5). Asmara is the single largest site to receive World Heritage listing. The paper discusses "Eritrea's decision to conserve Asmara's early colonial era architecture represents a profoundly different attitude towards architectural heritage and its interpretation and treatment compared with many other post-colonial settings" (Denison, Teklemariam, & Abraha, 2017, p. 11). The city plans to employ its heritage status to define and direct its future development and conservation.

Figure 2.5: Then and now. Strict preservation policies have ensured the conservation of Asmara's modernist architecture including the Ministry of Health building. © Edward Denison

Urban master planning

Master planning is a long-established field of expertise in architectural practice and often informed by expansive data and research that focuses on the many facets of urban development including social and environmental resilience, responsive master planning, land use, urban interventions, the implications of health and well-being at the city scale, transport infrastructure, and station design, and the role of green infrastructure and public space in cities.

Historic England commissioned Allies and Morrison to conduct a London-wide analysis of the character of Greater London and its development over 1,000 years, to inform their 'Keep it London' campaign and later submission to the London Plan Review. The team reviewed historic and current maps, land use, street structure, transport infrastructure, existing densities, and heritage designations to develop a new map using Geographical Information System (GIS) software. The final report, *Locating London's Local Character and Density*, recommended a rethink of the central, urban and suburban approach to characterising the city to view places at a more individual basis that would retain the character of each area while allowing for future growth (Allies and Morrison, 2016; Manning et al., 2018).

Although work in this area might be considered to be the preserve of large practice, several smaller studios including Architectural Research Office (see Chapter Eight), LOLA and Stoss demonstrate that this is not the case. Rotterdam-based LOLA (LOst LAndscapes) focuses on abandoned sites in the city, suburban areas, and countryside. For one project, the research team reviewed 370 city edges in southern Holland with 20 case studies examined in further detail. The practice developed a new typology and a new strategic map published in the Zuidvleugel city border atlas (LOLA Architects, 2013). While Boston practice Stoss conducted a whole city assessment of land use choices over the short and long term in New Orleans including job creation, affordable housing and identify developable land. The final report, for New Orleans Redevelopment Association + Van Alen Institute Future Ground, presented a conceptual strategy aimed at "unlock[ing] the economic value of vacant land, putting it to work economically, socially, and environmentally" (Stoss, 2015).

2.4.2 Cross sector research

Building performance and environmental resilience

Long before the climate crisis was acknowledged across the architecture profession and beyond, environmental issues were an established area of research focus for practice and academia, and the breadth of research in this field is extensive. Work under this umbrella includes building and building fabric performance including interstitial moisture behaviour and moisture risk, heat loss through fabric and air leakage, indoor air quality and comfort conditions, the performance of the building fabric, energy efficiency in new housing, embodied carbon and energy, carbon emission reduction strategies, operational energy, flooding, and water resiliency, overheating and ventilation, Modern Methods of Construction focussing on sustainable building materials, the circular economy, internal and external air quality and different scales the resiliency of resource supply chains. These issues and research that underpins them runs across all sectors and across geographic boundaries (Chen, Marshall, & Imam, 2020; Morphogenesis, 2020; Pomeroy, 2016).

For Dr. Marylis Ramos, Director of Sustainability and Research at PRP Architects, clients need assurances, and research to better understand how buildings perform and the effective communication of this work to clients is essential (Dollard, 2019; Ramos & Burrows, 2015). However, post occupancy studies in housing, particularly those investigating the impact of retrofit on overheating and energy bills, are uncommon and those that do exist are largely anecdotal, supporting Ramos' position and highlighting the research gap.

Since the launch of Architect's Declare in 2019, the global manifesto focused on building to a higher environmental standard as set out in 11 aims, practices have reported a greater interest in conducting research in this field. To reflect this, there has been a pronounced increase in the recruitment of sustainability specialists, seen on employment websites, rather than short-term subcontracts through consultants such as Max Fordham. Feilden Clegg Bradley Studios, one of the organising signatories of the UK's Architect's Declare movement, have continued this leadership role publishing a climate change guide for other architects (Fielden Clegg Bradley Studios, 2019a) and hosting an exhibition at their central London studio. The 'Carbon Counts' exhibition assessed the environmental impact of the extraction and processing of 12 key materials, linking each to work by the practice and "focused on carbon, as the most immediate consideration affecting climate change... pollution, water use, biodegradation of extraction sites, and working conditions all have impacts" (Fielden Clegg Bradley Studios, 2019b). This has been followed by a free whole-life carbon calculation tool FCBS CARBON (Fielden Clegg Bradley Studios, 2020).

Post occupancy evaluation

Occasionally referred to as a life-cycle assessment, a maintenance inspection, energy or environmental audit, Post Occupancy Evaluation (POE), understanding the performance of a building, comparing the design against the final building, plays a significant role in the research at many practices (Hay, Bradbury, Martindale, Samuel, & Tait, 2017). Although its potential and benefits cannot be overstated, as discussed above, barriers to its use remain. The widely acknowledged benefits of POE include a clearer understanding of project aims and challenges, ongoing engagement with the client and the potential, establish whether a building matches the design ambitions, and provide enhanced knowledge for an ongoing process and the next project. While applicable across sectors, POE is regularly used for commercial developments, public sector buildings, and education facilities but less frequently in housing with occupancy and ownership providing access and interest issues (Carthey, 2006; Enright, 2002; Lackney & Zajfen, 2005; Wener, 1994).

British practice Architype specialise in Passivhaus design and have adopted an extensive POE schedule with all designs with the short to medium term aim of meeting their design ambitions and with the longer-term goal of providing guarantees or warranties for their buildings. This rigorous analytical approach, applied to their school buildings for primary-aged children and children with special educational needs, has secured ongoing architectural commissions. Mark Lumley remarked that "the POE process is a learning process that has helped to resolve problems, helped move future design forward" and secure ongoing commissions from the same client (Martindale, 2016).

Materials, development and testing

Developing new materials and innovating the application of exiting materials is one of the fields of research most commonly associated with, and often expected of, architecture both in practice and in schools working with a broad range of materials from low to high-tech. AL_A's Pitch/Pitch stackable sports field system required a load-bearing, lightweight structure that could be assembled easily. In collaboration with ARUP, the practice developed fibreglass composite posts as part of the temporary and semi-permanent facilities while offering a 25 year estimated lifespan (AL_A, 2020).

The development of traditional materials led conservation specialists Purcell are engaged in the development of new, more durable materials for use in the restoration of stained glass, stonework, lime and lead work (Purcell, 2020). C-re-aid, a not-for-profit architectural studio with offices in Tanzania and Belgium, promotes responsible building practices and materials to address Tanzania's socio-economic and environmental challenges. This ethos has led to the development of compressed earth blocks (CEB) made from local materials in a system that can be used by anyone (Figures 2.6–2.8). The design includes an interlocking option for the blocks, "represent[ing] a considerable improvement over traditional earth building techniques", helping to persuade builders and

Figure 2.6: Fabrication of the Compressed Earth Blocks using materials and press developed by the practice in close collaboration with partners in Tanzania. © C-re-aid

Figure 2.7: Materials research has refined the formula of the Compressed Earth Blocks while making them ecologically sustainable and affordable. © C-re-aid

Figure 2.8: The completed home constructed using Compressed Earth Blocks. © C-re-aid

the community that CEB can be as environmentally resilient as cement block or fired bricks that need to be transported great distances and can use polluting production methods (C-re-aid, 2018).

Modern Methods of Construction

Modern Methods of Construction (MMC), off-site construction, particularly the use of structural and Cross Laminated Timber (CLT), has attracted increasing attention from both academic and practice-based researchers (Jayalath et al., 2020; Martindale, 2020; Ramage et al., 2017; Walter, 2020). Its benefits including reduced structural weight, cost savings, reduction in waste materials, safer construction process, healthier interior environment, and higher environmental sustainability standards are regularly cited as a means of addressing the environmental impact of construction and, where housing delivery is described as being in crisis, the expediency of construction.

Figure 2.9: Redevelopment of the former Läkerol Pastille factory includes Cross Laminated Timber and renewable energy technologies across the site. © Pomeroy Studio

Figure 2.10: The Candy Factory's mixed use and residential tower includes larger balconies than are typical in Sweden, with wintergardens extending their usability in both summer and winter. © Pomeroy Studio

While the implications of the Grenfell Tower fire have acutely impacted the use of CLT, although not the interest, in the United Kingdom (Martindale, 2020), this hasn't affected research and construction of tall timber buildings outside of the United Kingdom with schemes in various stages of development from Toronto to Rotterdam to Melbourne. Drawing on their extensive sustainability research, the redevelopment of the former Läkerol Pastille factory site in Gävle, Sweden by Singapore-based Pomeroy Studio, includes a 15 storey mixed-use and housing tower in CLT (Figures 2.9 and 2.10). Lendlease Australia's feasibility and technical research into the capacity for CLT construction on unstable ground, delivered Australia's first tall timber building in collaboration with Bates Smart (Lendlease, 2018) and are partners in The Future Timber Hub, a university-led research centre with government and industry partners (University of Queensland, 2020).

Digital technologies and robotics

The introduction of new technologies has encouraged many practices to invest time and resources in the research and application of AR and VR, streamlining the BIM process, robotic construction, 3D printing including printing with different media and large scale printing, autonomous drone surveys, and digitisation of the custom build process. The expense associated with some of the necessary equipment and the space required, particularly with robotics, leads to collaborations with universities. Foster + Partners, for example, have established collaborations with Cranfield University and ten companies in a £5m EU funded project to develop artificial intelligence for welding, with Loughborough University, Skanska and ABB for 3D concrete printing, and Imperial College London and Dyson Lab for autonomous drone mapping of construction sites, part-funded by Innovate UK (Foster + Partners, 2016).

Flow Architecture, a small east London practice has employed digital data sources and mapping for several projects. They used social media tags and open-source data generated along hiking routes in Iceland to develop strategies for the tourism board and applied content analysis and grading of tweets geotagged in Hackney to identify sentiment about the location to create the Hackney Mega Picture. The practice tested a digital system that tracked the movement of visitors to their exhibition for the 2016 London Festival of Architecture. This process was replicated in Heartbit Walks, a project combining the movements of 25 participants around the Olympic regeneration landscape in Hackney with Galvanic Skin Response data in a psychogeographic mapping project, exhibited at the 2018 London Festival of Architecture (FLOW Architecture, 2018).

Engaging with communities

It is evident across several sectors that engaging with different groups within communities both as a process and a means of delivering inclusive architecture that responds to the diversity of community needs, is significant to architectural practice. Research by practices in this area includes empowering excluded communities, working with young people, designing for neuro-diverse groups, addressing issues of socio-economic inequalities and sustainability, working with older people in different residential settings, and engaging children in the design and building process.

Engagement as a means to designing with children and their diverse needs is an expanding area of interest for practice (Bornat & Shaw, 2019; Greater London Authority, 2020; Lipscomb & Stewart, 2020; Young, Cleveland, & Imms, 2020). Erect Architecture director Barbara Kaucky reported that they, working with Lambeth Early Action Partnership, had secured a portion of £40 million lottery funding shared among five cities and their local authorities over ten years, to investigate the impact of capital works and wayfinding strategies in efforts to deliver the child-friendly city. Australian practice Architectus conducted an assessment of the needs of different aged children in libraries for the redevelopment of the State Library of Victoria in Melbourne, Australia. The team interviewed parents and held co-design workshops with children with the resulting drawings produced combined with the interview data that informed the final design that included a two-story castle with sensory play areas at ground level for babies and toddlers and a mezzanine level above for older children (Wilson, 2019).

2.5 Conclusions

The breadth of architectural research conducted in practice confounds many. Too often the assumption is that it is limited only to large practice and to materials research, takes too long to complete, and, particularly if it is aligned to academic research, is irrelevant to practice and their design work. All of these presuppositions can be rejected. The size of practice is no barrier to establishing a research agenda in any field and projects can be tailored in duration, aligned to a project or not, and conducted with collaborators from any field, location or professional affiliation. Research conducted in a practice should be tailored to the needs of that practice.

However, while practice-based research is not without its challenges, if established with a clear vision for the subject area, purpose, senior-level support, funding, staffing and potential collaborations, it can be a highly effective tool for many practices. The research conducted in most practices is a reflection of the sectors in which those practices work or aspire to work, and use research projects to develop that knowledge and expertise that informs their architectural work with projects in multiple sectors. Depending on resources, time and funding, most practices are involved in more than one field of research although there is the capacity for cross-sector research and collaboration across design teams. The evolution of research within practice from small internally funded projects to commissioned research and larger collaborative projects is more often a reflection of their integration in design projects rather than stand-alone research projects with ongoing research attracting further funding, collaborators, colleagues and clients.

Chapter Three

Funding research in practice

3.1 Introduction

The most frequently asked questions by practitioners relate to funding research in practice. This chapter sets out to discuss different sources of funding to support research activity including international Research and Development tax schemes and their associated government agencies, client-based commissions, establishing academic collaborations including Knowledge Transfer Partnerships and academic funding mechanisms, and concludes with a list of grant sources that practices have been successful in securing funding from.

While every effort has been made to ensure that the information presented in this section is correct and accurate, it is intended to provide general indications of potential sources of funding for practice rather than specific instruction. It is imperative, particularly with reference to the section on Research and Development tax schemes, that guidance is sought from appropriate professionals. The information contained in this chapter was correct at the time of publication but as research funds, eligibility requirements, policies, and internet addresses can all change at any time or be withdrawn, professional financial guidance should be sought.

3.2 Research and development tax schemes

Research and Development (R&D) tax schemes can provide the most consistent form of financing for some research in practice, with around half of those interviewed for the case studies in Chapter Eight confirming that they use such schemes. It is an activity within business that governments are keen to encourage as Appelt, Galindo-Rueda, and González Cabral (2019) note: "[i]nvestment in research and experimental development is an important driver of innovation and economic growth... tax incentives have become a key policy instrument for promoting business R&D." However, not all activities conducted in practice under the research banner are considered eligible by the administering government agencies.

The eligibility of work conducted varies between countries although the foundation for many R&D schemes lies in scientific research with the phrase 'to seek to resolve a scientific or technological uncertainty' repeated throughout the guidance provided by governments internationally. This is reflected in a bias towards the scientific and technology research work supported, meaning that in some instances research conducted in the social sciences may not be eligible. Guidance from the New York State Society of Certified Professional Accountants is typical when it states that the US Government expects that R&D should "rely on a hard science, such as engineering, computer science, biological science, or physical science" (Holtzman, 2017). For architectural practitioners, this may mean that not all of their research will attract this tax relief. Some practices that conduct more social or cultural rather than technical research have reported challenges in perception about their eligibility to claim R&D tax relief while others have submitted successful claims. Specialist tax accountants should be able to provide potential claimants with clear guidance on their eligibility and their research work and seeking this before commencing a research project can help improve the likelihood of scheme compliance.

There is a consistency to the accepted definition and structure of research that governments offering tax relief for research activities, draw on when determining the validity and rigour of research submitted for R&D tax relief schemes. In almost all cases this is based on the Frascati Manual which states that R&D is "creative work undertaken on a systematic basis in order to increase the stock of knowledge, including knowledge of man, culture and society, and the use of this stock of knowledge to devise new applications" (OECD Publications, 2002).

This scientific approach to research continues with a classification of research intent, scope and process. "The term R&D covers three activities: basic research, applied research and experimental development" (OECD, 2015). Basic research is that which is conducted without a specific practical application. Applied research is work undertaken with a view to a specific practical application, and experimental development research aims to create or improve materials, devices, products or processes. Besides the broader social sciences or the humanities topics, research that does not fall under these headings such as market research and routine data collection for a project is generally considered ineligible.

3.2.1 Three pitfalls to avoid when applying for R&D tax credits

The first point for consideration is the expectation that this research has not been conducted before. It is essential to determine what research has already been carried out before commencing the project. With the lack of published practice-based research, this is not always easy to achieve and requires a broad knowledge of the field. Even where this work has been conducted elsewhere, that does not automatically determine that further studies in different environmental conditions, geographic locations, or communities, testing the findings of or expanding an earlier study, are not worthwhile or ineligible. A statement confirming that such a review has been conducted and the gaps that have been discovered in existing knowledge and justifying the motives for replicating the study, if applicable, should be included in any claim. Chapters Four and Five discuss this in greater detail.

Adopting a systematic research process, including accepted design methods, techniques, procedures, and protocols in the process, is the second essential requirement of a successful R&D claim. As the OECD notes R&D "work undertaken on a systematic basis in order to increase the stock of knowledge, including knowledge of man, culture and society, and the use of this stock of knowledge to devise new applications" (2015). The Canadian Government states that "problems are solved by following established procedures and standards. In other words, a systematic approach is used to carry out work" (Government of Canada, 2015). They continue, noting that it is imperative to distinguish

> between a systematic approach to carrying out work and the approach…
> The latter approach includes defining a problem, advancing a hypothesis towards resolving that problem, planning and testing the hypothesis by experiment or analysis, and developing logical conclusions based on the results.
>
> (Invest in Canada, 2020)

The importance of documenting work, particularly as the research is conducted, is the third requirement for R&D projects. This includes identifying and justifying the expenditure incurred on eligible R&D activity in accordance with the appropriate government's eligibility criteria. It is crucially important to document all aspects of the research process when considering making a claim for R&D tax credits, as you would for any other tax claim or process. Documenting the process including hypotheses, tests, data sources, and results, as well as expenses and time spent by staff on various tasks. This should provide sufficient detail that demonstrates that the work could be replicated, and so establishing this early in this process is hugely beneficial.

3.2.2 R&D tax schemes by country

Below are the R&D tax schemes of selected countries. As discussed above, the expectation of the standard of research conducted is consistent but there are variations in name, motivation, geographic scope, approach, claimant, limits, and eligibility, some of which are covered below and regularly updated by the OECD (2019). In all cases, interested parties should seek advice from the relevant government agency, and links have been included, or financial specialist as the information provided below is indicative of the schemes and offered as general guidance.

Australia

The Australian scheme, known as the R&D Tax Incentive replaced the R&D Tax Concession on 1 July 2011. The scheme is intended to encourage companies, particularly small businesses, to engage in R&D activities that increase competitiveness and productivity across the Australian economy. The scheme is administered by the Australian Tax Office and the Department of Industry, Innovation and Science, on behalf of Innovation and Science Australia. It is essential that R&D activities are registered before submitting a claim to determine eligibility, every year a claim is to be made (Australian Government, 2017).

To be eligible, claimants must have incurred at least A$20,000 expenditure on eligible R&D activities and be determined to be an R&D entity – a company that is liable to pay income tax in Australia. Individuals, a corporate limited partnership, most trusts, those whose income is entirely exempt from income tax are ineligible. The rate of the R&D tax offset varies depending on turnover. Claimants with an aggregated turnover of less than $20 million per annum are eligible for a slightly higher refundable tax offset.

Further details are available at
https://www.ato.gov.au/Business/Research-and-development-tax-incentive/

Canada

Accompanied by the slogan "Do Your R&D in Canada: It Pays off!" (Invest in Canada, 2020), the Scientific Research and Experimental Development Tax Incentive Program (SR&ED), is a cross-sector tax incentive that provides either an income tax deduction, an investment tax credit or a refund and is administered by the Canada Revenue Agency. The scheme allows applicants to amass SR&ED expenditure to reduce current-year income or apply it to a following year, up to 20 years later, and employ the SR&ED investment tax credit to reduce income tax. Canadian-based businesses can claim 35% on SR&ED expenditure of CA$3 million and this drops to 15% on any amount over $3 million.

Further details are available at
https://www.canada.ca/en/revenue-agency/services/scientific-research-experimental-development-tax-incentive-program.html

Denmark

There are three options for R&D support in Denmark. First, is a deduction for taxpayers for expenses associated with taxpayer's profession of 105% in 2021–2022 and increasing to 108% in 2023–2025 and to 110% in 2026, in line with Section 8 B of the Tax Assessment Act (Ligningsloven). Second, is the Danish Depreciation Act that stipulates that buildings used for business can be depreciated up to 4% per year, although this is not specifically related to R&D costs and there is a higher depreciation for machinery and equipment used for R&D. Finally, companies can claim R&D tax credits of 22% for any deficit related to R&D expenses up to DKK 5.5 million per year (22% of DKK 25 million), in accordance with Section 8 X of the Tax Assessment Act (Ligningsloven).

Further details are available at
https://skat.dk/skat.aspx?lang=da

Ireland

Referred to as the R&D Tax Credit, the scheme reduces a company's Corporation Tax liability and is calculated at 25% of qualifying expenditure made through the Revenue Online Service. Businesses are eligible to apply if their qualifying R&D activities are conducted in Ireland or the European Economic Area, their expenditure does not qualify for a tax deduction in another country and is within the charge of Corporation Tax in Ireland. The Research and Development Tax Credit manual qualifying activities and the types of expenditure that qualify for the credit (Office of Revenue Commissioners, 2019).

Further details are available at
https://www.revenue.ie/en/companies-and-charities/reliefs-and-exemptions/research-and-development-rd-tax-credit/index.aspx

and
https://www.revenue.ie/en/tax-professionals/tdm/income-tax-capital-gains-tax-corporation-tax/part-29/29-02-03.pdf

New Zealand

The R&D tax incentive provides a tax credit at a rate of 15% of eligible R&D spend up to $120 million. There is a minimum, annual spend on eligible R&D expenses of NZ$50,000. However, those with a lower expenditure using an approved research provider to conduct R&D may still be eligible although the claim can only include eligible expenditure on pre-approved research providers. Additionally, while 10% of the total eligible spend can relate to overseas work, all other R&D work must be conducted in New Zealand.

Further details are available at
https://www.classic.ird.govt.nz/research-development/rdti/approved-research-provider-list/

and
https://www.business.govt.nz/news/r-and-d-tax-incentive-2019/

Singapore

The Singaporean Government invested S$16 billion between 2011 and 2015, to establish Singapore's knowledge economy and support domestic innovation and enterprise, with the aim of establishing the country as a destination for international research and development collaborations. This expenditure increased to S$19 billion for the 2016 to 2020 period (Research, Innovation and Enterprise Secretariat, 2016). The government operates several specific international R&D partnerships that attract financial assistance and several formal schemes, two of which may be more relevant to practice. The Industry Alignment Fund is administered by A*STAR, the Agency for Science, Technology and Research, and the Singapore Economic Development Board (EDB) with the intention of facilitating public sector research that responds to industry challenges and the potential to establish collaborative research partnerships. Also administered by the EDB, the Research Incentive Scheme for Companies was established to support the development and expansion of private-sector research laboratories in private companies in Singapore with tax offsets of 30–50% of eligible research expenses. R&D tax claims are processed by the Inland Revenue Authority of Singapore and companies of all sizes are eligible to apply although most are small and medium-sized enterprises.

Further details are available at
https://www.iras.gov.sg/irashome/Businesses/Companies/Working-out-Corporate-Income-Taxes/Specific-topics/Research-and-Development--R-D---How-to-claim-R-D-tax-benefits/

and
https://www.edb.gov.sg/en/how-we-help/incentives-and-schemes.html

South Africa

The Research and Development Incentive was introduced into the South Africa Income Tax Act in 2006 with the aim of encouraging South African companies to invest in R&D across all sectors and company sizes. The South African Revenue Service administers the scheme which allows for two deductions; an accelerated depreciation for capital expenditure incurred on machinery or plant, and 150% of the R&D eligible expenditure. Claims can be approved if they have been pre-approved by the R&D Adjudication Committee, the Department of Science and Technology has issued an approval letter in support of the applicant, and expenditure has incurred for R&D activity directly, generated income, and is an ongoing business.

Further details are available at
https://www.dst.gov.za/rdtax/

Sweden

As the government hopes to stimulate increased investment in the business sector, R&D conducted in Sweden should be for a commercial purpose. The total deduction for all R&D staff cannot exceed SEK 230,000, equivalent to a total research deduction from employers' contributions of a maximum of SEK 2,760,000 for one year. Companies operating in Support Area A, which includes municipalities in inner Norrland and the northern parts of Värmland and Dalarna counties, may be eligible for further deductions.

An employer may make deductions from the employer's contributions by 10% of the basis for the contributions on compensation to a person working with research or development. This applies to both Swedish and foreign companies that pay employer contributions in Sweden, although the Swedish National Tax Board can grant a higher exemption of 25% for international researchers. The person working with research or development can be employed in a company of any size or be a consultant but should be between 26 and 65 otherwise a lower deduction is applied. To be eligible, researchers should spend a minimum of 75% of at least one month and at least 15 hours of their actual working time on R&D projects.

Further details are available at
https://www4.skatteverket.se/rattsligvagledning/edition/2014.1/1334.html

United Kingdom

For UK companies, R&D Tax relief is applied to Corporation Tax and so can only be claimed if your company is liable for Corporation Tax. It is also possible to claim a tax credit even if the company is loss-making. The tax relief operates differently depending on company size and structure and is only available to small or medium-sized enterprises (those with fewer than 500 staff and a limit set on annual turnover or company balance sheet). If the business has external investors, whether the practice is either a connected or partner company, all affect SME status and associated calculations. Those subcontracted to another company or in receipt of notifiable state aid are ineligible to claim but may be entitled to R&D Expenditure Credit.

Companies claiming for the first time can apply for Advance Assurance. R&D claims submitted in the first three accounting periods will be accepted if the claims are in line with what was discussed and agreed with HMRC. A claim period runs from the point at which work to resolve the uncertainty starts until a resolution has been found or the project is stopped. The level of detail to be submitted depends on the number of projects included in the claim. If a claim includes fewer than four projects all should be detailed, while claims with four to ten projects (the maximum) should detail 50% or at least three of the projects.

Further details are available at
https://www.gov.uk/guidance/corporation-tax-research-and-development-tax-relief-for-small-and-medium-sized-enterprises

The RIBA's guide to R&D Tax in the United Kingdom is available at
https://www.architecture.com/knowledge-and-resources/resources-landing-page/guide-to-research-and-development-tax-credits

United States

The Research and Experimentation (R&E) tax credit, first introduced in 1981 as a two-year incentive, is a federal tax credit under Internal Revenue Code (IRC) section 41. Unlike other schemes, its intention is considered to be a 'reward' for US companies increasing their investment in R&E. Although some exclusions apply, it is available to any business or taxpayers who have attempted to develop new, improved or technologically advanced products or trade processes or have improved upon the performance, functionality, reliability or quality of existing products or trade processes for expenses incurred for performing Qualified Research Activities in the United States.

Eleven research-related activities are excluded from claims including market research, testing, or development and routine data collection, surveys, studies, or activities related to management functions or techniques, routine or ordinary testing or inspection for quality control, funded research, and any research in social sciences or research conducted outside of the United States. Variations in the process apply depending on the size of business, ownership structure, and legal structure of the company.

Qualified Research Expenses include wages paid to employees for qualified services, depreciable supplies used or consumed in the R&E process, 65% of the cost of third-party contract research expenses, and 75% of the cost of basic research payments to qualified educational institutions and various scientific research organisations.

Further details are available at
https://www.irs.gov/pub/irs-pdf/p535.pdf, pp. 100–117.

Guidance on this from the American Institute of Architects is available at
https://www.aia.org/articles/6206410-do-you-qualify-for-rd-tax-cred

3.3 Client commissioned research

Research projects commissioned by clients are less common than many practices would like. Several of the practices interviewed for Chapter Eight conduct research directly for clients including Baca Architects, Architecture Research Office, White Arkitekter, and ZCD Architects. Client commissions in the form of subcontracted research work for other architects were the starting point for Counterspace Studio. Where there exists the option of research for a client, the work typically takes one of three forms; direct funding for research only projects, a portion of a design project designated for a research component, and no attributable fee for the research component of the design project, but it is covered in other costs or 'written off' with the costs of conducting the research project, including staff fees, overheads and expenses, absorbed elsewhere in the project balance sheet.

The success of these approaches often depends upon the relationship with the client. Finding clients who are interested in commissioning research is a persistent and significant challenge for most. White Arkitekter, for example, clients rarely approach the practice with a research project in mind. Usually, the team develops a research component to be included in the architectural project following initial conversations with design clients. Others have been successful in winning contracts through government procurement and while the value of some of these contracts can be low, they can provide a route into further work with the client and similar projects for authorities elsewhere.

3.4 Academic collaborations

Many practitioners have established connections with academic institutions, often through teaching, mentoring and examining roles. There is a natural progression for some to expand that work to include research-based either within a school of architecture or allied faculty, or within their own practice through a joint project. However, most practices engaged in collaborative research with a university without a teaching component or connection, tend to be attached to engineering departments. For many practices, identifying a faculty or individual academic to work with often starts with alumni links or through existing links with the practice to a nearby university. The best contact points at universities are often the Dean of Research within the relevant faculty or the university's research support office, whose staff are experts in locating research funding, submitting funding applications, and establishing and supporting research partnerships.

Beyond the usual issues of working relationships, the key to delivering successful academic, practice research collaborations lies in understanding and managing the pace of the project. Academic research often operates on a long-term programme punctuated by publications and presentations at key stages, and this is not often the case for practice. While Foster + Partners have long-term research projects, including supporting PhD students in their practice, at several universities including the Royal Veterinary College, Loughborough and Cranfield, PLP Architecture formed a three-month partnership with the University of Cambridge for their Super Tall Timber project that has led to a longer-term working relationship. But, as Adam Yarinsky of Architecture Research Office noted in interview, if a research project is linked to a design project then timing is critical. Even without an academic partner, not starting a project early enough can be problematic with research findings delivered too late to inform the design process. As the preparation and processing of research grant applications can easily take more than a year, and the university research conducted in a manner that adheres to academic protocols often operates at a slower pace than in practice, frustrating both parties.

University researchers have access to research funds that are not available to practitioners but in some instances offer opportunities to collaborate with non-academic researchers. Although it is possible to be included on research grants there are often limits and few research grants exist to cover all expenses, such as salaries, overheads, external consultants, travel, research expenses, and consumables such as new equipment. Different agencies offer varying levels of funding support or cover specific research expenses, such as salaries or conference attendance. In some circumstances, it is possible to hold more than one grant for the same project, although typically it is to cover different aspects of a project or different research expenses such as conference costs or inter-national travel. In almost all cases, partnerships need to be established before funding applications are submitted to take account of all expenses. Joining a funded project later may require a separate funding application.

The body responsible for administering research grants is specific to each country such as the Australian Research Council (ARC) in, unsurprisingly, Australia, the National Science Fund for the United States, and the UK Research and Innovation (UKRI) in the United Kingdom. A government agency, the UKRI is split into seven research councils including the Arts and Humanities Research Council, Economic and Social Research Council, Engineering and Physical Sciences Research Council, and Natural Environment Research Council, along with Innovate UK and Research England. UKRI's Gateway to Research website also provides information on over 42,000 funded research projects from more than 33,000 researchers (UK Research and Innovation, 2020).

The final option for academic engagement is through a Knowledge Transfer Partnership (KTP). KTPs are a mechanism that funds research collaborations between academia and practice. The aim of the government-backed scheme is to support businesses to innovate and develop research expertise. The scheme establishes research partnerships between universities, research organisations, and graduates with businesses to develop and conduct research within the business. As discussed in the previous chapter, KTPs are available in the United Kingdom and Australia. In the United Kingdom, the scheme is part-funded by a grant and part by business that contribute between £35,000 and £55,000 per year depending on the project and size of the practice to cover the salary of the practice-based graduate researcher, referred to as an Associate, and their academic supervisor. Depending on the scope of the work and needs of the business, projects are expected to last between 12 and 36 months.

KTPs, funded by the ARC, are available in Australia but currently only in the state of Queensland. The scheme provides funding of up to A$50,000 to Queensland businesses, representing two-thirds of the cost of hiring a graduate, to work with universities on innovative projects. To be eligible, the business must have fewer than 200 full-time equivalent employees, have been operating for at least two years, be a registered company in Australia, hold an Australian Business Number, be registered for Goods and Services Tax (GST) before commencing the project, have the finances to cover the remaining costs of the graduate student, have already established an academic partnership, and have an innovative project defined.

Further details of the UK scheme are available at
https://www.gov.uk/guidance/knowledge-transfer-partnerships-what-they-are-and-how-to-apply and http://ktp.innovateuk.org

Further details of the programme in Queensland are available at
https://www.business.gov.au/Grants-and-Programs/Knowledge-Transfer-Partnerships-QLD

3.5 Funding sources

Below is an annotated list of grants, scholarships and awards available to architectural practices, from a range of organisations to which architectural researchers have successfully applied. Some of these funds may appear small but are worth considering as winning even a small grant inspires trust, reduces perceived risk, attracts additional funds for a later phase or a future project, and can be accompanied by press coverage and further promotion including speaking opportunities.

These details, including links, were correct at the time of publication. Those interested in applying for funding through these sources should confirm that the fund is available and determine their own suitability. Contacting the funding agency directly is often an effective first step. Other funding sources that have previously supported research in practice included the BRE Trust, Centre for London, Higher Education Design Quality Forum, Homes England, The World Bank, and UNHabitat. These sources have not been included below as their funding was either not available at the time of writing or secured through an invitation to participate, a procurement advertisement, or initiated by a unique event.

3.5.1 American Institute of Architects – Upjohn Research Initiative

The primary aim of the American Institute of Architects (AIA) Upjohn Research Initiative is to 'enhance the value of design and professional practice knowledge'. This is reflected in the evaluation of proposed projects with almost a third of the grading awarded to proposals that demonstrate how the research project delivers on this ambition. The scheme funds up to six projects of US$15,000 to US$30,000 each year with the caveat that the value sought from the AIA must be fully matched with 'hard dollars'. Applications should reflect the AIA's priorities for the year of application and projects are expected to be 6–18 months in duration. There are no restrictions on an applicant's geographic location. Final reports and findings are published on the AIA website.

Further details are available at
https://www.aia.org/pages/11911-aia-upjohn-research-initiative-grant

3.5.2 Arts Council England

Funded by the National Lottery, Arts Council offers several Project Grants to arts, museums and libraries projects. They include:

- Creative media and digital activity for artistic and cultural works and content created for digital platforms, and/or are distributed digitally to engage the public;
- Project Grants for music projects from individuals, groups and organisations working in the music sector;
- Literature projects, to support writers create new work and reach audiences, through a range of publication options including digital distribution and production, and live events; and
- Libraries and Project Grants, to develop libraries' role as cultural providers in their communities.

Grant proposals are expected to be innovative, experimental and show creative risk-taking, and present clear plans for effective audience engagement. Applications for £15,000 or less are determined in six weeks, while decisions for those of £15,000 take 12 weeks.

Further details are available at
https://www.artscouncil.org.uk/funding/funding-finder

and
https://www.artscouncil.org.uk/funding/other-sources-funding

3.5.3 Ashden Awards

Ashden Award recipients receive a £20,000 prize for completed work that demonstrates an innovative approach to sustainable energy with a demonstrable impact. Alongside the potential to improve a range of factors including health and wellbeing outcomes, air quality and job creation, applications should discuss and be able to demonstrate their contribution to:

- Radical decarbonisation – how the work can contribute to reducing carbon emissions without compromising quality of life.

- Reducing inequality – how the project works towards creating a fairer, more sustainable society and reducing inequality.
- Participation and democratisation – demonstrate how inclusive the work has been in its engagement and consultation across different community groups and sectors and stakeholders.
- Resilience – indicate how the work supports environmental, economic and social resilience.

Further details are available at
https://www.ashden.org/awards/ashden-awards

3.5.4 Australian Department of Industry, Innovation and Science

The Australian Government site provides a list of funding sources including the Global Innovation Linkages and the Global Connections Fund, the Australia-India Strategic Research Fund, Australia-China Science and Research Fund, the Prime Minister's Prizes for Science, and the Regional Collaborations Programme. In most cases, the applicant is expected to be an Australian resident or an Australian business.

Further details are available at
https://www.industry.gov.au/topic/funding-and-incentives

3.5.5 Australian Institute of Architects – David Lindner Prize

The David Lindner Prize seeks to inspire graduates and emerging architects through research in significant and challenging design issues involving the public realm relevant to Australian cities. Recipients of the annual award are expected to present proposals to address these challenges and offer a contribution to the architecture profession that indicates societal benefits. Applicants must be Australian citizens or permanent residents, members of the Australian Institute of Architects, or be nominated by a member, and have graduated from an architecture degree course within 15 years of application.

Further details are available at
https://wp.architecture.com.au/nswawards/david-lindner-prize/

3.5.6 British Council: Newton Fund Institutional Links Grant

Newton Fund Institutional Links Grants offer £30,000–£300,000 over two to three years for collaborative projects submitted in response to calls published on their website. The scheme aims to support the development of research collaborations between universities, researchers and institutions and the exchange of expertise and research knowledge. Calls vary in their study location and focus and welcome contributions from the arts, humanities and social sciences.

Eligible applicants must be leading researchers or established researchers, as defined by the European Commission, and are likely to be PhD holders (European Commission Directorate General for Research and Innovation, 2011). Each funding call specifies the locational or residency requirements for applicants but usually, this is focussed on those in the United Kingdom and European Union. The fund covers expenses related to research activities such as hosting meetings or seminars, research expenses, and some staff costs.

Further details are available at
https://www.britishcouncil.org/education/science/current-opportunities

3.5.7 Global Challenges Research Fund

The Global Challenges Research Fund (GCRF) is a £1.5 billion fund that supports research addressing the challenges faced by developing countries. The scheme is keen to engage researchers who may not previously have considered the applicability of their work to development issues, support research that provides an agile response to emergencies, and strengthen collaborative research partnerships between the United Kingdom and developing countries.

The GCRF has three challenge areas. First, to facilitate equitable access to sustainable development, such as secure and resilient food systems, inclusive and equitable quality education, clean air, water and sanitation, and affordable, reliable and sustainable energy. The second focuses on sustainable economies and societies which covers sustainable production and consumption of materials, inclusive economic growth and innovation, and short and long-term environmental resilience. The third considers human rights, good governance and social justice, which includes displacement and refugee crises, reducing poverty and gender inequalities.

Further details are available at
https://www.ukri.org/research/global-challenges-research-fund/

3.5.8 Heritage Lottery Fund

The Heritage Lottery Fund supports projects that consider heritage in its broadest definition and in its application to architecture, landscapes, the built environment and its community. Not all projects are required to be exclusively research but would attract funding if research was a component of the work. Heritage projects could include:

- countryside, nature and habitat conservation, and restoration;
- conservation of designed landscapes including public parks, historic gardens and botanical gardens;
- oral history, documenting stories, memories and songs, commemorations and celebrations that convey these social histories and specific times and dates;
- cultural traditions including dance, theatre, food, clothing, languages and dialects;
- community engagement in archaeology;
- historic buildings, monuments and the historic environment including industrial, maritime and transport sites; or
- improving access to museums, libraries their collections, and archives.

Funding ranges from £3,000 to £10,000 for a one-year project, to £5 million and above for those lasting five to seven years and can be used for community activities, repairs and conservation, digital outputs, new staff posts including paid training placements, and professional fees. Proposals should clearly define the project outcomes, addressing those set out in the guidelines and a statement detailing how the project will attract a broad audience.

Further details are available at
https://www.heritagefund.org.uk/funding

3.5.9 Historic England

Historic England is a charitable organisation that offers funding for strategic research, skills development in the historic environment, and work that helps them better understand how people use historic environments and their future through the Heritage Protection Commissions. Local authorities, universities, charitable trusts, limited companies and registered self-employed researchers are all eligible to apply through three routes. First, is the Open Proposals Programme which accepts applications on a rolling basis. The second is through calls for proposals with defined subject areas and, last, by tender which defines the specific project requirements, both advertised on the website throughout the year. All proposals should be aligned with their Corporate Plan. In its status as Independent Research Organisation, Historic England is able to apply for research funding from the relevant UKRI bodies and partner with industry and academic partners to conduct research.

Further details are available at
https://historicengland.org.uk/services-skills/grants/our-grant-schemes/hpc/

3.5.10 Horizon Europe

Horizon Europe is the replacement for Horizon 2020. It is a fund for members of the EU and was the most frequently cited source of funding for UK architecture practices. The scheme was established to ensure Europe produces world-class science, removes barriers to innovation, and makes it easier for the public and private sectors to work together in delivering innovation. The scheme supports European partnerships with EU countries, the private sector, foundations and other stakeholders.

There are five mission areas covered by the €100 billion research and innovation programme, of which the most relevant to the architecture industry are adaptation to climate change including societal transformation, and climate-neutral and smart cities. The scheme has been overhauled with the aim of widening participation, making the process faster and more transparent, and strengthening the European Research Area. Most calls require a team of at least three partners. Two-year work programmes are announced on the Funding and Tender Opportunities page and the EU's Official Journal and published throughout the year.

Further details are available at
https://ec.europa.eu/info/horizon-europe_en

3.5.11 Leverhulme Trust Research Fellowships

The Trust offers research fellowships for projects lasting between three months to two years. Fellowships of up to £55,0000 are awarded to experienced UK resident researchers in both academia and practice "to complete a piece of research" across a wide range of disciplines. Applications require completion of a detailed online application form including a financial breakdown for the project. Eligible costs include economy standard travel, subsistence, research assistant salary costs, photographic costs and consumables, and either the costs of a temporary replacement and, if a sabbatical is taken from usual duties, loss of earnings except where the applicant is self-employed.

Further details are available at
https://www.leverhulme.ac.uk/research-fellowships

3.5.12 National Endowment for Science, Technology and the Arts

The National Endowment for Science, Technology and the Arts, NESTA, is an independent charity and innovation foundation focused on addressing big challenges facing society. The organisation has several priority areas including health and the health care system, education for the future, the creative economy, arts and culture, innovative government, and innovation policy. The agency offers a range of funding options that in themselves are not direct research funding but projects that have research components, they include;

- Democracy Pioneers, a £100,000 award, funds up to 10 innovations addressing ways to re-energise civic participation and everyday democracy in the United Kingdom.
- The £5.75 million CareerTech Challenge aims to encourage bold solutions to improve people's working lives and unlock future employment opportunities.
- Funded by the AAL Programme, Smart Ageing is a €50,000 challenge prize for solutions that support, empower and inspire older adults to engage in entrepreneurship.

Further details are available at
https://www.nesta.org.uk/help-me-innovate/

3.5.13 National House Building Council Foundation

Submissions to the National House Building Council Foundation are accepted that address their published objectives which include the performance of new homes and guidance for new occupants, technical guidance for designers and house builders, and proposals debating challenges facing housing supply. Applications are taken on a rolling basis throughout the year by submitting either a 200–300 word research idea by email or an outline research proposal including cost estimates via an online form or by email. If approved at this stage, applicants are then invited to submit a more detailed proposal.

Further details are available at
https://www.nhbcfoundation.org/research/

3.5.14 National Science Foundation

Established in 1950 "to promote the progress of science; to advance the national health, prosperity, and welfare; to secure the national defense" (National Science Foundation, 2020), the National Science Foundation (NSF) has an annual budget of US$8.3 billion (FY 2020). The Foundation funds just over a quarter of the 40,000 proposals it receives each year from colleges, universities, school systems, businesses, informal science, and other research organisations in the United States across ten fields. Those most relevant to architectural practice include:

- Biological sciences including environmental biology;
- Education and human resources which includes research on learning in formal and informal settings;
- Engineering which includes environmental and transport systems and industrial innovation and partnerships;
- Environmental research and education;
- Mathematical and physical sciences which includes materials research; and
- Social, behavioural and economic sciences including behavioural and cognitive sciences, and social and economic sciences.

The NSF offers funding through two mechanisms in the Programs for Small Businesses scheme. First, the Office of Small and Disadvantaged Business

Utilization identifies businesses to work with to "increase contract and subcontract awards to small and disadvantaged businesses". The second is through the Small Business Innovation Research or Small Business Technology Transfer program which provides US$190 million annually to small businesses and startups. To be eligible, companies need to be located in the United States with a minimum of 50% owned by US citizens or permanent residents, and have fewer than 500 employees. The proposed project should demonstrate sector need, its potential to effect a global impact, be conducted in the United States, and be led by a researcher who is an employee. Applications are accepted across 24 categories including advanced materials, Artificial Intelligence, energy and environmental technologies, the Internet of Things, and robotics. For research proposals that do not fall into one of these themes, there is provision in the 'Other Topics' category.

Further details on the Office of Small and Disadvantaged Business Utilization are available at
https://www.nsf.gov/about/contracting/osdbu.jsp

Further details on Programmes for Small Businesses are available at
https://seedfund.nsf.gov

3.5.15 New South Wales Architects Registration Board – Byera Hadley Travelling Scholarship

Administered by the Architects Registration Board, the Byera Hadley Travelling Scholarship provides small grants to graduates of the schools of architecture in the Australian state of New South Wales. The scheme is open to both current students and graduates wishing to conduct a short research project which includes travel either within Australia or overseas. The maximum scholarship available is A$5,000 for students and A$15,000 for graduates, and previous Scholarship recipients are eligible to reapply five years after the completion of their previous award.

Further details are available at
https://www.architects.nsw.gov.au/public-resources/byera-hadley-travelling-scholarships1

3.5.16 Royal Institute of British Architects – Boyd Auger Scholarship

Awarded annually, the Boyd Auger scholarship was established to support international travel for a 6–12 month research project. Eligibility for the £6,000 scholarship is linked to RIBA studentship. Only applicants who are either enrolled in a RIBA Part 1, 2 or 3 course in the United Kingdom or overseas, have secured a place on a RIBA Part 2 course, or have graduated from a RIBA Part 1 or 2 course in the preceding five years, are considered eligible.

Further details are available at
https://www.architecture.com/education-cpd-and-careers/studying-architecture/advice-on-funding-your-architectural-studies/funding-opportunities-for-students-of-architecture/riba-boyd-auger-scholarship

3.5.17 Royal Institute of British Architects Research Trust

Established to support research "relevant to the advancement of architecture, and connected arts and sciences, in the United Kingdom", reflecting the Institute's Royal Charter, applications are open to independent researchers, practitioners and academics. Multiple, annual grants of up to £10,000 are paid to individuals rather than a business or an academic institution, but cannot be used for costs such as course fees, expenses, and subsistence costs by research students.

Further details are available at
https://www.architecture.com/education-cpd-and-careers/studying-architecture/advice-on-funding-your-architectural-studies/funding-opportunities-for-students-of-architecture/riba-research-trust-awards

3.5.18 Royal Institution of Chartered Surveyors Research Trust

The RICS Research Trust is open to all qualified researchers, not just chartered surveyors, and accepts applications for large research proposals from established researchers to smaller projects from emerging researchers in response to defined calls published on the website in May and November each year. In addition, the Trust will consider proposals submitted as 'open calls' for proposals that fall outside the defined calls. Grants are usually for

£5,000–£10,000 but can be more for exceptional proposals from established researchers. For both options, applications should be submitted at the start of March and October for consideration in the May and December grant awarding rounds, respectively.

Further details are available at
https://www.rics.org/uk/news-insight/research/research-trust/

3.5.19 Royal Society Research Grant

This annual grant is aimed at UK-based scientists. While the scheme does not support work in the social sciences or humanities, one subject group focuses on engineering and technology so may be relevant to those practices with an existing research interest in those fields. Applicants must hold a PhD.

Further details are available at
https://royalsociety.org/grants-schemes-awards/grants/research-grants/

3.5.20 UK Research and Innovation

Formerly known as Innovate UK, UK Research and Innovation (UKRI) supports research across the full range of academic disciplines including engineering, social sciences, environmental sciences, economics, and the arts and human-ities. While they are responsible for the academic funding agencies, they are also charged with engaging with business and industry to support their research by offering a diverse range of funding opportunities, fostering international collabo-rations, providing access to high-level facilities and infrastructure, and providing training and career development to researchers.

The strategic interests of the agency are liable to change but the long list of fields of specific interest relevant to architectural practice include, creative industries clusters, digital security by design, healthy ageing, decarbonisation, prospering from the energy revolution, robots for a safer world, self-driving cars and transforming construction, including making buildings more affordable, efficient, safer and healthier.

UKRI supports research through four schemes. The Strategic Priorities Fund targets 'high quality research and development' with researchers and businesses at the cutting edge of research and innovation, with priorities across multidisciplinary and interdisciplinary programmes. The UKRI Future Leaders Fellowships aims to develop UK-based researchers while the Strength in Places Fund supports regional growth through a place-based approach to research and innovation funding. Finally, the Industrial Strategy Challenge Fund, part of the UK Government's Industrial Strategy, is intended to increase funding in research and development by £4.7 billion over 4 years by addressing the most significant industrial and societal challenges.

Further details are available at
https://www.ukri.org/funding/

3.5.21 Winston Churchill Memorial Trust

The Memorial Trust aims to provide the opportunity for individuals to travel overseas to conduct research in their chosen field. The scheme is available in the United Kingdom, Australia and New Zealand. In the UK fellowships are available in ten categories including arts for the built environment, enterprise supporting social impact, environment, conservation and sustainable living, rural living including strengthening countryside communities, and science, technology and engineering. The Australian scheme covers 27 categories including architecture, technology and the environment, while the New Zealand programme is looking to fund more fellowships in agriculture, science or technology and learning from cultures in the Pacific and Asian regions. Funding for all three counties' schemes covers four to eight weeks of international travel in one trip and applications are open to all UK resident citizens for the UK scheme, Australian citizens for the Australian scheme, and New Zealand resident citizens for the New Zealand scheme, over 18 years of age.

Further details on the UK scheme are available at
https://www.wcmt.org.uk

Further details on the Australian scheme are available at
https://www.churchilltrust.com.au

Further details on the New Zealand scheme are available at
https://www.communitymatters.govt.nz/winston-churchill-memorial-trust-2/

3.6 Conclusions

Identifying external funding available to practice is key to facilitating research in practice. Depending on the focus of the research and methodology adopted, R&D tax relief schemes can be considered to offer the most consistent approach to financing practice research. Securing advice from a specialist accountant at the outset should assist in identifying eligible expenses, clarify documentation requirements and refine the scope of the research to align with R&D requirements.

Securing funding for research in practice through published research funding and grants can appear to be a challenging or disheartening option to pursue as they often offer limited funds and attract a high number of applicants, and commissions from design clients can be sparse. However, as is discussed by some of the interviewees in Chapter Eight, early small successes can inspire confidence in future funding agencies and clients establishing longer-term partnerships and the publicity around them elevates the practice profile. Establishing collaborations with universities can offer a level of research support, including funding advice and resources, that would be inaccessible without it, again developing ongoing associations with further teaching, student engagement and research opportunities.

Chapter Four

Developing the research proposal

4.1 Introduction

From established academics to practitioners and independent researchers, anyone conducting research will have, at some point, written a research proposal. Several of the architecture practices interviewed here, including Perkins&Will, White Arkitekter and Hayball Architecture, operate internal research funding schemes for their employees that can form a substantial part of the research activity of the practice. As part of the application process, staff members submit a research proposal, responding to internal guidance documents and defined calls. The requirements for proposals vary between agencies, event organisers, universities, and publishers, some of whom will provide guidance on the expected content and scope of the proposal. This chapter sets out and discusses the components of a research proposal, and the structure and content of an abstract that accompanies most proposals.

4.2 Writing an abstract

Abstracts are the elevator pitch of research. Usually no more than one or two paragraphs, or 150 to 350 words, abstracts are submitted for consideration for conference presentations or event talks, included in research proposals, as part of an edited book of collated works by multiple authors, and always precede the full text of a paper in academic journals. There are, however, two distinct types of abstracts; those written before the research commences as part of the proposal (see below), and those that are submitted to a conference or journal, or book editors for publication. The difference in their intention is reflected in their content. Abstracts written for publication or presentation are usually written towards the end or following completion of a project and include mention of the data and findings of the work, an element absent from abstracts included in proposals given that the research has not yet commenced.

The basic structure of research proposal is composed of four or five key components, requiring a sentence or two on each.

- Context
  Discuss the problem or challenge the research relates to and previous work in this area, drawing on academic research, policy and industry publications where available.
- Aims and research questions
  State the purpose of the research and the challenges it seeks to address, that follow on from the background as summarised above.
- Methodology and data sources
  Outline the main data sources including case studies, and primary methodological approaches and analytical techniques.

An abstract for publication following completion or near completion, of the project would also include;

- Data analysis and discussion
  Present and evaluate the key results or preliminary findings from the research.
- Conclusions
  State the relevance of the findings to the industry and existing thinking. If the research is yet to be completed, indicate what stage the project is at and work that is outstanding.

While an abstract for a research proposal would conclude with;

- Significance and relevance of the proposal
  State how this research is pertinent to the industry and existing knowledge in the area.

While the length of the abstract varies, dictating the extent of the detail and discussion to be provided, the brevity of the abstract necessitates a clearly articulated and succinct presentation of the project. Achieving a balance of the information is critical as spending half of the allocated word allowance discussing the context and the problem, for example, leaves insufficient space to present the purpose and process of the research project.

4.3 Setting out a research proposal

A good research proposal used for research grant applications submitted to a range of organisations, comprises the same components and structure as a well-written research report or paper. This structure can be adapted to present a research proposal to clients, selecting the most relevant sections to suit the proposal's recipient and be applied to an in-house research scheme similar to those at larger firms. In addition, and relevant for applications to funding agencies such as those discussed in Chapter Three, a proposal should include a statement defining the relevance of the proposed project to the funding body that clearly aligns the research proposal to the interests of the agency.

- Title and subtitle
    As with all titles it is important to convey the focus on the research in an engaging manner. Employing keywords used in database searches in the title can help future readers to locate the publication, award notice or presentation.

- Abstract
    An abstract (see above) to be included in a research proposal differs from those submitted when a project has been completed or is nearing completion. For a proposal, the abstract should state the aims and questions for the research, the context and existing research in the field, the methodology and data sources to be used including any case studies, and the relevance of the research to the industry, and to existing understanding across practice, policy and academia.

- Project synopsis
    Typically 1,000–3,000 words in length, synopses are essentially a longer version of the abstract and should follow the same structure as the abstract, as laid out above. It should discuss the background and relevant literature,

aims and questions of the project, the data sources and methodologies, and the relevance of the proposal to industry and beyond. If an application does not specifically identify space on the application for statements for industry relevance, ethics, and a schedule and deliverables, those topics should also be addressed in the synopsis.

- Context or background and literature review

  For the research proposal, the background of the research proposal should include a review of existing academic research, past and current government and industry policy, best practice guidance, industry journals, and publications from industry bodies and practice. The gaps that exist in each that this proposal seeks to address should be identified as this relates to the aims and research questions in your proposal.

- Aims and research questions

  Formulating a research question or identifying a problem is essentially the same process as identifying a design problem. So this section should state the aim, or aims, of the research and the challenges or gaps in existing knowledge, that it seek to address, that follow on from the background as summarised above.

- Data collection and analysis methods

  Although there is no expectation that the work will have been conducted at this point, the purpose of this section is to demonstrate that the applicant has identified appropriate data sources to address the aims and answer the research questions, and how and why those data sources have been specified. The selection of any case studies should be justified, with an explanation of how they relate to the aims and why they have been nominated over other options.

- Concluding comments

  The synopsis should conclude with a statement considering the relevance of the proposed research to the industry and beyond, and existing knowledge on the subject.

- Industry relevance

  Demonstrating that the research and its findings are relevant beyond your interest and that of your practice, but for many applications it is essential.

Proposals should describe how the project findings will add to existing industry knowledge, specifically which groups, organisations and potentially university courses would benefit, and discuss existing professional networks and methods of dissemination of the acquired knowledge.

- Funding

    Most funding bodies will state the limit of the funding available for a project and permitted costs. Typically these may include research expenses, local and international travel and subsistence, any visa costs, salary replacement costs, other staff costs, and the purchase of specific technical equipment and consumables. Where costs include foreign currencies, exchange rates and the dates of the conversions should be included. The level of detail required varies between agencies, and funding competitions with more than one round many only ask for a detailed breakdown at the second stage. Most funding sources will expect a statement justifying costs, why a particular piece of equipment is required or why a car was used to visit a site rather than public transport, and almost all sources expect that standard class travel is the cost quoted.

    If the proposal is not intended for a funding agency or only part-funding of the project, it is likely that you will need to demonstrate, and usually evidence, how the project is being funded. This is also the case for salary costs as some funds do not extend to cover salaries. Where this is the case, applicants may be asked to confirm the source of salary. In addition, any conflicts of interest that might arise should be identified.

- Timeline

    The project schedule indicate anticipated start and completion dates. It should indicate when key phases and aspects of the work, such as fieldwork or interviews, will be conducted, and key deliverables including draft reports, final submissions, publications including website and social media posts, and conference presentations or industry event talks. Most funding agencies will define a timetable or at least identify a date by which a final report should be submitted to them.

- Research dissemination

    Discussing how and with whom the research will be shared is essential to any proposal. This can include in-house presentations to colleagues, industry talks, conference presentations, papers published in conference proceedings or academic journals, books, chapters, short articles for industry publications, and website and social media posts. The specificity of information provided here is important and, where possible, identify the journal or the conference and provide event dates. Where there is the opportunity for direct engagement with a wider audience, particularly with the public, government or other industries, these should be included as they are considered a benefit to the funding agency, the research, and other researchers.

- Referees
  Provide the contact details of, usually, up to three referees who can attest to your knowledge and research experience, and potential to deliver the research project successfully. Some proposal forms may require these to be drawn from outside of your practice while others may require confirmation of colleague support.

- Team biographies
  It is rarely the case that the space allocated to research team biographies provides ample space for full resumés. Typically they range from short paragraphs of 150 words to one page and should focus on research skills and experience, industry links, presentations, exhibitions, academic links such as teaching, and output including published written and design work. This section should also set out the relevant experience and structure of the research team, identifying the role of each person within the team and the relevant skills that they bring to the project, any key research-related output or contributions to policy, practice, industry knowledge, technological innovation, or product discovery and development.

Although not common, some agencies may seek further information.

- Ethics
  Any ethical considerations for the research process should be outlined here. These may include working with children or vulnerable adults and measures and protocols in place to protect them, any health and safety issues, how interviewees are approached, and their rights to their data. Any potential or already identified conflicts of interest should be discussed, particularly as they relate to a funding agency. For example, health-related academic journals, including those with interests in urban health issues, will not accept for publication any work that has received funding linked to tobacco companies, regardless of the value of the grant.

Where output from the project is to be published, particular reference should be made to any interviewees and the information they have shared, and how they will be kept informed following the publication of any report or material using their responses especially if the data is not anonymised or an image that could be used to identify them is included. It is also important to declare where there are any connections to third parties, such as consultancy engagements, that might be considered to present a conflict of interest. Ethics are discussed in further detail in Chapter Seven.

- Data management

    This section typically requires a statement specifying the security of data collected, particularly in relation to interviewees, who has access to that data, and the measures in place should those measures be breached. The ethics relating to the management of interview data is discussed further in Chapter Six.

- Equity statement

    A statement detailing the measure taken to ensure diversity across the research team and that opportunities are provided on an equitable basis is becoming increasingly common particularly for government procurement submissions. This can extend to providing employment opportunities for residents local to the project and identifying longer-term benefits to the community.

- Bibliography and references

    This section would require details of significant peer-reviewed publications, policy documents, industry publications, media sources, newspaper articles, and other research materials that have influenced your thinking, leading to this proposal. Although publications by the applicant can be included it is preferable that they do not dominate the list and that the references are directly related to the subject matter of the proposal rather than being general or from an allied subject.

- Funded projects

    The details of previous and relevant research projects including the value of funds received, the funding agency, dates of the project, title of the project, team members and outputs, and any available digital links should be included here.

- Professional or personal statement

  This statement should describe why this project is of interest to the applicant and how this research, and research grant, will benefit the applicant and support their future career ambitions in both the immediate and long term. Where there is more than one applicant, the statement should include all members of the team rather than just the lead researcher.

- Issues of intellectual property

  Copyright and intellectual property information require a statement considering innovations in new materials and digital tools and platforms, for example, that might be subject to intellectual property protection including patents, and other funding agents or research partners and team members with affiliations that might raise intellectual property issues.

  Other requests for information may include ORCID iD (a digital code used to identify researchers and academic authors), specific information regarding career breaks, teaching and mentoring activity, participation in professional training, details of other sponsorship and funding, and a second non-technical abstract or summary to be used outside of the expert field and for marketing purposes.

4.4 Conclusions

Research proposals differ in scope and often require a significant level of detail. The information requested is usually straightforward and those practices used to submitting procurement documents, for example, will be family with the scope and content required. Most funding bodies will specify their requirements either on the application form or occasionally with a separate, extended guidance document. For practices seeing to collaborate with university researchers, a basic internet search can provide pages from a range of academic institutions aimed at current and future research students, which could indicate what that institution and similar organisations require.

Chapter Five

The research process

5.1 Introduction

Chapter Five discusses the overall process and various stages of research, starting with establishing the research context and gaps in the literature, a guide to referencing, and creating citations. The chapter introduces the different data collection methods and analysis techniques most commonly used by practice that has been compiled following interviews and analysis of research publications from practice.

With all data collection, ensuring that the information is accurate and reliable is paramount, and so this continues with a discussion verifying data sources including reliability and triangulation, and dealing with fake news and false or misleading data. The final section addresses the writing-up process from establishing the context, setting out aims, questions and arguments, through the presentation and discussion of data and methodologies, the significance and impact of the work, and approaches for selecting images to accompany the text.

As an introduction to these methods and processes, each section is accompanied by recommendations for further reading that, where possible, are free to download or access online. These are drawn from sources that include research methods books, university library research guides, academic journals, publisher's encyclopaedia and practice guides, from the breadth of built environment specialisms and occasionally from other sectors such as healthcare that offer an external perspective on the subject while demonstrating an aspect the research method, notably its applicability across many fields.

5.2 Reviewing existing knowledge, writing a literature review

Including a review of existing research, academic and practice-based architectural knowledge, policy documents and publications, is usually dependent on the type of document that is being written. It is essential for research work and a required part of research and development (R&D) claims as evidence that the new work does not replicate existing knowledge. A review of existing knowledge and literature is important. It demonstrates an understanding of the fields in which a project is founded, identifies what has been done and understood, methods applied, identifies common themes and arguments, the evolution of ideas and knowledge, and any gaps from which to develop research questions and new research. Reading around the literature and producing a review also presents the opportunity to identify potential collaborators and experts to work with.

Sources for a literature review could include books and monographs, reports from government, think tanks, industry bodies and other research institutes, journal articles, papers published in conference proceedings, guidebooks, academic dissertations and theses, professional publications and industry publications and journals. Industry publications can provide a helpful indicator in identifying existing limits to knowledge and identifying gaps and methodologies. Effort should always be invested to confirm the validity and authenticity of all sources to avoid inaccurate, false, misleading, or poorly researched work (see Section 5.5).

University library catalogues offer the best starting point for searches, otherwise, the most efficient method of finding academic publications is via Google Scholar. A cursory search for community architecture will generate millions of responses that range from studies in algal communities and bacterial infection rates to ethnographic research of geographically remote populations and digital communications systems. Refining keywords and their combinations, and using quotation marks around key phrases, reduces and focuses the responses generated. Identifying relevant references is a process that continues throughout the research process as the work develops and to ensure that recent publications are included in the review.

In writing up, the review can be arranged chronologically if, for example, the evolution of knowledge in a field or development of a process, or thematically in order to analyse sources with shared issues. A review of the literature should avoid being an annotated list of every publication located and read in the process, but should present only the most relevant works that are significant to the research project, discussed in a cohesive manner setting out the key arguments and knowledge relating to the research proposed. As Hart notes, producing a good literature review

> means appropriate breadth and depth, rigour and consistency, clarity and brevity, and effective analysis and synthesis; in other words, the use of the ideas in the literature to justify the particular approach to the topic, the selection of methods, and the demonstration that this research contributes something new.
>
> (2018, p. 1)

It is important when reviewing the literature to be aware of individual political, social, and cultural bias, ensuring an ethical, considered, and unbiased assessment of the literature. Ethics across the research process are discussed in further detail in Chapter Six.

Further reading

Ridley, D. (2012). *The literature review: A step-by-step guide for students*. Thousand Oaks, CA: Sage.
University of Reading. (2019). *Study advice study guides: Literature reviews*. Author.

5.3 Referencing and citations

Referencing is a well-established practice in academic publishing but not always commonplace in practice-based research. Occasionally, it is argued by practitioners that as an architect or practice seeks to demonstrate their expertise in a particular field, with the aim of winning clients and commissions, referring to other practices implies a lack of original thought or creativity in their work, or theft of concept or design, and will drive clients to the 'original' architects. Citing existing research or publications demonstrates knowledge of the field both in terms of academic research as well as professional work. It identifies gaps in that knowledge and, therefore, the opportunities to innovate and contribute to a wider understanding of the subject. Not citing other's work, identifying their ideas, research and data, risks allegations of plagiarism, and theft of copyright.

Protocols for referring to published works include academic and conference papers, books, emails, policy documents, websites, films, documentaries, podcasts, pieces of music, or software, exist in established referencing systems referred to as styles. They provide guidance on layout for a document and specify everything from the indentation of paragraphs to presentation of quotations, but these are generally reserved for use in academic publications such as books and journals, rather than reports and professional publications.

Although there are differences in the placement of parentheses, whether titles appear italicised or not and the order of the information, each of the reference styles presents, essentially, the same information. All references should include:

- surname(s) and initial(s) of the author(s)
- the date of publication
- the title of the paper, chapter
- the publisher and place of publication

If it is a paper you will also need

- the title of the journal, volume and issue number, and page numbers for the article

If it is a chapter of an edited book you will also need

- the book's title, names of the editor(s), and page numbers for the chapter

If it is an online source, it requires

- the URL and the date you last accessed the page

The most common referencing styles used in academic writing, policy documents, and professional publications in the built environment are the American Psychological Association, Chicago, and Harvard. Typically, a publisher will specify which referencing style they require. As they provide the same information and no one is more acclaimed than another, writers only need to be consistent in their use. Below are examples of the presentation of the required information for the three most common styles that all appear in built environment publications.

5.3.1 American Psychological Association

The APA (American Psychological Association) referencing style was developed in 1929 for use in the humanities, social, behavioural and natural sciences, healthcare including psychology and nursing, research fields, but its use extends to some business, communications and engineering journals (American Psychological Association, 2019).

For authored book or reports
   Family name, INITIAL(S) (of editor). ed(s). Year. *Title*. Edition (if not first edition). Place of publication: Publisher.
For edited books and reports
   Family name, INITIAL(S) (of editor). ed(s). Year. *Title*. Edition (if not first edition). Place of publication: Publisher.
For chapters in an edited book
   Family name, INITIAL(S) of author. Year. *Title*. Edition (if not first edition). Family name, INITIAL(S) of editor. ed(s). Place of publication: Publisher.
For single-authored journal articles
   Family name, INITIAL(S). Year. Title of article. *Journal Title*. Volume(issue number), page numbers.
For webpage
   Family name, INITIAL(S) (of author or company name). Year. *Title*. [Online]. [Date accessed]. Available from: URL

5.3.2 The Chicago Manual of Style

Unlike other referencing styles, the Chicago Manual of Style is always listed with an edition, for example, Chicago 15th. The system is updated as referencing requirements evolve and new forms of publication, such as the inclusion of web-based documents, are included (University of Chicago Press, 2017).

For authored book or reports
   Family name, INITIAL(S) (of editor). ed(s). Year. *Title*. Edition (if not first edition). Place of publication: Publisher.
For edited books and reports
   Family name, INITIAL(S) (of editor). ed(s). Year. *Title*. Edition (if not first edition). Place of publication: Publisher.

For chapters in an edited book
    Family name, INITIAL(S) of author. Year. *Title*. Edition (if not first edition).
    Family name, INITIAL(S) of editor. ed(s). Place of publication: Publisher.
For single-authored journal articles
    Family name, INITIAL(S). Year. Title of article. *Journal Title*. Volume(issue
    number), page numbers.
For webpage
    Family name, INITIAL(S) (of author or company name). Year. *Title*. [Online].
    [Date accessed]. Available from: URL

5.3.3 The Harvard referencing system

The Harvard referencing system was established by Edward Mark Director of
the Zoological Laboratory of the Harvard University for use in the biological
sciences (Mark, 1881) but has since been adopted across fields.

For authored book or reports
    Family name, INITIAL(S) (of editor). ed(s). Year. *Title*. Edition (if not first
    edition). Place of publication: Publisher.
For edited books and reports
    Family name, INITIAL(S) (of editor). ed(s). Year. *Title*. Edition (if not first
    edition). Place of publication: Publisher.
For chapters in an edited book
    Family name, INITIAL(S) of author. Year. *Title*. Edition (if not first edition).
    Family name, INITIAL(S) of editor. ed(s). Place of publication: Publisher.
For single-authored journal articles
    Family name, INITIAL(S). Year. Title of article. Journal Title. Volume(issue
    number), page numbers.
For webpage
    Family name, INITIAL(S) (of author or company name). Year. *Title*. [Online].
    [Date accessed]. Available from: URL

When using more than one publication from the same author, or co-authors, in
the same year, they should be distinguished by adding a lower-case letter after the
year (a, b, c, d, etc.) in the order in which they are referenced in the body of the text.
In-text citations should appear as (surname, year) or (surname & surname, year).
    Typing these individually can be laborious, particularly if the list of references
is extensive. Online reference generators that will produce references for all

the main style systems using ISBNs and URLs for most published output from books and reports to webpages and sound recordings and films. By clicking on the quotation mark under the reference, Google Scholar generates references in several styles that can copied and transferred to another document or directly into reference management software including BibTeX, EndNote, RefMan and RefWorks. Of these software packages RefMan and EndNote and the most commonly used.

Further reading

Bodleian Libraries. (2020). *Oxford LibGuides: Managing your references.* https:// libguides.bodleian.ox.ac.uk/reference-management
Pears, R., & Shields, G. J. (2019). *Cite them right: The essential referencing guide.* London: Macmillan International Higher Education.

5.4 Data collection methodologies

Research methodologies fall into two categories. The qualitative method refers to the in-depth data often involving or observing human participants, which seeks to understand the drivers and motivations of behaviour and relationships typically through interviews or observation techniques. Quantitative methods focus on numerical data often in large sets and are often used to identify trends across a population or set, using questionnaires, statistics and large sets of digital data. Mixed methods, as the name suggests, employ a tailored cross-section of qualitative and quantitative methods to address the same research problem or question. A project could start with archival research, then draw on large census data sets to identify a trend before embarking on interviews, so using the archive and census data to identify a research question and provide the context for the interviews.

Likewise, data collection methods are divides into two groups; primary and secondary. Primary data sources are those the researcher gathers themselves directly from the participant or source usually from interviews, observation and surveys. Secondary data sources are those generated by others and includes newspapers, archives, videos, existing research, reports and documents, for review by the researcher, and many research projects draw on both sources.

Often researching a particular design sector will dictate and establish a consistent methodology for data collection, testing and analysis for a practice such as Gensler's workplace surveys and Gehl Architects' observational research. Collecting data on a longitudinal basis, as both of these practices demonstrate, requires consistent, replicable data collection building to a body of work that circumvents concerns regarding confidentiality by allowing the researcher to discuss larger issues and long-term trends. However, it is impossible to draw comparisons or identify trends across a body of work or project sector if the data is collected on an ad hoc basis. While the focus and information needs may change and evolve over time or even a project, it is beneficial to establish data collection protocols for longitudinal studies at the start of the project. One example of adapting a process is the census, where variations necessitated by changing lifestyles such as car ownership and internet access, are reflected in the questions posed while many of the questions like age and number of persons in the household, are consistent and appear on each edition.

Further reading

Creswell, J. W., & Creswell, J. D. (2017). *Research design: Qualitative, quantitative, and mixed methods approaches.* Oxford: Sage.
Fraser, M. (2013). *Design research in architecture: An overview.* Oxford: Routledge.
Groat, L., & Wang, D. (2013). *Architectural research methods.* London: Wiley.
Lucas, R. (2016). *Research methods for architecture.* London: Laurence King Publishing.
Vaughan, L. (2017). *Practice-based design research.* London: Bloomsbury.

5.4.1 Gathering data from people

With a profession that is focused on improving the human condition, it should not be surprising that engaging with different user groups is the most commonly employed data-gathering technique in architectural research for both academics and practitioners. There are four key techniques employed that are discussed below; they are, participant and naturalistic observation, interviews, roundtables and focus groups, and surveys and questionnaires. Used individually or in concert, each is deployed for different purposes and consequentially generates different data.

Participant and naturalistic observation

Allen defines participant observation as a

> process of entering a group of people with a shared identity to gain an understanding of their community... Through the experience of spending time with a group of people and closely observing their actions, speech patterns, and norms, researchers can gain an understanding of the group.
>
> (2017, p. 1187)

It is a method favoured by urbanists and William H. Whyte (1980), Jane Jacobs and Jan Gehl (see Chapter 8), and William Foote Whyte who moved to Boston to live among and observe the Italian community (2012). Originally published in 1943, his account of the process and findings has become the benchmark for participant observation where the observer is engaged or embedded with those being observed. Where this level of engagement is not feasible or desirable, remote observation, the sort of 'watching from afar' that we do when people watching while seated in a cafe, is referred to as naturalistic observation. As the researcher is removed from the group, in difficult circumstances avoids any risk to the researcher and reduces any influence the researcher may have over a group being observed.

The main purpose of participant observation is to understand how people use and interact in spaces. Researchers focus on patterns of movement and behaviours by different people or groups through and in a space, avoidance or engagement with other groups or individuals, and any impact this space may have on users and occupants. This can be a time-consuming process and can require more than one researcher and more than one visit. Small studies can focus on one particular group and one particular space with a contained timeframe, larger studies will include multiple viewing periods at various times of the day or night, on different days of the week or times of the year. The schedule is dictated by the groups the study intends to observe.

Regardless of the scale of the project, recording this data should comprise detailed note-taking including diagrams, and potentially filming or photographing the encounter. This would require the consent of those involved or, in the case of children or vulnerable adults, a third party, usually a responsible adult such as a parent, carer or teacher. Before commencing observation it is critical to identify and map out objectives. If the observation process takes place on private property, it is usual to seek permission to film or photograph from the property owner.

Further reading

Gehl, J., & Svarre, B. (2013). *How to study public life*. Washington, DC: Island Press. Iowa State University Library. (2020). *Library guides: Research methodologies guide: Participant observation*. Author.

Interviews

While this is the most commonly conducted data collection method, and a process that almost everyone will have participated in, in some form, it is worth noting some key considerations. First, where interviews are to be conducted in person, it is important to consider where the interviews will take place. Inviting an interviewee an individual in their own environment, whether that is their home, place of work, recreational or social space, may make them more comfortable and generate better responses. This also provides the researcher with the opportunity to observe the interviewee in that setting, offering discussion points. For example, if the purpose of the interview is to discuss housing conditions, it may be more productive to conduct the interview in a domestic location, using aspects of the home to lead and stimulate the discussion.

Constructing an interviewee list is the second issue requiring additional scrutiny. The occasions for which only one interviewee is required are exceptionally rare, so the challenge for researchers is in ensuring that their interviewees are drawn from a cross-section of the group of interest which will be dictated by the research question. Where clients specify groups, it is the role of the researcher to consider if that focus will deliver the responses and information required, and adjust accordingly. There are many examples in which key stakeholders, typically meaning those with a controlling or financial interest, have been the only interviewees to the exclusion of others. That all groups in society are provided the opportunity to present their point of view has become increasingly important. Identifying and connecting with groups and individuals is often a time-consuming process. There is a responsibility on the researcher to invest the effort in this, as the information shared by interviewees will inevitably shape the landscape of the research, its validity and applicability. Although a single research project cannot cover every aspect, unintentionally or deliberately limiting the interviewees only serves to limit the research and can impact its value.

The third point relates to interview questions. Questions for interviews should start with easy, comfortable subjects and move through to the more involved and taxing issues. They should be open-ended rather than leading, as this generates more valuable and interesting responses. The three main styles for interviewing are structured, where the questioning follows a specific list of questions closely, semistructured, in which the questions form a conversation, and unstructured, or a guided conversation around topics rather than specific questions. As a qualitative research process, interviewing requires the interviewer to control the direction of the conversation, ensuring that all the necessary questions are addressed, and respond to the answers to develop the conversation without interrupting or limiting the information shared by the interviewee.

Without extensive funding, large-scale interviewing is difficult to achieve and if responses from a large cross section of a community are required, questionnaires might be a more effective approach. Where there are barriers to conducting an interview face to face, interviews conducted via email, telephone or video link do not diminish the validity of the method. All interviewees should be provided with the questions prior to the interview to allow them to prepare and highlight any points of concern, and a Participation Information Statement (see Section 6.4).

The final consideration is the ethical conduct of the researcher, from selecting and contacting potential participants, through conducting the interview, to the presentation and sharing of the data. This includes recording the interview and all participants should be informed when they are being recorded. There are obvious benefits to recording an interview, including to improve accuracy when taking notes as it not always easy to take notes while trying to maintain a conversation with an interviewee. Each part of this process requires careful consideration and this, along with a section highlighting the additional attention when working with vulnerable people and children, is discussed in greater detail in Chapter Six.

Further reading

McGrath, C., Palmgren, P. J., & Liljedahl, M. (2019). Twelve tips for conducting qualitative research interviews. *Medical Teacher*, 41(9), 1002–1006.

McLeod, S. A. (2014). *The interview research method*. Simply Psychology.

Qu, S. Q., & Dumay, J. (2011). The qualitative research interview. *Qualitative Research in Accounting & Management*, 8(3), 238–264.

Rubin, H. J., & Rubin, I. S. (2012). *Qualitative interviewing: The art of hearing data*. Thousand Oaks, CA: Sage.

Roundtables and focus groups

The principal difference between interviews and focus groups is the number of people in a single session, and so many of the considerations discussed above are applicable here also. Focus groups and roundtables can be a time-effective method and useful when observing interactions within a group but transcribing and analysis is more time-consuming. Skilful session management by the researcher is required to ensure that both the conversation responds to the questions or points for discussion, and that everyone invited is afforded the opportunity to speak again requiring skilful management by the researcher. The number of people speaking can make note-taking a challenge and can be addressed by recording the session and limiting the number of participants in a group.

The most important aspect of this method is the group's composition and this should be considered from the outset. A balanced mix fosters trust and encourages engagement, while an imbalance can have the opposite effect. For example, in workplace analysis, holding focus groups by job role allows participants to share their experiences openly without fear of criticism by a manager.

Further reading

Breen, R. L. (2006). A practical guide to focus-group research. *Journal of Geography in Higher Education, 30*(3), 463–475.

New York Library Association. (2020). *Toolkit for conducting focus groups*. New York: Author.

Surveys and questionnaires

As a quantitative data collection method, surveys and questionnaires are commonly used to gauge responses from a larger number of people than is possible with interviews, it is an efficient process and can be conducted over the phone, in person, by post, email or online. The introduction of online survey tools, such as Survey Monkey, has made the construction, dissemination and analysis of this method far more accessible and can be replicated easily for longitudinal studies, in the same way as the census.

Questions in surveys can be closed, requiring short responses often with limited options provided, or open which includes empty boxes for respondents to complete. For both options, responses can be problematic. If too many questions are posed for either there is the risk that respondents will become disinterested, and either ignore or answer the remaining questions inaccurately or even abandon the questionnaire. The accuracy of responses can present an issue but a large number of survey responses can compensate for individual inaccuracies, bias or responses, and repeating questions, phrased differently, provides a point of comparison.

Without direct engagement with the researcher, response rates can be quite low in comparison to interviews or roundtables. A response rate of around a third is widely accepted as statistically significant but that depends on the number of people or households invited to participate in the first place. Where cosmetic companies, for example, announce that 94% of those surveyed agreed with the claim being promoted in the advertisement, it is worth noting that often their sample sizes are usually quite small, sometimes fewer than 50 people, raising questions about the validity of their claim.

Further reading

Emerald Publishing. (2020). *How to... use questionnaires effectively*. Author.

Harkness, J. A., Braun, M., Edwards, B., Johnson, T. P., & Lyberg, L. E. (2010). *Survey methods in multicultural, multinational, and multiregional contexts*. Hoboken, NJ: John Wiley & Sons.

McHanwell, S., Humphrey, R., & Appleby, J. C. (2006). *Guidelines for question- naire design and use*. Newcastle: Newcastle University.

5.4.2 Case studies

The case study is a qualitative research method that employs data from a wide range of sources to examine one case, or make comparisons between a small number of cases, the focus of which could be a single building, street, city, country, an individual, or community, and set in within a particular timeframe. Interviews, surveys, oral histories, census data, archival research, policy analysis, and site surveys are among some of the most commonly used data sources used in case studies, although this should be tied to each case and research question. Using such a broad selection of sources can be a time-consuming process but is a much-used approach for the depth of understanding brought to the case. Other benefits include its real-world context, making it appropriate for architectural research, and the multi-layered, inclusive approach that accommodates and accepts data that might be dismissed as weak or irrelevant by other methods.

Critics of this technique highlight that examining single cases prohibits or limits its generalisability, consequently invalidating the value of the research findings. Where the purpose of the research is to fully understand a single case, this point is irrelevant and the weight of the argument is diminished when multiple cases are examined to understand a particular issue, policy or phenomenon. When selecting a case study, their selection should be justified. When multiple case studies are employed, this explanation should identify their relevance to the research question or issue, and how they relate to one another.

Further reading

Baxter, P., & Jack, S. (2008). Qualitative case study methodology: Study design and implementation for novice researchers. *The Qualitative Report, 13*(4), 544–559.
Yin, R. K. (2003). *Case study research: Design and methods* (Vol. 5). Thousand Oaks, CA: Sage.

5.4.3 Archival data collection

Typically, archival research is the process of identifying and examining data primary resources collected and held by a third party such as a library, museum, historic societies, libraries, universities or government offices. While the name may conjure images of piles of dusty pages in cold stone libraries, the definition of archival material extends to include manuscripts, documents, electronic records, photographs, films, sound recordings, newspapers, magazines and other printed or physical material which could also be contemporary as age does not define an archive. The materials held by the RIBA Collections in London, for example, range from documents and watercolours by Andrea Palladio to the design archives of contemporary architects and their practices, donated throughout the twentieth century.

Archives can be a time-consuming resource to access, particularly when their contents are not available online as digitising collections is expensive and labour-intensive process. However, there is the fantastic prospect of discovering an item, document or image that has lain hidden for years that might expand the understanding of a particular field, resolve a design problem or present a precedent to prove an argument. In challenging the planning decisions for their new gallery for the Victoria and Albert Museum in London, AL_A uncovered archived drawings of the original Aston Webb screen fronting Exhibition Road that supported their design to remove parts of the later wall previously used to hide the boilers that no longer existed (V&A, 2020), opening access to the courtyard from the street (Figures 5.1 and 5.2).

Figure 5.1: The Sackler Courtyard featuring 11,000 handmade porcelain tiles, a new cafe, roof light above the new subterranean gallery space, and the restored Aston Webb Screen. © Hufton+Crow

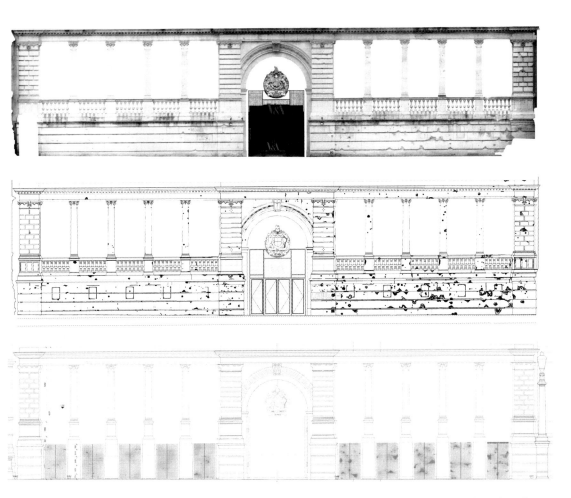

Figure 5.2: The transformation of the Aston Webb Screen. Previously obscuring the boiler house yard from view, the stone plinth was removed, replaced by metal gates that depict the bomb blast damage inflicted on the stonework, opening up the Sackler Courtyard to Exhibition Road. © AL_A

The cataloguing of items and collections can vary with different keywords and descriptions, sometimes making searching a challenging process that requires a creative process of refining and evolving search terms. Engaging the archivist or librarian attached to the collection is a helpful approach to overcoming both of these issues, making the process more efficient.

It is imperative that any researcher is aware of their own bias and that of the authors of the original document and mindful of any omissions. Historical accounts were not always created with future research in mind and can present a curated and narrow perspective of events.

Further reading

Schmidt, L. (2020). *Using archives: A guide to effective research.*
Tesar, M. (2015). Ethics and truth in archival research. *History of Education, 44*(1), 101–114.

5.4.4 Digital data

Digital design and use of digital data have become ubiquitous in practice, matched by increasingly sophisticated analytical software. It is common for practices to develop their own project-specific software, such as RAPIERe by Architype (see Section 8.4.1) and SPEED at Perkins&Will (Perkins&Will, 2020a), or develop smaller-scale projects such as Heartbit Walks by Flow Architecture (see Section 2.3).

Data in digital formats can arise from a multiplicity of sources including social media, online surveys, geographic data through Geographic Information Systems (GIS) software, post occupancy studies, and generated by architectural software packages. Collecting digital data can be an efficient process, particularly when using open-source data that has been collected by others and is already freely available or when conducting longitudinal research as the process can be easily replicated. The propensity is to collect vast amounts of information, although without sufficient resources this can raise challenges for its synthesis.

However, as Jurkiewicz (2018) discusses, this raises ethical concerns around the collection and use of digital data, noting that existing legal frameworks have failed and that "industry and professional ethical codes have not worked either" (s52). This is in part, a reflection of the pace at which technology is developing. It is imperative, therefore, that researchers make every effort to ensure that digital data is collected, analysed and stored ethically with protocols established at the outset of the project to the same standard as data collected by other means.

In late 2015, Transport for London ran a four-week pilot research project aimed at understanding how passengers navigate station platforms when switching tube lines, and how crowding develops. The project used WiFi connections data, collecting 509 million pieces of data from 5.6 million mobile devices taking 42 million journeys across 54 stations within Zones 1–4 (Transport for London, 2016). The results showed specifically how and where crowding occurs on platforms or around escalators, how people move around stations, and the variety of route options people took between stations. While digital ticketing data can identify station arrivals and departures, this offered an insight into passenger movements that could not have been achieved through other methods. This project allowed passengers to opt out of the research and consulted the Information Commissioner's Office, privacy campaigners and consumer groups to consider establishing a permanent data collection process across the entire Tube network and how this data could be shared with customers for ongoing research.

Further reading

Barns, S. (2018). Smart cities and urban data platforms: Designing interfaces for smart governance. *City, Culture and Society*, 12, 5–12.

Grey, T., Dyer, M., & Gleeson, D. (2017). Using big and small urban data for collaborative urbanism. *Citizen empowerment and innovation in the data-rich city* (pp. 31–54). Cham: Springer.

Kitchin, R. (2016). The ethics of smart cities and urban science. *Philosophical Transactions of the Royal Society A: Mathematical, Physical and Engineering Sciences*, 374(2083), 20160115.

5.5 Verifying data, dealing with false data and fake news, and triangulation

Reliability of data and the verifiability of sources have always been a problem for researchers. In the early 2000s, the highest profile source of inaccurate or false data was Wikipedia but this has been superseded by a global trade in deliberately false information disseminated through social media, blogs and alternative news sites. Although the phrase 'fake news' has been around since the late 1800s, its recent adoption into everyday conversation epitomises its escalation. However, identifying honest sources of information is not straightforward.

Media outlets such as *The Washington Post, New York Times, Sydney Morning Herald, The Guardian*, CNN and the BBC, are generally considered reliable sources of information but, as with all sources, all have a bias and filters. Before it is published, any data presented will have travelled through the article's author and at least one editor, each with their own perspective, contained within the interest and viewed through the lens of the organisation. Not only can information be misused and misinterpreted, but when an author or editor is focused on developing an article, some information may be diminished or excluded altogether if they are beyond the focus of the piece.

The further away from the original source data articles become, the greater the number of reinterpretations, and the more likely it is that the data will be misrepresented or inaccurately portrayed. This dilution of the impact of the original work or information is not the preserve of the news media and can occur with all secondary sources, emphasising the importance of locating the original source material. In addition to checking the original source, researchers should consider establishing the author's credibility, motivations and influences, and critically examining the quality of the original source data, research methodology, and funding sources. Funding sources can attach conditions that influence or limit the scope or direction of the research, potentially compromising its validity or applicability.

Twelve years after its publication, the medical journal *The Lancet* withdrew a paper published in 1998 that claimed the MMR vaccine had caused autism in children. Despite earlier concerns regarding the small sample size of only 12 children, it was the UK General Medical Council's discovery that the study was "funded by lawyers acting for parents who were involved in lawsuits against vaccine manufacturers", that prompted the discrediting of the research and its authors (Eggertson, 2010). In certain circumstances poorly conducted or unethical research can have far-reaching implications, and this case demonstrates the need to question funding sources, a statistically small study, and contrived participant selection.

Where it is not possible to validate a single study, or it is too specific or small, triangulation is another means by which data can be verified. The approach uses either multiple, independent data sources to verify a single fact, issue or piece of data. For example, the sources might agree that an event took place on a date in history or offer several versions of events on a particular day that the researcher needs to interpret. Searching for several sources that all state the same fact can be troublesome if, in the process, other conflicting studies are dismissed. Where sources do not confirm all aspects of an event, the variations should be included in the research for discussion.

Further reading

Hastings, S. L., & Salkind, N. J. (2010). Triangulation. *Encyclopaedia of Research Design*.
Morse, J. M., Barrett, M., Mayan, M., Olson, K., & Spiers, J. (2002). Verification strategies for establishing reliability and validity in qualitative research. *International Journal of Qualitative Methods*, 1(2), 13–22.

5.6 Analytical methods

5.6.1 Comparative analysis

Comparative analysis is the process of drawing on and analysing the similarities and differences between two or more phenomena, objects, locations, cases, etc., using primary or secondary data or combining both. There are four reasons for selecting this method. The first is to better understand the relationship between two cases such as the impacts of different housing policies between two neighbouring states. The second is to identify a key trend or identify a pattern by using multiple cases, clarifying, for example, the reasons for differences in housing vacancy rates between cities. The third is to establish whether the phenomenon in one case is relative only to that case and if that can be exported to influence another. For example, is the housing vacancy rate in one city due to specific policies that could be applied elsewhere, or do they only work in that circumstance for other reasons as economic, cultural or climatic? Finally, the fourth reason is to better understand the underlying causes of these similarities or differences, which may be economic, historic, social or political.

The strength of comparative analysis lies in the careful, considered selection of the cases to be examined presented with a clear defence of their inclusion in the study but this also presents the greatest challenges. Where the differences between the selected cases being compared are so significant and varied it makes it difficult to justify the comparison, with the possibility of invalidating the study. It would be difficult to make a comparison between contemporary British housing policy and its impacts and those of another country in another era, as the cultural, economic, political and geographic disparities are substantial.

Further reading

Pickvance, C. G. (2001). Four varieties of comparative analysis. *Journal of Housing and the Built Environment, 16,* 7–28.

Walk, K. (1998). *How to write a comparative analysis.* https://writingcenter.fas.harvard.edu/pages/how-write-comparative-analysis

5.6.2 Content analysis

Organising, sorting and identifying patterns in data derived from qualitative sources such as interviews and quantitative methods including questionnaires or other text-based artefacts, is referred to as content, thematic or textual analysis and used to demonstrate the significance of an issue by identifying the frequency with which predetermined words and phrases arise in the data. Although some authors may propose more (Castleberry and Nolen, 2018), the process of analysing the data can be broken down into four broad steps.

First is a familiarisation with the subject area in order to establish the categories or theories to be applied, leading to a list of words that are expected to arise. Counting words or phrases from surveys and interview transcripts using the prepared list is the second step. Also referred to as coding, it is typical for the list to expand at this point as new topics or synonyms arise. While for large data sets content analysis software may be an efficient process, manual analysis provides a more nuanced evaluation of the data, particularly where synonyms and colloquial phrasing might be overlooked by the software. Step three is the thematic categorising or mapping of words and phrases. Where word maps are used, the size of the text should represent the frequency with which words or phrases appear in the data. The final step reviews the data with a view to refining categories and drawing associations between groups and individual words and phrases to identify the most influential concepts and significant responses.

Further reading

Bengtsson, M. (2016). How to plan and perform a qualitative study using content analysis. *NursingPlus Open, 2*, 8–14.

Neuendorf, K. A. (2017). *The content analysis guidebook* (2nd ed.). Thousand Oaks, CA: Sage.

5.6.3 Gap analysis

As the name suggests gap analysis seeks to identify what is missing from a particular data set, inverting other analytical processes which establish the most common or most significant element, issue or response. It is the process that researchers apply when conducting a literature review to identify a missing aspect within existing knowledge that their work can address. Where this process is used to identify gaps in knowledge or awareness with interviewees or in historic documents, for example, the method is effectively the same as content analysis in that the researcher searchers for expected words or terms within the data, or missing links between two phenomena whose presence might be expected. It is also used regularly by businesses looking for an opportunity to innovate in a market or assess skills within the workplace and in environmental assessments of the building where comparisons are drawn between the expected and actual data, identifying the gaps.

Further reading

Robinson, J. F., Foxon, T. J., & Taylor, P. G. (2015). Performance gap analysis case study of a non-domestic building. *Proceedings of the Institution of Civil Engineers-Engineering Sustainability, 169*(1), 31–38.

Robinson, K. A., Akinyede, O., Dutta, T., Sawin, V. I., Li, T., Spencer, M. R.,... Weston, C. (2013). *Framework for determining research gaps during systematic review: Evaluation methods report.* Rockville, MD: Agency for Healthcare Research and Quality.

5.6.4 Social network analysis

Predating the digital social networks and their applications by around 70 years, social network analysis (SNA) identifies the connections and relationships between actors or nodes, and the power and influence exerted by each, knowledge flows between them, and the patterns generated. Used across several fields including biology, politics, sports science and criminology, this is an effective tool to explore decision making in the built environment, explaining why, for example, community groups may be unlikely to influence planning outcomes, how protest groups organise and mobilise, and assess whether those making decisions actually wield the influence we assume they do.

This is multi-method analysis can include data collected from participant observation, focus groups, interviews, news media, and archive material, used to identify and understand individual participants, identify relationships and knowledge flows. This process can be conducted manually for a qualitative approach or quantitatively using specific SNA and data visualisation software that can analyse patterns in large data sets. Typically, data for both the qualitative and quantitative is mapped with data visualisation software used to generate graphic representations of complex networks.

Further reading

Sailer, K., & McCulloh, I. (2012). Social networks and spatial configuration— How office layouts drive social interaction. *Social Networks, 34*(1), 47–58.

Yang, S., Keller, F. B., & Zheng, L. (2016). *Social network analysis: Methods and examples.* Thousand Oaks, CA: Sage.

5.6.5 Policy analysis

As a profession that is defined by often complex and interconnected government policies, policy analysis is often a starting point for research in practice, with housing policy a global concern both with practice and academia (Maina, 2014; ZCD Architects, 2016). Policy analysis may be conducted in six steps. First, define the problem then, second, the evaluation criteria. The third and fourth steps identify and then evaluate alternative policies, after which the final steps involve selecting and then implementing the preferred policy (Patton, Sawicki, & Clark, 2013). Where an alternative policy isn't apparent, an obvious option would be to propose amendments to existing or new policies. It is typical for researchers to identify and include alternative policies drawn from other countries or sectors as an alternative or to provide context to the discussion.

Narrative Policy Analysis uses responses from interviews and focus groups to evaluate the value and success of complex policies and better understand the debates surrounding them (Hampton, 2009; Roe, 1994), and depending on the data, operate at three levels. First, the micro-level uses narratives from a range of sources including media interviews or surveys, meso-level is concerned with policy actors such as politicians, groups and organisations, and finally, the macro-level narrative operates at the large, conceptual scale, focussing on historic events, cultural and political debates (Shanahan et al., 2018). The process is not dissimilar to Content Analysis (see above), in which key themes and issues are identified or coded, drawing out the connection between individuals and policies, and their motivations responses to the policy.

Further reading

Browne, J., Coffey, B., Cook, K., Meiklejohn, S., & Palermo, C. (2019). A guide to policy analysis as a research method. *Health Promotion International, 34*(5), 1032–1044.

Open University. (2020). *An introduction to technology and innovation policy research: Narrative policy analysis.* Retrieved January 16, 2020, from https://www.open.edu/openlearncreate/mod/oucontent/view.php?id=13636&section=5.1

Weimer, D. L., & Vining, A. R. (2017). *Policy analysis: Concepts and practice.* Oxford: Taylor & Francis.

5.6.6 Post occupancy evaluation

POE refers to the collection and analysis of data that, as discussed in Chapter 2, reviews both a building's performance and the organisational use of the space, using a mixed-methods approach that compares the findings to predetermined indicators. Evaluating building performance employs predominately quantitative data collection through a range of specialist sensors measuring temperature, humidity, lighting, acoustic performance, water use, air quality including CO_2 and VOC levels, ventilation, energy consumption, and structural movement in the building (Candido et al., 2016), with occupant surveys, interviews, focus groups and surveys (Barlex, 2006; Vischer, 2001) lending a richer understanding of the building and its use, and explaining anomalies in the data.

Qualitative POE methods are frequently used in commercial settings and educational facilities to establish the wellbeing and organisational benefits of the space through questionnaires, interviews and focus groups, and often conducted separately to evaluating the environmental performance of the building (Sailer, Pomeroy, & Haslem, 2015). Questions focus on perceptions, productivity, satisfaction with the space, its design including its fixtures, comfort levels including thermal, light, acoustics and air quality, and overall working practices.

Further reading

Leaman, A., Stevenson, F., & Bordass, B. (2010). Building evaluation: Practice and principles. *Building Research & Information, 38*(5), 564–577.
Stevenson, F. (2019). Embedding building performance evaluation in UK architectural practice and beyond. *Building Research & Information, 47*(3), 305–317.

5.6.7 Spatial analysis

Also referred to as geospatial or geographical analysis, spatial analysis uses quantitative data to generate maps, graphs and other statistics with the aim of identifying patterns, and understanding existing and predicting future relationships between objects. This method has been adopted for use in urban design, urban development, ecology and environmental studies, migration studies, geography, healthcare and crime analysis.

Data sources can include mobile devices, social media sites, photographs and videos, location and tracking sensors, questionnaires, observation studies, patient and school records, traffic and census data, and species population distribution, to create graphs, maps and plans that explore social, political and economic dynamics, and identify their relationships, patterns and anomalies, and reflect on their relationship to space.

Analyses can be complex, using software including GIS, and different mathematical models and methods to collecting analyse the data which can then be applied at macro, meso and micro scales to understand whole cities (Abrantes et al., 2019; Cheng & Masser, 2003) or scaled down to assess a smaller space at street level (Jalaladdini & Oktay, 2012; Yoon & Srinivasan, 2015).

Further reading

Cappelli, C. (2013). *The language of spatial analysis.* New York: Esri. https://www.esri.com/library/books/the-language-of-spatial-analysis.pdf
Fotheringham, A. S., & Rogerson, P. A. (Eds.). (2008). *The SAGE handbook of spatial analysis.* Thousand Oaks, CA: Sage.

5.6.8 Space syntax

Established at the Space Syntax Laboratory at The Bartlett School of Architecture at University College London, space syntax is the urban analysis research method based on mathematical algorithms and geospatial computer technology and developed by Bill Hillier and Julienne Hanson that seeks to understand the links between human behaviour, movement patterns, and spatial layouts (Hillier & Hanson, 1989). This method has been applied to identify the influence of design on security, the relationship between spatial segregation and social disadvantage, land densities, and land values, and the organisational cultures of buildings (Space Syntax Network, 2020a).

A scaleable process, it can be applied to individual rooms, buildings or streets (Kishimoto & Taguchi, 2014; Sailer & Thomas, 2019; Van Nes & López, 2007) to entire cities (Major, 2018; Serra & Pinho, 2013). The method uses data from interviews, ethnographic analysis, building function analysis, and spatial assessments overlaid onto observation and tracking patterns of pedestrian movements through and behaviours within a space to create maps at different scales. Software designed specifically for the use of this approach is available on the Space Syntax website (Space Syntax Network, 2020b).

Further reading

Sailer, K., & McCulloh, I. (2012). Social networks and spatial configuration— How office layouts drive social interaction. *Social Networks, 34*(1), 47–58.
Space Syntax Laboratory. (2020). *Space Syntax – Online training platform.* The Bartlett, University College London. https://www.spacesyntax.online
UCL. (2020). *Journal of Space Syntax.* http://joss.bartlett.ucl.ac.uk/index.php/joss/

5.7 Writing up and image selection

The structure for writing up a piece of research comprises five components: the context of the research; the questions, arguments and aims to be posed and debated; the research data, its sources and collection; the analysis of the data; and the research findings and their significance. Where the work requires a lengthy written response, it can be beneficial to set out the purpose of the research, such as its aims, questions or the problem to be addressed, at the start to frame the discussion that follows.

  As the introduction sets up the publication for the reader, with the following text and images exploring this in greater detail, this should be the last section to be written. As such, it is much easier to write this at the end of the writing process when the rest of the publication and the conclusions have been worked out. The introduction does not need to be lengthy but should reflect all of the components of the work, setting out the aims, how they fit within the context of the literature, the methods and data used, and the significance of the work. The findings and their implications should be discussed in the conclusion.

5.7.1 Background and context to the research

Referring to research or built work demonstrates an understanding of the scope of existing research and knowledge of the industry, and the gaps that research by others can address. This section provides the foundation upon which to build an argument by discussing the key issues and themes relevant to the research and how the project relates to the field. All publications, websites and work cited in this and later sections, should be referenced in a bibliography, reference list or footnotes.

5.7.2 Research arguments, questions and project aims

The second part should present the questions that have arisen from the existing literature and practice knowledge, the arguments to be debated, and the overall and specific aims of the research project. Usually, this section requires a short introduction, a list of questions relative to the scope of the project. It is feasible to have both questions and aims for a project as these serve different purposes. The questions, aims and arguments should be focussed, clearly articulated, and address the problems they seek to resolve. Including too many questions or aims risks diluting the depth and quality of the work to be carried out, the outcomes, and its impact.

5.7.3 Data sources and research methodology

The third section identifies data sources and discusses and justifies the research methods employed to collect and analyse the data. This should include a review of the primary and secondary data sources, where relevant, and why they were selected against other options, and how they address the research questions and aims. If any ethical concerns related to the data collection, and its later use, were raised they should be discussed here along with the measures taken to address those issues.

5.7.4 Data analysis and findings

Following on from the discussion of the research methods and data sources, the fourth section should present the findings of the data, including a discussion of any challenges experienced, analysis of the data, and how that relates to and answers the research aims, questions and hypotheses set out above.

It is as important to examine what the data does not show and the problems experienced as the positive side. These can include low response rates to invitations to participate in interviews or questionnaires, data that didn't provide the anticipated result, and inaccessible or inaccurate data. This demonstrates an ethical approach to handling the data and allows other researchers to continue your work, develop new strategies or technologies, or uncover alternative data sources that could advance knowledge in the field.

5.7.5 Conclusions, impacts and significance

This section addresses the aims and research questions presented at the start, discusses the potential impact of the work, its relevance to the wider industry and beyond, who might benefit from this research, and where this work might continue. This section should not include any new data or findings but reflect on that already presented in the previous section of the publication. Any impact and broader significance that has already been established or anticipated, such as ongoing research or presentations, should be included here.

5.7.6 Image selection

The role of images in research publication differs from that of design work. Each image should be included to illustrate a concept or finding, or communicate data or the research process, and should earn its place in the work rather than being illustrative. As image rights and production can be expensive, particularly when using colour or a large number of images that increase the number of pages, many publications and publishers will place a limit on the number of images. It is not usual for additional restrictions to be in place for the use of colour. Many academic journals will publish in colour for an online edition but only in black and white for the print version unless additional charges are levied for colour images in print. So understanding what each image adds to the research and its communication and which reproduce well in monochrome, will aid the image selection process.

5.8 Conclusions

This chapter aimed to set out the key processes, methods, data sources, and referencing protocols, while highlighting the benefits, challenges and potential solutions, illustrated with case studies and reading recommendations. This is by way of introduction to the research process and its components. As a profession focussed on improving the built environment for communities and visitors, there is a great focus on the practice of data gathering from people and drawing on historic references and archives, so the methods presented here reflect this as well including some of the more technical analysis methods. The component parts of a research project are likely to vary with every project, but the process and rigour with which it is conducted are paramount, not only as a means of adding value to knowledge within the studio and the value that research can have for design work, but also for its potential to attract funding and R&D tax relief and for its contribution to wider industry knowledge.

Chapter Six
_____

Research ethics

6.1 Introduction

Ethical conduct has an established role in architectural practice. In their Code of Ethics and Professional Conduct, the American Institute of Architects asserts that "[m]embers should continually seek to raise the standards of aesthetic excellence, architectural education, research, training, and practice" (AIA Office of General Counsel, 2020). In practice this includes mentoring students and young architects, pro bono work and work for charitable organisations, advocating for and delivering sustainable development (United Nations General Assembly, 2015; Webster-Mannison, 2013), and establishing and maintaining ethical supply chains including both people and products, respectful relationships with clients, inclusive and supportive working environments (Johnson & Gore, 2016; RIBA, 2019; The Ethics Centre, 2019; Wasserman, Sullivan, & Palermo, 2000).

This chapter discusses how those ethical practices and codes extend to include research practices and protocols, both to the benefit of the researcher and their practice and to research participants (Iphofen, 2016). Ethics in research spans a wide range of issues including the origins of research funding, the collection, use and storage of data, every aspect of engaging with interviewees, particularly vulnerable adults and children.

6.2 Established research ethics

The most extensive research ethics frameworks, protocols and guidelines have been established by universities and the agencies that fund their work, to ensure that research is conducted to consistently high standards and that the rights of those that participate and conduct research are protected. All academic institutions have ethics panels or committees to which academic researchers and students must apply for approval before commencing any research that involves interviews or participation. However, they are not exhaustive and cannot plan for every eventuality and, particularly in practice, need to be tailored to each project.

> Research projects are designed and thought through in advance; getting ethical clearance is part of the process. My impression when completing our ethics application for our work... was that the process of gaining institutional ethical clearance fails to prepare us for unexpected or complex situations: the muddles, or mess, of human interactions, the dilemmas posed by 'everyday ethics'.
>
> (Rendell & Padan, 2019, p. 6)

Although ethics applications are unlikely to cover every situation, compiling such a document will have established protocols and processes that allow researchers to respond to unforeseen situations in an ethical manner.

As Israel and Hay (2006) have identified, the approach to research ethics varies between countries. Those that are 'top-down' include the United States, Canada, Australia and Norway with government bodies and research agencies setting out research and ethics protocols while a 'bottom-up' approach is followed in the United Kingdom, New Zealand, South Africa and Denmark.

> Professional organisations and individual institutions (and even individual researchers in the case of Denmark) drive a multiplicity of ethical approaches. However, recent developments in South Africa and the United Kingdom suggest a shift away from 'bottom-up' arrangements to more uniform national regulation.
>
> (Israel & Hay, 2006, p. 40)

Aside from the drivers, funding agencies for each country are consistent in their expectations of ethics and their application throughout the research process. For practices familiar with risk assessments and internal codes of documents, ethics applications are likely to be an extension of those documents and processes.

6.3 Applying for ethics approval

Within academic environments, ethics approval is required for all research "that involves human participants; their tissue and /or data to ensure that the dignity, rights, safety and well-being of all participants are the primary consideration of the research project" (Imperial College London, 2020). Although it is unlikely that architectural research will include the use of human tissue, many research projects involve some form of participant engagement and will therefore require a review of ethical procedures. The process of gaining ethics approval for research activity is less common outside of academia. All academic institutions have research offices staffed by experts in submitted research applications to funding agencies and applying for ethics approval. While university partners or their research office are likely to take responsibility for the completion and submission of the application to their ethics committee for collaborative projects, external parties are still expected to contribute to that process. For example, any external agency intending to engage University College London is required "to ensure that the research is of the same ethical standards as that carried out by UCL staff and students" which includes submitting copies of the ethics documentation (UCL, 2020a), and any graduate architecture or PhD student based in practice will be responsible for submitting their own ethics application. This approach is not unusual.

Typically, the application process involves a detailed application form and statement submitted to a specialist ethics committee, which will either accept or reject the proposal, request amendments or seek clarifications before making a final decision. This can be a lengthy process particularly if committees meet infrequently. Although application requirements, such as the details and length of each section, vary between institutions and funding bodies, most should be expected to cover the following information.

- Basic details of the project including title, anticipated start and finish dates.
- A synopsis of the project that states the need for the research, details of the methodology, and analytical approach.
- Details relating to any case study locations used in the research and the justi-fication for their selection.
- Information about all researchers involved in the application including a nominated lead, or principal researcher, and their contact details.

- Details about any collaborations connected to the research, the extent of their role in the project, and their contact details.
- Details of any and all funding agencies supporting the project, their contact details, the value applied for, or awarded, and the progress of that decision.
- How and where the findings will be disseminated, including conference and other presentations, exhibitions, reports, academic and conference papers, articles for industry publications, and social media content.
- A statement of the ethical implications of the project including details about participants such as the number of participants, their ages, participants considered to be vulnerable and measures established to protect them, a description indicating what might upset or negatively impact a participant and measures in place to address this, their likely motivations to participate and benefits for doing so, and whether there will be any further engagement following the completion of the project. Any remuneration or compensation afforded to participants should be detailed also.
- Details of how permissions and consent will be sought from participants, and copies of letters used for invitations including interview questions.

Further consideration may be required regarding how data will be recorded, particularly if this includes photographs, video and sound recordings, and how the data will be stored as well as the security of that storage system, protocols in place should there be a data breach, who will have access to the data, how long it will be retained and how it will be disposed of. Reference should also be made to any relevant legal documents or acts this applies to. This list of typical requirements would be relevant for consideration by practice seeking to establish in-house research ethics protocols and guide-lines. Examples of ethics application forms can be found on most university websites.

Practices that have collaborated with university researchers raised three challenges that they have faced in the ethics process. The first was in identifying the level of risk posed by the research process to the parties involved although, typically, this applied only to first proposals. Where concerns were discussed and addressed with the academic partner, this was not reported to have been an ongoing issue. Where multiple collaborators were involved, the second point of concern related to identifying the lead party in the project who typically carries any risk identified. This was addressed through relevant insurance cover and clear delineation of roles and responsibilities in the project, often with a written agreement or contract. The final matter of concern, achieving approvals from an academic Ethics Board within a timeframe that aligned with the design process, created a persistent challenge. The most effective method of addressing all scheduling concerns when working with universities is, as discussed earlier in Section 3.3, to identify the university schedules. This is obviously less problematic when joining a university research project that has already obtained ethics approval, or for research that is not linked to a design project.

6.4 Interview ethics

6.4.1 Identifying potential participants

In drawing up lists of potential interviewees, there are five points to take into consideration.

- Determine how many participants are required, including additional candidates to compensate for the inevitability that not everyone will accept the invitation to participate. The anticipated rejection rate for a questionnaire can be as high as 65% but is usually lower, around 30%, for interviews. If those being interviewed are part of a group, for example, a school class or employee group, it is worth debating whether additional groups are required for comparative purposes, and whether they will offer sufficient responses for the data required.
- Provide a clear justification for the selection of these individuals or groups. Where groups are to be used, consideration should be given to the selection of that group with shared characteristics, such as age, gender, location, etc., or whether a greater cross section is required. In some circumstances it is helpful in the recruitment of participants, to include details of the selection process so that participants understand why they have been selected.
- Any contact details including telephone numbers and email addresses obtained through former engagement, such as a previous and separate research project or when employed by a different organisation, should not be used unless explicit permission has been granted or they exist in the public domain such as a website or social media profile.

- When issuing an open call for responses, through social media platforms or distributed by a third party, for example, it is important to acknowledge that those who self-select may not be able to provide all of the information you require or their bias may skew the data. Where this occurs it should be reflected in the data gathering and analysis with the methods adapted accordingly (see Chapter Five).
- Digital engagement has addressed, although not entirely resolved, many of the problems with engagement. Two key issues remain. As some sectors in society may have restricted or no access to the internet or are not used to using online resources. Where surveys are distributed electronically, but only one response is required per household, it is possible for respondents to circumvent these restrictions given the prevalence of multiple digital devices in households. There are measures that can be adopted to address these, sending invitations by email that permit only one response or hosting group sessions for example. Where this is not possible, statistical variations should be adopted that account for this.

6.4.2 Contacting potential participants

In the first instance, particularly when the interviewee is unknown to the researcher, sending an introductory email can elicit a more positive response. This email should include brief details regarding the project including the title of the research project, the names of team leaders and their affiliations, what information is being sought and how this will be used to contribute to the objectives of the research, and why they are being invited to take part. If links to previous, relevant projects and publications are available these should be included also. Once the invitation has been accepted, this should be followed by a more detailed email including the Participant Information Statement.

A Participant Information Statement details an interviewee's rights, the interviewer's obligations, how their information will be used and stored and complies with any legal, ethical, institutional and funding obligations. All communications should be concise and clearly written, information sheets should avoid abbreviations where practicably possible, jargon or technical terminology. The information sheet should be dated and state that the participant will be given a copy of the information sheet and a signed consent form to keep.

The Participant Information Statement should include;

- your contact details at the practice including your position, the names of all other research team members and their affiliations.
- an outline of the research project, including the title of the research project, its context, the research methods being used, the project's duration, and who is funding the work.
- the purpose of the research.
- when the session(s) is (are) to occur and, therefore, by when the participant should respond to the invitation.
- details of the use of data, who will have access to it, how it will be stored, whether it will be treated as confidential, and whether data will be anonymised. For example, "All the information that we collect about you during the course of the research will be kept strictly confidential. You will not be able to be identified in any reports or publications."
- if the session is to be recorded, what equipment is to be used, whether this will be used or broadcast in which case an additional consent form may be required that details how and where the broadcast will occur, such as at a conference or on a website or via social media.
- identify whether additional support for the participants is required and who, a family member, support worker or teacher, for example, would fulfil that role.
- what the output of the research will be and where it will be published, such as the practice website, industry publications, report, academic or conference paper, etc.
- a sentence or two stating why the participant is being invited, how they and other invitees were selected.
- an indication of the duration of participation and number of sessions, if applicable.
- an outline of what will happen at the session, such as one to one interview, roundtable discussion, or walking tour.
- a synopsis of the interview questions or discussion topics or a list of the questions.
- an indication either to the participant or others of any risks or benefits to participating.
- whether this research will, or may, be used for additional research. If this is the case then this should be explicit on the participant consent form.

- a note if are you including refreshments such as lunch and covering any costs such as travel expenses.
- specify whether any payment, voucher or benefit will be offered for participation. This is not always an option and some funding agencies and universities prohibit what may be interpreted as incentives, as they can be considered to unduly influence participants.
- information about the staff members the participants will encounter and their affiliations.

The Statement should be clearly stated that participation is voluntary and their agreement to participate can be withdrawn at any time without having to provide any justification and that they can seek further information or clarification on any aspect of the process at any point. This is particularly pertinent as some individuals and members of a group can feel pressured to participate.

6.4.3 The interview

While conducting the interview there are three key ethical considerations. First, is the location in which the interview will take place. Interviews should take place in locations that accommodate any access requirements for both the interviewer and interviewee (Halej, 2017). Some interviewees may be more comfortable in a space they know well, such as their own home, but this may in turn raise safety concerns for the interviewer. For some projects, it is advantageous to the researcher to conduct the interviews in a location that is the focus of the project, as the environment can be employed as part of the discussion. The second issue is concerned with the participant's welfare, namely that they are comfortable with the environment in which the interview is taking place, with the process, the interviewer, and recording of responses. The final concern relates to the safety and well-being of the interviewer. This highlights any issues that might jeopardise their safety when undertaking an interview. This might include, for example, the decision to employ two researchers to conduct an interview where the location is a private dwelling or remote location. The contact details of interviewees and a list of locations should be lodged with a colleague, usually another member of the research team.

6.5 Working with vulnerable groups and children

The legal definition of vulnerable people centres on adults with physical or mental disabilities, have a substance dependency issue, those in custody, resident in a healthcare facility or sheltered accommodation (ACNC, 2020; HM Government, 2006; Minnesota Legislature, 2019). In social sciences research, this is often expanded to include any individual or group who may feel unduly pressured into participating and includes, but is not limited to, the homeless, elderly people, refugees and ethnic minorities, or any group where there is an imbalance of power with the interviewer or third party.

As the Economic and Social Research Council (ESRC) continues,

[v]ulnerability may be defined in different ways and may arise as a result of being in an abusive relationship, vulnerability due to age, potential marginalisation, disability, and due to disadvantageous power relationships within personal and professional roles. Participants may not be conventionally 'vulnerable', but may be in a dependent relationship that means they can feel coerced or pressured into taking part, so extra care is needed to ensure their participation is truly voluntary.

(ESRC, 2020)

The ESRC considers a more robust review of research involving vulnerable people or groups, including children and young people, including those with a learning disability or cognitive impairment, should be conducted and that "vulnerability should be considered on a case-by-case basis" (ESRC, 2020). It is critically important to acknowledge and address this when seeking consent for participation in research projects.

Besides a review of documentation and records relating to children, active research involving children is likely to be either observational analysis or participatory research. When engaging in participatory research, the National Society for the Prevention of Cruelty to Children (NSPCC) in the United Kingdom identifies four aspects of potential harm that should be addressed, stating that "individuals can find participating in research stressful, especially if they are vulnerable; hidden or suppressed feelings or memories may be uncovered; additional concerns may come up; and participants may worry about what they have shared" (NSPCC, 2020). In some cases, these anxieties may be mitigated by interviewing in a group, in a familiar environment, or with a trusted adult nearby.

Where a child is under the legal age for consenting to participate in a research process, a guardian or parent will be required to provide this consent on top of any discussion with the child regarding the research to be conducted. Skånfors (2009) suggests that researchers should also be aware of any signals, particularly non-verbal signals, a child may express in wanting to withdraw from the process. Powell, Taylor, Fitzgerald, Graham, and Anderson (2013) propose a seven point charter for ethical research involving children that stipulates that a child's "consent must always be sought, alongside parental consent and̸ [that] indications of children's dissent or withdrawal must always be respected."

Many architecture practices will already have experience working with vulnerable groups and children as participants in design and participation in research through the collection of data using cameras, mobile phones, drawing and writing. Of those actively involved in engaging with children and young people for their projects, none reported having to provide formal ethics statements, but all stated that this was an issue that was overdue for consideration. The only exception to this was the occasion of a collaboration with an academic institution. However, there is a distinction to be made between this activity and the observation or participation of children as part of a research project which will alter the necessity and extent to which ethics responses are required. Fiona MacDonald, Co-Founder of educational design and engagement specialists Matt+Fiona, questions whether there is "any distinction [between being observed and a participant] from the child's perspective" suggesting that at least an awareness of ethical concerns with children, and other vulnerable groups, should always be considered when working in relevant sectors. A practice's code of conduct documentation may cover these issues including vulnerable person and child protection policies, as well as specifically identifying a duty of care to those participating in the research.

6.6 Data storage and management

The secure storage and management of all data collected during the research process should be afforded the same consideration as the practice of gathering data. Summers and Corti (2020) discuss the perils of failing to establish and adhere to sound data storage and management protocols, citing cases in which data was lost due to fire, failure to create secure copies and degraded digital hardware, and occasions when portable flash drives holding sensitive UK government data was lost and then discovered in public places. Besides the data collected during the research process, protocols for data storage should extend to personal information including names, addresses, professional affiliations, social media profiles, and other contact information compiled throughout the research period, even for those who, ultimately, did not participate in the project.

To establish secure data storage and management, there are six key questions to address.

1. How will participant data be collected and recorded?

   When conducting interviews and recording them, there exists in most countries a legal obligation to inform the participant and, if relevant, their carer, support worker, parent or teacher, that they are being recorded. This applies also to creating photographs, video and sound recordings in which participants are included.

2. How will the information be stored?

   Best practice in data storage recommends producing a copy of each item and storing each collection in separate locations. For digital data, there are several alternatives including small portable storage devices, networks or remote or cloud-based options. Of these, concerns remain for cloud-based storage for the security of a site and the potential that the site could close, terms could change, and access be restricted or blocked completely. The preservation of hard copies including paper-based material, photographs should be considered along with storage conditions that avoid direct sunlight, humidity and dramatic temperature changes. While there are obvious space advantages to digitising all data, hard copies of original sources can be more stable and last longer than digital copies. Where possible, original data should be preserved particularly where this includes historic artefacts. The costs of data storage and preservation should be included in any project budget.

3. Who will have access to that data?

   If the research project is a collaboration or employs contractors it is necessary to clearly define who will have access to that data after the completion of the project and under what circumstances, and when and who will subsequently inherit the data, and when that handover will occur.

4. What protocols are in place should there be a data breach?

The access, theft, accidental sharing, or unauthorised alterations made to data are all considered a breach of data. Depending on location and field of work it may also be necessary to report the data breach to an official body such as the UK's Information Commissioner's Office. This is a requirement for any organisation collecting data in the EU and is subject to General Data Protection Regulation (GDPR) regardless of the location of the researcher, and breaches much be reported to the relevant authorities within 72 hours of the breach being detected. It is necessary, therefore, to establish who is to be informed of the breach, how they will be contacted, of what they will be informed, the implications of this, and any identified solution. Appointing a data protection officer within the practice, who will be a point of contact for participants and collaborators should a breach occur, will help support this process.

5. How long will the data be retained?

Funding bodies and universities adopt specific guidelines detailing data retention periods which will have implications for collaborative projects but with the rapid accumulation of digital data in practice and space in studios at a premium, it is worth considering what data should be retained and for how long and what can be disposed of and when.

6. How will the data be disposed of?

Hard copies of documents should be destroyed by shredding or burning, while digital documents, wherever they exist, should be erased used specific software.

Research institutes, universities and funding bodies have established protocols relating to specific aspects of seeking consent, privacy notices, data storage, ownership, deletion dates, and data breach conventions to which all collaborating parties will be expected to adhere.

6.7 Plagiarism, copyright and referencing

Plagiarism is defined as "presenting someone else's work or ideas as your own, with or without their consent, by incorporating it into your work without full acknowledgement" (University of Oxford, 2020). However, there are two forms, that which is deliberate and intended to mislead, and that which is unintentional and arises from missing referencing and citation indicators either through lack of care, awareness or misunderstanding. With the high standards of professionalism across the architecture industry it is more likely that where plagiarism occurs, it is unintentional usually because either text, an image, or other data has not been correctly referenced. Every photograph, table, drawing, sketch or illustration, should include in footnotes or endnotes, or as a list of image sources at the end of a document, the name of the copyright owner for each item used.

Copyright is afforded

> automatically to authors of original literary, musical, visual, dramatic, artistic and other creative works and productions — to control copying, and therefore exploitation and activities such as publishing and posting on the web, of their works. This includes books, articles, reports, poetry, plays, music, paintings, photographs, illustrations, sculptures, text messages, games, web pages, videos and computer programs.
>
> (British Copyright Council, 2019)

In most instances, copyright "endures for a term consisting of the life of the author and 70 years after the author's death" (U.S. Copyright Office, 2020). Although there are exemptions, including non-commercial research, teaching or when conducting a review, it is important therefore that permission to reproduce the item is sought from the copyright owner and this may incur charges depending on the publication and copyright owner.

Established in 2001, Creative Commons is a not-for-profit organisation based in the United States that provides six licenses allowing creators of images, music, reports, research data, books, videos and educational materials to share their work without charge to the user. While a Creative Commons licence grants the user permission to reproduce, distribute or use the selected material for free, it should still receive a formal attribution in the same way as a copyrighted item.

Where quotations are included in a section of writing or citations have been used in support of a statement made, both should be referenced in the text and then in a bibliography or reference list at the end of the document. As is discussed in greater detail in the previous chapter, including referencing style guides, appropriately referenced research demonstrates a knowledge of the field and intent to contribute further to the understanding of the subject area. It is required when applying for research funding, particularly in relation to academic funding applications, and for R&D claims where statements discussing the context or background to the research proposed are essential.

6.8 Conclusions

This chapter is intended to highlight some of the ethical considerations for researchers in practice and where they exist across all aspects of the research process. While the foundation of research ethics protocols and application processes may lie with universities and academic funding bodies, they, along with guidance presented by professional architecture bodies and network organisations, such as the United Nations Development Program, can provide the frameworks for practices to establish their own, extending existing codes of conduct, particularly where they relate to engagement with stakeholders and community groups. Most practices will have in place data security measures for their design work and information relating to clients, collaborators, contracts and colleagues, although the specificity of funding, and some government, agencies can require exacting detail. Responding to requests for such information requires an awareness of security concerns and a straightforward strategy for approaching them and responding to breaches. A recognition of unintentional plagiarism through a lack of correct referencing and copyright is a matter of increasing concern as the internet and social media make sharing unattributed images and data easier than it ever has been. It is incumbent on all researchers, therefore, to take all necessary steps to ensure that all work is appropriately attributed to its creator, which will in addition meet the expectations set out by R&D tax agencies and all funding bodies, both academic and professional.

Chapter Seven
_____

Publishing your research

7.1 Introduction

Publishing research work, and particularly findings, can be a contentious issue for practice. This is exacerbated where time is a limiting factor, resources are scarce or there are concerns about a client's response, confidentiality or loss of proprietary knowledge that are expected to diminish the competitive advantage. There are, however, four key motivations for publishing practice-based research; to demonstrate expertise, win new clients, to share the outcomes of their work with a wider audience across the built environment industry and academia. As Tom Dollard of Pollard Thomas Edwards notes, "[i]t is important that architects understand how important research is, and the significance of marketing and disseminating that research." This chapter discusses the options for disseminating research through self-publishing, traditional book publishers, and academic sources, along with the traditional territory of exhibitions, industry publications, and exhibitions, supported by content creation for practice websites and social media accounts, and the processes of capturing and managing research knowledge for use within practice.

   To determine the best publication option is it worth asking five questions.

1. Who is the intended audience?
2. What does the publication hope to achieve?
3. How will it be used?
4. How long will it be required?
5. When will the information be updated?

7.2 Knowledge capture and management in practice

As Kayaçetin and Tanyer note, "[k]nowledge is a critical factor in choosing the right projects, preparing the winning bids and successfully realizing projects" (2009, p. 279), and documenting, disseminating and managing that knowledge becomes critical for that success. As Kayaçetin and Tanyer discovered, many architecture practices, including many of those profiled in Chapter Eight, share their research and knowledge with colleagues at regular in-house presentation sessions. This not only forms the primary path for knowledge dissemination between projects but also forms a key part of training and induction for recent graduates and new recruits. Australian practice Hayball hosts monthly 'CONNECT sessions' orientated to providing professional development, while White Arkitekter collates research outputs and project updates for presentations that tour their studios across Scandinavia and beyond.

Less commonplace is the written documentation of research projects for an internal audience that sits alongside publications, such as reports, produced for an external party including clients.

Writing up the findings from a research project may appear to be an onerous task for what might be non-billable time, particularly in a busy studio. However, interview responses show that those architects who do write up, have identified this as a means of avoiding accidental duplication, and loss of knowledge, particularly when a staff member leaves the practice. Although written knowledge capture doesn't always mean long thesis-like publications, it can range from intranet blog posts to more detailed reports and books. UK practice Levitt Bernstein, for example, publish single A3-sized, quick reference guides on a range of design-related research topics that are used across the practice.

With all documented work, videos, photographs, illustrations and written work, ensuring that it is accessible is critical. Although knowledge management software is available it is not always necessary, particularly for practices with established information management systems already in place for use with design projects. Where these don't exist or cannot be adapted to suit establishing a knowledge management system requires four stages.

1. Planning

    Set out what aspects of the research should be documented including name(s) of the researcher(s), establish a document that can be easily populated, establish document naming protocols, create a list of key search terms, how access will be determined and who will be able to access documents (particularly where the information is sensitive or confidential), identify the person responsible for the management of the system, how large files including original data files will be stored, how and whether documents should be linked, and identify any training required for users.

2. Capture and process

Deliver any required training, identify a person within a project responsible for data capture and populating documents created in the planning phase, and ensure the stages at which data should be collected and logged liaising with the knowledge manager.

3. Organisation and dissemination

Assemble and arrange the documentation submitted, link to internal notification through email, intranet blog post, short video, or live presentation, ensuring that these are also documented and linked and available thereafter.

4. Storage, management and access

Ensure that the information is easily searchable using the keywords and research names established in the planning phase, that documents are easy to update should the research need to be replicated to reflect a change in policy or standards, or repeated on another project. Determine how large files are stored and the backup systems required, and decide what documents should be retained in hard copy and where they should be stored.

7.3 Self-publishing

Self-publishing provides the opportunity to control every aspect of the publication and with options to publish ranging from short reports to full-length books in both hard copy and digital formats, it is a common option for practices publishing research work as well as catalogues of their design work. In-house publishing provides the greatest control over the document, its content and design, and while specialist publishing houses and online templates provide a tailored service and so can be costly, most practices produce documents in-house initially.

Scott Brownrigg's Design Research Unit has published *Intelligent Architecture* on a biannual basis since 2013 (Scott Brownrigg, 2020) prompted by the realisation that existing research required a coordinated method of dissemination available both to clients and within the practice, essential with eight studios in five countries. The compact, A4-sized publications provide a glimpse of the research work, proposals and projections, and competition responses in digital and hard copy. Illustrated articles range from 250 to 2,000 words in length delivered in an accessible, conversational style with technical detail when needed, and cover a wide range of subjects including school design, airport design, POE, the circular economy, BIM, and carbon reduction strategies in construction. Neil MacOmish, Board Director at Scott Brownrigg, remarked in interview that he sees the publications as celebrating the practice, as it "highlights the work of groups and individuals that may in the everyday working of the practice, be missed or over-looked and blurs the boundaries between our sector structures".

Although this route offers several benefits, there are two disadvantages. First, books published without going through the peer review process do not carry the same academic weight as those that do, placing self-publication at a disadvantage when applying for larger research grants and academic grants with academic partners. Second, and more minor point of concern, is the lack of the familiar 10 or 13 digit ISBN and barcode that features on the back of most books which doesn't often appear on self-published books. Used to identify a book in physical and online bookstores, collate and analyse data on sales and ensure that all details related to the publication and its authors on databases are accurate, The 13 digit number, required on books published after January 2007, cannot be applied to a publication retrospectively. Not all self-publishing companies provide ISBNs as part of their services but can be bought online in bulk or individually directly from the International ISBN Agency or one of their representatives.

7.4 Publishing books

The second option for publishing a substantial manuscript is adopting the more traditional model using an established publisher such as Routledge Taylor and Francis, Wiley, Phaidon, Thames and Hudson, or one of the many publishing houses attached to academic institutions internationally. Selecting a publisher from an almost overwhelming list of options should start with a review of their back catalogue. Identifying who already publishes books in the same field and by similar authors is an effective starting point. These publishing houses, unlike those who support self-publishing, manage the process from proposal to distribution and cover the production and print costs, marketing and editing. However, it is rare to be offered an advance and typically royalties are small. Although this is likely to deliver an operating loss, it delivers higher credibility, profile and distribution, and several of the case studies in Chapter Eight, including Baca Architects, PLP Architects, Architecture Research Office and White Arkitekter, have published books using this route.

With the exception of only a small number of publishing houses who either only accept submissions from agents or have a limited capacity restricting the number they can publish, all other publishers have both contacts and guidelines for submissions on their websites. While there are variations in the specific submission requirements of different publishers there are common, key components of a book proposal.

The timeline from submitted a proposal to publication of the book can be 12 months or longer depending on the availability of reviewers, the frequency with which editorial boards meet to decide on new commissions, the length of the book, and the time taken to write and submit the manuscript.

- A title and subtitle

    Including a title, and potentially a subtitle, may seem obvious but both are an important marketing tool. Having the right title will allow prospective purchasers to find your book when using keywords in any internet search, and it will link it to similar books in the field.

- Abstract

    A 150 to 350 word paragraph of the book provides your potential editor with a snapshot of the proposal. An abstract typically includes the key arguments, research questions and aims, data sources, data collection and analysis methodologies used, findings and conclusions, and relevance to the field of research. This statement may also form the basis of the marketing material produced by the publisher.

- A detailed synopsis

    Essentially a longer version of the abstract, this statement outlines the rationale behind the book. Most publishers will specify the length but usually this should be no longer than three to four paragraphs or a page long, and state the aims, concept, key arguments, data sources, methodologies, findings, significance to the literature, and existing thinking. It is important to discuss why a book proposal is important, relevant or needed by the audience and who that audience is.

- Table of contents

    This section may request only a list of chapter headings and subheadings or require annotated sections with a few short sentences to a paragraph outlining the content of each chapter and subsection. If the book is a collection of papers of chapters each by a different author, you should provide a synopsis of 150–250 words for each chapter.

- A description of the target market and market need

    All proposals need to detail the professional and academic audiences, and students, providing details of undergraduate, graduate and research courses. It is critically important that you are able to demonstrate that there will be demand for your book and that you understand the market. By clearly identifying the market, it will be evident to the publisher that you not only understand the audience you are writing for but you have also identified the audience they will focus on when promoting the book.

- The key selling points features of the book

    This section should include three to five key features or benefits of the book such as identifying what the book offers that other publications in the same field do not, explaining the relevance of a new methodological approach, or the innovation that this work offers.

- A review of the main competing titles

    As it is unlikely that your book will be the first in the field, it is important to know which other books are available in the field. This provides the editor and proposal review panel with an idea of the market for your proposal if others have sold particularly well, or not, where the gaps lie that your proposal could address, what distinguishes your proposal from other books, and helps to establish an appropriate price point for your book. With a brief analysis of the strengths and weaknesses of the competition titles and how your book is different, details here should include the full citation, ISBN and price.

- The format of the proposed publication

    This will include an estimated number of words which does not usually including footnotes, image captions, references or the index. A publisher will also expect you to estimate the number of illustrations and images to be used, how many would be in colour or black and white, and the number of tables, line drawings, charts, maps and other illustrations. When you submit the manuscript you will also be required to have obtained copyright release for each image, illustration and map and you will be responsible for any fees associated with their use.

- A timeline and delivery schedule

  Typically this section requires an author to specify how long it will take them to produce the manuscript and its images. It can take two to six months to secure an agreement and contract from a publisher, and around six months from submission of the complete manuscript to publication. So it is worth considering the overall length of publication the publication date as this will assist in identifying a publication date that may correspond with an event, such as an anniversary or event launch.

- Marketing and promotion

  Authors are as responsible for the marketing and promotion of the book as the publishers, demonstrating that you have a marketing and communications strategy including a website, social media and professional contacts and how you might use your existing networks to promote the book will support your proposal.

- Online resources or companion website

  Not all publishers require this section, however, if you are writing a textbook you should provide a paragraph on any online resources that will support the book.

- Profile for all authors

  You should provide the curriculum vitae and contact details for each author and editor for the book, and include digital links to professional websites and social media apps such as Twitter and LinkedIn.

- Referees/peer reviewers suggestions

  All proposals will need to include the names and contact details of three to five independent referees. They should be experts in the field to which your book is best suited and able to assess your proposal.

- Submissions to other publishers

  Not all publishers will ask whether you have submitted, or intend to submit, your proposal to more than one publisher and who that is. Articles or papers submitted to academic journals can only be submitted to one publisher at a time but this does not apply to books.

- Sample material

  Having a chapter already completed with any relevant images included in your submissions is a great benefit to the proposal, particularly for first-time authors and writing partnerships. If you have more than one chapter to choose from or are planning to write a chapter to accompany the proposal, select a core chapter rather than the introduction or conclusion.

7.5 Academic journals and university publications

Each academic journal provides a detailed submission, style guide, and a statement specifying the topics of interest to the publication. Unless an author is responding to a 'Call for Papers' which specifies the submission of a shorter proposal or an abstract, papers are submitted when completed with all images or diagrams and copyright releases for all third parties. Articles are reviewed by editors before being anonymised and sent to two to three reviewers. Submissions to a journal are usually free, regardless of the author's affiliation, but no royalties are paid to the author upon publication.

It is uncommon for practitioners to submit papers to academic peer-reviewed journals as the audience is mostly academic, but far more common when there is a university partner. Academics are expected to publish by these means to retain their existing role, win a new job, or secure grant funding. Many university departments publish their own reports and journals in-house and these are usually available online with no access fees. This an effective method of demonstrating a school's expertise and disseminating their work, and is much faster than publishing in academic journals which can take 12 months to two years from submission to publication.

Another drawback of academic journals is that their content is often locked behind a paywall, with most journals charging readers around US$35 to access each article, although this beginning to change. While university libraries have free access to journals through subscriptions, this structure is prohibitively expensive for practice and their clients. In addition to subscriptions, some universities will pay for all papers authored by their staff to be open access which may be of benefit to those seeking an academic partner. Alternatively, journals offer the option to provide open access to a specific article, and fees are specified on the publisher's website.

7.6 Industry media and journals

The challenge for researchers seeking to publish research work in industry publications, in print or online, is the prevailing preference for image-based architecture stories over those which focus exclusively on research. Data visualisation communicated through an impressive array of graphics does not currently carry the same weight or authority as photography, renderings, technical drawings or even sketches. Interview responses from the practices feature in Chapter Eight suggests that a more successful option is to pitch a project with a research component.

7.7 Conference and event presentations

All of the case studies in the following chapter, and many others referenced elsewhere in this book, most frequently share their research work at talks within their own practice and at professional events to a wide range of audiences. The significance of delivering talks and presentations was highlighted by the judges for the AJ100 Sustainable Practice of the Year in 2019. In awarding the title to PassivHaus specialists Architype for an unprecedented third time, the judges remarked on Architype's "generous approach to industry knowledge-sharing" having "delivered more than 50 talks during the year" (Hartman, 2019). But industry talks are not the only option.

Academic conferences are not always exclusively academic and with a growing interest in collaborative research and engagement, presentations from practitioners are welcome. Most conferences will publish at least a book of abstracts online on an open-access basis, while others produce full proceedings containing complete written papers for all or selected presentations and keynotes. Just as the papers published by academic journals are peer-reviewed, so too are papers, abstracts and panel proposals submitted to academic conferences. With the exception of keynote speakers, most presenters and delegates at academic conferences pay to attend and sometimes submit their papers as these events rarely attract the level of sponsorship that is common in industry events, if at any at all.

Talks are transitory and building up an evidence base to demonstrate knowledge and expertise requires some form of documentation. For those events, including industry talks, where the organisers do not produce a publication, it is worth considering documenting not just attendance but the content of the presentation including video and audio recordings if available, or a copy of the slides or paper presented. Papers delivered at events and that are not published by organisers can be submitted for publication elsewhere, such as in academic journals.

7.8 Exhibitions

From displays in a studio window or entrance to large events such as the Summer Exhibition at the Royal Academy of the Arts and the Venice Biennale, and urban architecture and design festivals and spaces showcase the translation of research into design. Níall McLaughlin Architects were selected to represent Ireland at the Venice Biennale Architettura in 2016 with a project entitled *Losing Myself* (Arthur, McLaughlin, & Manolopoulou, 2017). Working with Dr. Yeoryia Manolopoulou from the Bartlett School of Architecture, their installation, a drawing representing the movement over 24 hours around an Alzheimer's Respite Centre in Dublin designed by the practice, was an "attempt to communicate and interpret some of the changes to spatial perception caused by dementia" (Níall McLaughlin Architects, 2016).

Tonkin Liu has exhibited architectural models at several Royal Academy of Arts Summer Exhibitions. Founding Director Mike Tonkin believes that while they highlighted the practice profile, it was their show in the practice exhibition space at the RIBA's main building at 66 Portland Place, although small, that led to further commissions and design competition wins. He identified it as the perfect location to be viewed by passing RIBA members and the Institution's President, who often compose design competition panels. While the physical exhibition may provide impact and engagement, they are almost always temporary, posing the same challenges in capturing and documenting this knowledge as experienced with conference presentations and industry talks. Exhibition catalogues offer a tangible format to legacy to support the exhibition. In both examples here, the practice produced their own publications to document their research and exhibition work (Arthur, McLaughlin, & Manolopoulou, 2017; Tonkin, Liu, & Clark, 2013).

7.9 Content for website and social media

The most obvious location to publish research work is clearly the practice website. For most practices, the section on their site headed 'Publications' hosts trade journal articles in which their work has appeared rather than their own written work including books, reports and papers but it is worth distinguishing between the two. The websites of many of the practices in Chapter Eight host distinct research pages with separate landing pages for publications coordinated with social media links including the use of hashtags.

The potential and benefits of social media to architectural practice are well-acknowledged, particularly for image-driven Instagram (Goldreich, 2020; Waite, 2017). Alexandra Lange argues that "social media can do more for architecture than showcase pretty faces and soundbites. Architects need to start thinking of social media as the first draft of history" (2014). However, there is no distinction made between different aspects of architectural work, which benefits to a greater or lesser extent. Dinah Bornat of ZCD Architects credits social media, and Twitter specifically, with connecting their practice to experts around the globe, establishing an ongoing international network of researchers that has supported and facilitated their research work.

Ben Morgan, Co-Founder of BowerBird, sees the benefits of focussing on LinkedIn and Instagram, and the 'vital' role they play in attracting new clients, although he points out that they will attract different audiences. As an image-focussed platform, Instagram lends itself well to the architectural profession and connects practitioners to individuals. For this reason, he recommended, in interview, that small practices and those with a single residential focus should establish an Instagram account, noting that the platform is frequently referred to as 'the Google of architecture' as "people will often go straight to Instagram, before even googling your practice name. If they can't find you on Instagram, you may as well not exist". He advocates a different approach with LinkedIn where the emphasis is on professional development, discussing ideas, and engaging with "a lot of people with the means to hire an architect" for larger projects in commercial, retail, education, and public sectors.

Morgan is less convinced by the coordinated website and social media approach, commenting that unless a practice has more than 100,000 social media followers and comparable visits to their website it is unimportant. Instead, referencing Dave Sharp of Vanity Projects, Morgan recommends commissioning

as many professional architectural photographs as you can afford. If you finish four projects per year, and you get 50 photos for each project, that's four social media posts per week with a different photo, a different angle, and another part of your story.

Although he cautions that "what works today might stop working tomorrow, so adaptation and research are important".

7.10 Conclusions

Architects report that there are clear benefits to publishing research work. In the first instance, and most frequently cited, it provides practice with the opportunity to demonstrate their expertise in an enduring format to future collaborators, colleagues, clients and funding agencies. Second, it provides a focus for conversations with clients, providing them with an insight into the practice beyond architectural and design work. And finally, it retains knowledge within a practice providing a reference point for design projects and a foundation for future research work, both within the practice and researchers elsewhere both including academic researchers and students.

Chapter Eight

Case studies

8.1 Introduction

This chapter presents 12 international architecture practices includes a practice profile and illustrated project profile. Case studies were selected based on their established and published record of research and the scope of their work and geographic spread also a consideration. The information presented in the profiles below has been drawn from interviews with key staff, often at directorial or principal level, in research posts or research-led design roles within the practice. The semi-structured interview questions, and their responses, were broadly grouped into five main categories. First, how the practice is structured and the role that research plays in the practice. Second, the acknowledged benefits of research to the practice and its influence on architectural design. The third part discussed the scope and focus of the research conducted, how each practice funded their research, and the professional and academic collaborations in which each was engaged. Finally, the practices discuss how they share their research knowledge, both within and to a wider audience, including their approach to publications.

In part, this chapter sets out to challenge the perception that research is the preserve of big practice. During the first two years following the restructured RIBA President's Award for Research, 2016 and 2017, only a third of those who submitted featured on the AJ100, while a further third came from practices of ten people or fewer (Martindale & Dixon, 2017; Martindale & Tait, 2016). Half of the case studies presented in this chapter are micro or small practices with the total number of staff (not just registered architects) ranging from two to thirty.

The micro practice section starts with the Johannesburg-based Counterspace Studio, who discuss the legacy of the city's gold mines and their research behind the 2020 Serpentine Pavilion. They are followed by ZCD Architects from London and an insight into their research that focusses on involving children in the design process. Also located in London are Baca Architects whose research focusses on water resilience, and Tonkin Liu whose nature-inspired Shell Lace structure has been developed beyond architecture for medical applications. The small practice section starts with sustainability and future-proofing focussed Pomeroy Studio in Singapore. They are followed by the American Institute of Architects' Practice of the Year for 2020, New York-based Architecture Research Office, who discuss three sustainability projects in New York.

In the mid-sized practice category are Passivhaus specialists Architype, located in the United Kingdom, who demonstrate how this approach can be applied across different design sectors, and the Copenhagen practice Gehl Architects, renowned for their observational analysis and urbanism, discuss a two city approach to foodscapes. Australian practice Hayball shares its strong research focus on education that drives design across the sector from pre-K to university building. The chapter concludes with three large practices. London-based PLP Architecture, White Arkitekter which has studios across Scandinavia and in the United Kingdom, and the US-based global practice Perkins&Will. The project profiles for all three offer an insight into the breadth of the research-led design work conducted in the practice and includes a new university campus in India, structural timber in a commercial building near Stockholm, and the 2040 Masterplan for Kuwait.

8.2 Micro practice case studies

8.2.1 Counterspace Studio   *Micro practice case study*

Johannesburg, South Africa

Practice structure

Counterspace is an inter-disciplinary and collaborative studio led by Sumayya Vally, established in 2015. Research has been integral to the practice's operation from the outset with some of their first work research conducted for other South African architecture studios. Their location and socio-political heritage are central to their purpose, and the search to define what it means to be an African architect, a new African architecture practice, and defining, or redefining, African architecture, at a city and continental scale, that accompanies an ambition to broaden the view and understanding of architecture in their context and beyond. "Architecture was used so violently against us," Vally observed. "Without understanding this, we are perpetuating this violence." To address this they feel compelled to engage across all sectors and with the widest possible demographic groups, using their research process as an engagement tool.

Vally's interest in providing mentorship to the next generation of architects is reflected in the practice structure with, at the time of interview, four students at different stages in their career, making up the team. They include one school leaver heading to architecture school, one undergraduate, one part-time graduate student embarking on an architectural journey to Japan, and one full-time graduate of Vally's who now teaches at the University of Johannesburg School of Architecture. The practice, its structure, and methods of process and collaboration are under constant evaluation and evolution which accommodates for the imagination of new forms of practice, that are reflective of a changing concept of practice and which encompass a greater awareness of gender, race, and the environment.

The benefits of research and its influence on design

Each design project starts as a research project that operates at four speeds and intensities depending on the project and context. First is the academic-based research, in which Vally, her team and collaborators are engaged through ongoing teaching responsibilities, and can be both in-depth and longitudinal. This is followed by writing which can be slow and meandering or occupy intense bursts, depending on the output and project. Third are the long-term practice-based research project interests that grow from observations, histories and obsessions around working with the context, Johannesburg (and more recently, London) that informs design projects. Finally, the small, temporary research projects that are sometimes translated as exhibitions or installations, which are periodic tests of deeper ideas and slower interests. All of these speeds overlap and test each other.

Critical to both Vally's research and design process is an understanding and acknowledgment that everything has an embedded history and an embedded bias. The practice has found that their research is a circular and interconnected process, where one project may plant the seed of an idea and evolve into another project, influencing their design work as they progress.

Research focus

Conceptualising the physical, social, political and ecological fabric of their environment is the mainspring of the practice. Much of Vally's work offers a detailed analysis of the impacts for the built environment at an individual level which is informed by performance and language and linguistics as storytelling as well as traditional research techniques. Vally's research process has emerged from frustrations around the architectural canon and context in South Africa, and deep fascinations with the histories and rituals of Johannesburg, leading the practice to identify and examine elements that stand out, which don't fit. Counterspace's research is interconnected and, collectively, presents a sense of their mission to understand how as architects they fit into and redefine their context, and the practice and understanding of architecture.

Funding and client commissions

Counterspace launched their practice with research commissions from two local architecture practices, Local Studio and Urban Works, and Wits University Campus Planning. The Wits University project analysed the movement of students around the Johannesburg campus, the dignity and fears of gender-based violence of women on campus, and questioned the democracy of the university's perimeter fencing, that occurred against a backdrop of the Cecil Rhodes and Fees Must Fall protests, extending the brief and engagement with student voices and protest movements. For Urban Works, the practice developed an understanding of the local economy and entrepreneurial roadside activity in Johannesburg.

Since these early projects, the practice has embedded research in their design process and developed ongoing relationships with clients such as the Johannesburg Development Agency for whom they conducted a profile of the historically coloured community of Fleurhof working with memory, oral histories, and present community rituals to develop a more nuanced and complex understanding of race and the community.

Collaborations

The practice is actively engaged with academia through research projects and teaching at graduate level. Vally leads a Masters studio at the University of Johannesburg that focusses on finding design expression for themes of African and hybrid identity and contested territory and history, and the development of research methodologies to understand and articulate these interests, working with performance, ritual, language and music. Vally also maintains active links with the Architectural Association in London, The Bartlett School of Architecture, University of Technology Sydney, and Gauteng City-Region Observatory.

Publishing and disseminating work

The practice views the dissemination of their work as vital and their determination to do things differently drives them to find new routes and languages to work with, 'decolonising' traditional forms of engagement. The practice conceptualises, hosts and participates in events that encourage dialogue and discourse around architecture in Johannesburg, reimagining the salon format, sometimes through occupying shopfront spaces in the inner city. Through Backstory, a shopfront in Braamfontein, the practice hosts a range of events that aims to change the narrative, in part through rearranging how people are seated together and conducting a non-traditional research process that includes performances by jazz musicians, presentations by student protest leaders, and poetry readings. Besides their own website, they often occupy physical spaces temporarily for projects to communicate with stakeholders and community members, and to publish the work their practice and of other practices. In 2020, Vally founded Counterparts, an initiative alongside Counterspace, that is focussed on collaborative working methods, interdisciplinary residencies, and publishing.

Counterspace Studio - Project profiles

Golden Plateaus

The bright, shimmering light of Johannesburg is filled with a fine dust that hangs in the atmosphere and blankets the city. It is a legacy of the city's gold mines (see Figure 8.1), an activity that continues, albeit in an informal manner, conducted by individuals referred to as the Zama Zamas, isiZulu for 'the ones who try and try' (Hutton, 2016). The toxic waste generated by the mines has created dumps historically employed as a "divisive urban tool – massive mountains of toxic separation between economically-suppressed races" (Vally, 2019), reinforcing treatment of these communities under apartheid.

In response to this, Vally and her colleagues collected the mine dust containing copper, cobalt, aluminium, and iron created during the blast mining process, examining the structure of its constituent elements (see Figures 8.2 and 8.3),

Figure 8.1: Aerial view of 'Top Star' mine dump in Johannesburg. © Counterspace Studio

Figure 8.2: Pigments grafted from mine waste in Johannesburg. © Sumayya Vally

Figure 8.3: Microscope view of ferrous crystalline structure, mine waste pigment. © Sumayya Vally

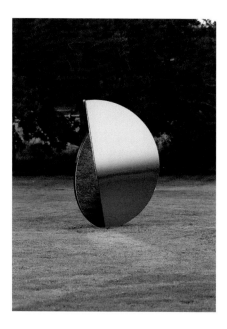

Figure 8.4: Folded Skies sculpture installed at the Spier Wine Estate in Stellenbosch. © Cait Warther

the paths taken through the waste sites, and documented how these sites are now used, which includes a play area for children and site of religious ceremony. The team's poetic translation of their findings is in capturing the light of Johannesburg at different points in the day and represented as sunrise, sunset and midnight, in mirrors coated with non-toxic versions of the minerals identified to form a three sculpture installation originally located in the grounds of a local winery, juxtaposing interconnected South African histories and legacies (see Figure 8.4).

2020/20 PLUS 1 Serpentine Pavilion

Inspired by the spaces, places and experiences of gathering, memory and care across London, notably those from migrant and marginalised communities. In developing the concept realised in the final design, the practice surveyed meeting places across London from Brixton in the south to Hackney, Peckham and Whitechapel in the east, Ealing and North Kensington in the west, and along Edgware Road in north London. The research included reading and learning from the archive and the city – configurations and forms of food vendors' pavilions

Figure 8.5: Street market traders in London. © Sumayya Vally

and canopies (see Figure 8.5), gathering spaces in the street and in restaurants in migrant neighbourhoods, and historically significant places of gathering and cultural production for migrant communities, influencing the final design.

The temporary pavilion, built adjacent to the Serpentine Pavilion in the grounds of Kensington Gardens, was scheduled to open in June 2020 but Covid delayed its physical construction and on-site events until 2021 (see Figures 8.6 and 8.7). The additional time has allowed for a deepening of the research and engagement with communities, with planned additional initiatives, physical and virtual, planned to launch alongside the pavilion programme.

Reflecting the climate emergency agenda and the Pavilion's role in the Serpentine's *Back to Earth* programme, the structure will be built using Kenoteq's K-Brik formed from recycled construction waste and cork blockwork. Parts of the pavilion's structure and programme will be located in communities across the city acting as the focus for events, before being returned to the Pavilion over the summer.

Figure 8.6: Interior detail of the Serpentine Pavilion. © Counterspace Studio

Figure 8.7: The proposed Pavilion with the Serpentine Gallery behind. © Counterspace Studio

8.2.2 ZCD Architects *Micro practice case study*

London, United Kingdom

Practice structure

Founded in 2013, ZCD is led by Cordula Weisser and Dinah Bornat who are both active researchers and teach at several universities across London. The studio is made up of around eight staff, depending on workload, with Dinah as the practice research lead. All staff are involved in research and the staff that have joined since its inception have been attracted by the research-led design agenda of the practice. There is an acknowledged need for up-skilling and research training, which is conducted in-house and includes training Part II architecture students starting with introductory data collection such as observational work and running workshops.

The research agenda was established shortly after the founding of the practice, and becoming involved in the play streets movement in East London in which demonstrated the lack of consideration for children in the built environment. The practice directors, confident that they "could do better" set out to develop an evidenced base to inform architectural thinking and resolve key problems in the built environment encountered by children, with particular reference to housing developments.

Research focus

ZCD's research work focusses exclusively on child-friendly design in the built environment. Bornat sees this "laser like focus" on this single issue as a strength for the practice as they expand their expertise and develop their designs in response. Their work has been well received not only among fellow architects and the community in East London that is the focus for several of their studies, but has received coverage in the national press that, on one occasion, led to a change of policy and engagement with the housing minister (Grant, 2019a, 2019b).

The influences on their research extend beyond architecture and urban design to incorporate other fields including psychology, colour, play, learning and child development. Interdisciplinary thinking, and adoption of research techniques allow their researchers to gather data through play and engagement with children.

The benefits of research and its influences on design

For its capacity to better understand the brief and to better design to better deliver, ZCD views research as the driving force behind their design work. More specifically, there have been two distinct and tangible benefits to conducting and publishing their research for the practice. First, is in establishing their credibility as experts in a crowded marketplace of architects and report that this investment in research-led output and engagement has led to an explosion in commissions for design work and consultancy work engaging with children, including the Greater London Authority (Bornat, 2020). The second benefit has been the practice's ability to charge higher rates for their design and consultancy services, a direct reflection of their acknowledged expertise.

Funding and client commissions

Despite their practice's fee structure for design and consultancy work, they face the same challenges as most when it comes to securing research funding. Early success in winning a research grant from the RIBA Research Trust established their credentials with future funding agencies although it is often a collection of research funds and supporters for each project rather than one single agency, and occasionally that is still not sufficient to cover all research project costs. As a small practice, ZCD are reluctant to bid for larger funding applications and competitions as they present a greater level of risk and leave the practice "very exposed", so investing in in-house research offers better value for money and time.

In a mix of grants, procurement, seed funding and invitation, the practice has previously secured funding from the Town and Country Planning Association, Sport England, New Direction Fund, NHBC Foundation, Royal Town Planning Association, and the Royal Institute of British Architects through the RIBA Research Trust. This has been underpinned by political support in their local area from the Mayor of Hackney which they feel has been invaluable in terms of lending credibility to the practice and their research and has inspired confidence in funding agencies.

Collaborations

The practice has created working partnerships with other smaller organisations but has not yet sought to establish collaborations with universities. This is due to concerns about funding disparities and the expectation to provide match funding from the university. This was highlighted when the practice investigated Knowledge Transfer Partnerships which they later dismissed as an option as they considered the scheme to great a challenge for small practice and its associated fees and costs.

Publishing and disseminating work

ZCD regularly publish their final reports both in hard copy and on their own website on an open-access basis. Where they have been commissioned by a client such as the Royal Town Planning Institution, the work appears there also. For ZCD Director Dinah Bornat, publishing their research, including methods and findings, is of paramount significance to the practice. "It is important to publish your research. It doesn't diminish your intellectual property or competitiveness. It allows you to showcase your expertise and win clients." Often, they are commissioned by clients who expect them to disseminate research findings in a report. Many of these reports are also published on their own website on an open-access basis.

    The practice has found that presenting research to different audiences helps to refine ideas and further develop knowledge within the practice. In addition, sharing their work and research findings on social media platforms including Twitter has not only facilitated knowledge sharing across the platform and beyond, but this has evolved into a global network based on shared interest allowing the practice to draw on best practice from international experts exchange ideas. While attending professional events has been straightforward, one of the key barriers to sharing work in an academic environment has been the lack of funding available to visit international conferences, and the fees charged by conference organisers to non-academics are usually much higher than academic fees, charged even when presenting.

ZCD Architects - Project profiles

Neighbourhood design: Working with children towards a child friendly city

In 2018 the practice collaborated with the University of Westminster to develop design guidance, noting that "[t]wenty-five per cent of London's population are under the age of 18. A significant proportion, but in spite of this, children are largely unrepresented in urban development policy and practice" (Bornat & Shaw, 2019, p. 2). This reflects the United Nations Convention on the Rights of the Child advocates that: "[p]arties recognize the right of the child to rest and leisure, to engage in play" and "encourage[s] the provision of appropriate and equal opportunities for cultural, artistic, recreational and leisure activity" (UNICEF, 1999). The overriding ambition of this project, and other research conducted by the practice, was to establish children as legitimate participants in the planning and design process, which they often find lacking.

In 2018, the practice involved fifth-year pupils and staff at De Beauvoir Primary School in the north London borough of Hackney to assess the De Beauvoir Estate, a multi-story residential development surrounding a large shared outdoor area (see Figure 8.8). This comprised 12 sessions designed to engage the children through photography, walking tours (see Figure 8.9), guided discussions and creative writing events, and concluding with an exhibition at the school. This was supported with 110 hours of observational analysis carried out across the estate, to producing a Heat Map (see Figure 8.10), that ranks usability of spaces, and a Networks and Connections map (see Figure 8.11). The Heat Map reveals "very few instances of the right spatial conditions that support children to play, meet friends and get around safely" (Bornat & Shaw, 2019, p. 84), and is echoed by the Networks and Connections map that reported poor highlight lines and connections for use by children.

Advocating for a more holistic approach to engagement than interventions aimed solely at addressing issues such as obesity or 'too much' screen time, the final report discusses the impact on children of issues including crime, alcohol and drug use, and traffic, and considers how the children read use and interact with the space. Besides the broader guidance relating to the benefits of involving children in the design process with outcomes that support independence and well-being, site-specific recommendations in the final report (Bornat & Shaw, 2019) includes addressing the intolerance toward children, their behaviours and play, the needs of different age groups from small children to teenagers, and gender differences. The project, which received support from Hackney's Mayor Phillip Glanville, received funding from the University of Westminster, the Royal Institute of British Architects, and childhood advocacy charity, A New Direction.

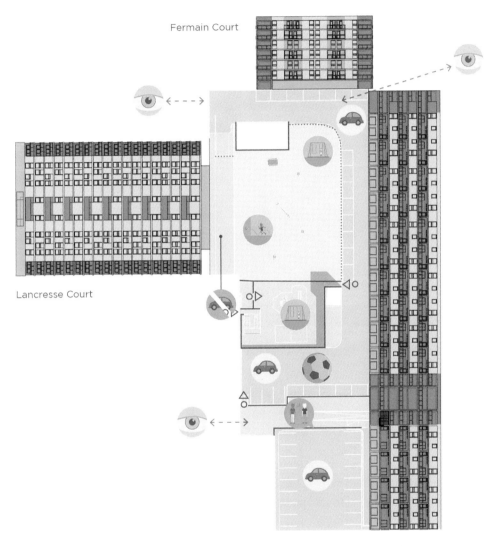

Fermain Court

Lancresse Court

Fermain Court

Figure 8.8: Fold out analysis of the De Beauvoir Estate. © ZCD Architects

Figure 8.9: Engagement session with pupils from De Beauvoir School. © ZCD Architects

Letchworth Garden City design proposal

ZCD's Letchworth Garden City proposal (see Figure 8.12) focussed on three themes to build a community; food production, transport and play. In the proposal, food production is a localised community activity supported by allotments and kitchen gardens accessed through shared gateways (see Figure 8.13), with shared al fresco eating and barbecue areas. With cars and parking restricted to the perimeter of the development and wide boulevards reserved for public transport, the emphasis on external space is in the provision of safe spaces that encourage walking and cycling for all ages groups linking homes, schools, gardens, and places of work, retail and markets. Shared, linked gardens with a naturalistic planting scheme featuring grassy mounds and trees are designed to

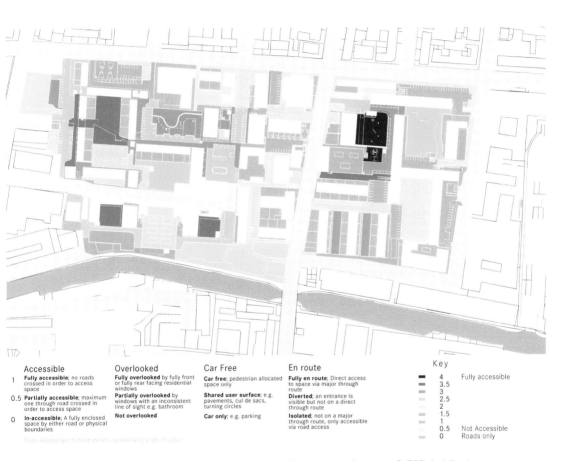

Accessible

1 **Fully accessible**; no roads crossed in order to access space

0.5 **Partially accessible**; maximum one through road crossed in order to access space

0 **In-accessible**; A fully enclosed space by either road or physical boundaries

Overlooked

Fully overlooked by fully front or fully rear facing residential windows

Partially overlooked by windows with an inconsistent line of sight e.g. bathroom

Not overlooked

Car Free

Car free; pedestrian allocated space only

Shared user surface; e.g. pavements, cul de sacs, turning circles

Car only; e.g. parking

En route

Fully en route; Direct access to space via major through route

Diverted; an entrance is visible but not on a direct through route

Isolated; not on a major through route, only accessible via road access

Key

4	Fully accessible
3.5	
3	
2.5	
2	
1.5	
1	
0.5	Not Accessible
0	Roads only

Figure 8.10: De Beauvoir estate Heat Map indicating and ranking the use of spaces. © ZCD Architects

Case studies

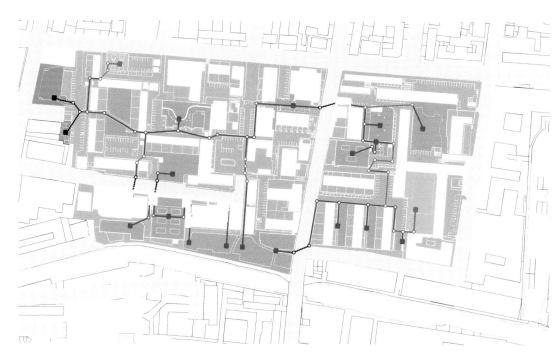

Figure 8.11: Network Plan of the De Beauvoir estate mapping the development's connectivity and barriers in the spaces used by the children. © ZCD Architects

Figure 8.12: Planometeric drawing of the Letchworth Garden City proposal. © ZCD Architects

encourage self-directed play and independence, all while being viewed from the houses that overlook both spaces and, largely, enclose them (see Figure 8.14).

The design proposal builds on their ongoing research into the provision of safe, supportive and flexible environments for children whose benefits, their work has revealed, supports a wider community that is inclusive of all age groups. In this case, removing cars from the central and main spaces, linking green spaces and encouraging play, shared experiences through food, and informal learning through serendipitous participation in growing food, cooking and eating in community gardens provide social as well as environmental sustainability to the benefit of all.

Figure 8.13: Sketch illustrating a gateway leading to the shared gardens, part of the Letchworth Garden City proposal. © ZCD Architects

Figure 8.14: View onto the shared gardens at the Letchworth Garden City proposal. © ZCD Architects

8.2.3 Baca Architects   *Micro practice case study*

London, United Kingdom

Practice structure

Founded in 2003, Baca Architects averages around ten people with Director John Napier, and Matt Sharman-Hayles and Hestia Maillet-Contoz making up the core research team, led by practice co-founder Richard Coutts. Embedding research within design projects has been part of their process since their formation. For Richard Coutts, this approach was actively encouraged during his architectural training at Sheffield University and previous professional experience in R&D-led practice environments including working with Dr. Ken Yeang (Malaysia and Australia) and Andrew Wright (former Head of Sustainability at Rogers Stirk Harbour + Partners).

All staff arrive at the practice with research training or experience in flood, sustainability or climate change research. The practice's first publication *Aquatecture* (Barker & Coutts, 2016) serves as a key research training tool for new recruits although finding time to offer more formal research training is challenging, as is often the case for all small practices. The practice also operates an active mentoring scheme with staff members spending between 10% and 20% of their time on research for architectural projects.

Research focus

Baca specialise in waterfront architecture and flood resilience, low carbon technology, and large-scale master planning on sensitive sites for projects in the United Kingdom and overseas. Their work is split between research for policy and research for architectural projects and includes work on innovative materials and their applications. Their design work includes place-making that considers the increasing significance and value placed on communal space as housing units become smaller, and how these spaces can address issues of climate change and water resilience as all of their urban design master planning work has a flood zone risk component to it.

This work has led to regular invitations to contribute to UK policy and building regulations and their publications including documents for the RIBA. However, the practice has found that calls for innovation and change are blocked by over-regulation and political intransigency. Baca has developed proposals for three sites with a realistic chance of delivering floating homes. To deliver these proposals the team is looking to establish Planning and Performance Guidelines in the United Kingdom which will, in turn, unlock further opportunities.

The benefits of research and its influence on design

For Coutts "research and the project are symbiotic" with the built work providing the proof of concept that he hopes will allow others to follow and develop this knowledge further, ultimately demonstrating the value that architects can add both to the built environment but also to knowledge and understanding of a subject. This approach, notably developing expertise through the focus on a single topic, has elevated Baca's profile resulting in invitations to contribute to government commissions and panels and opportunities to work with high-profile organisations such as The World Bank, and collaborate across disciplines.

Their research and design focus has also proved to be an effective tool for recruitment and regularly receive large numbers of applications for advertised vacancies. On one occasion, the practice had to withdraw the advertisement for a junior role after only 24 hours, having already received over 200 applications.

Funding and client commissions

The practice has successfully applied for funding from the Department for Environment, Food & Rural Affairs, Technology Strategy Board (now Innovate UK), and The World Bank, and in all cases, these were significant figures that funded substantial research projects. The single-minded focus of their research agenda expressed through these projects, self-initiated R&D work applied to real projects, and the publications arising from them attracts new clients. To allow the practice to continue to disseminate the research behind the projects as well as the project, all private clients agree to open publication of this work.

Collaborations

The practice is currently with working Professor Edmund Penning-Rowsell of Middlesex University focussing on three leisure projects in flood risk areas.

They have previously collaborated with the UK Building Research Establishment, University of East Anglia, GHK, University of Wolverhampton and, as a reflection of their policy focussed research, three UK Government departments – the Environment Agency, Department for Environment, Food & Rural Affairs, Department for Communities and Local Government (now Ministry of Housing, Communities and Local Government).

Publishing and disseminating work

The practice has been involved in several TV documentaries regarding their work including the construction of their Amphibious House project that was featured on an episode of the British edition of Grand Designs TV show (Vening, 2016). Although this research-driven project generated attention and was covered in several publications when the show aired, they have generally found it difficult to persuade industry publications to cover their research work even when it is linked to a project. As an aesthetically driven industry, greater emphasis is placed on the images associated with a project than the research. They feel that even if it is a good research project, without images considered sufficiently engaging, the editors regularly decline to publish the work.

To address this the practice has published books through established publishing houses including RIBA Publishing, and have contributed to other reports and documents such as the review of the National Planning Policy Framework, *World Flood Handbook* (Jha, Bloch, & Lamond, 2012), and *The Metric Handbook* (Barker & Coutts, 2015). They are active across several social media sites although focus on image-driven work on Instagram and publishing articles on LinkedIn, and are regularly invited to deliver presentations and talks to various audiences including cross-industry professional events, industry seminars and international conferences.

Baca Architects - Project profiles

Flood-resilient homes, Stratford upon Avon

Completed in late summer 2020 this small development of 11 houses on Shipston Road, a main road into Stratford upon Avon, replacing a derelict three-storey 1970s apartment block that had lain empty for over a decade following several unsuccessful planning applications. The site is designated Flood Zones 2 and 3 by the UK Environment Agency meaning that it has a more than 1% likelihood of flooding every year. The design challenge in building new dwellings with elevated floor levels without significantly increasing the height of the site and respecting neighbouring building heights, on a site at risk of surface water and flooding from the nearby River Avon.

Baca's response was to arrange the houses around a shared communal garden and amenity space with raised footpaths and cycle paths, allowing a route through the development and to the new houses even during flood events (see Figures 8.15 and 8.16). The dwellings are elevated by piles (see Figure 8.17) with a floodable area beneath with louvered screens preventing the accumulation of debris that risks impeding water movement. The overall design of the site allows large quantities of water to flow within the site in a controlled and planned manner, with a system of swales, gullies and relief pipes. The landscaped areas were designed as rain gardens with low walls that retain and control water run-off, with overall improvements to ground water permeability.

This approach builds on their expertise expressed in their publications (Barker, & Coutts, 2015, 2016) and ongoing consultation work for UK Government Department for the Environment, Farming and Rural Affairs (DEFRA), and addressed concerns from both the local council and Environment Agency regarding building in flood zones and historic locations.

Figure 8.15: Render of the housing development at Shipston Street with flood resilient planting. © Baca Architects

Figure 8.16: Render of the Shipston Street development showing the flooding capacity. © Baca Architects

Figure 8.17: View of the stilts at the Shipston Street development, elevating houses above likely flood level. © Baca Architects

Room for the River: Nijmegen and Lent Masterplan and Flood Mitigation Strategy

Flooding poses a significant and sustained risk to existing development and restricts new plans in Netherlands. Baca Architects' successful response to an international competition placed a 1 km-long flood relief channel between Nijmegen and Lent at the centre of the €365 million 'Room for the River' programme, aimed at managing not only the increased flood risk but also creating a destination site and encouraging new development in the wider area and transforming the site (see Figures 8.18 and 8.19).

Alongside the relocation of a major dyke, the masterplan incorporates three new bridges, a 70 m tall tower containing an eco-hotel, leisure facilities including an equestrian centre, a sailing club and an extreme sports centre, a camping site,

Figure 8.18: Aerial view of the 'Room for the River' site in Nijmegen before redevelopment. © Baca Architects

holiday accommodation, and 25,000 new homes (see Figure 8.20). Establishing a new activity-rich destination allows local residents and visitors to access the river and landscaped areas such as river dunes, embankments (see Figure 8.21).

This approach adopted at Nijmegen follows the principles laid out in The LifE Handbook which sets out principles aimed at developing new flood risk management strategies that are of advantage to the wider community and supports well-considered and sustainable development (Baca Architects, 2009). Working on a large-scale project allowed the practice to specify solar PVs, heat exchangers, rainwater harvesting units, reed beds, and complete lifecycle use of all materials, in their aim to deliver a carbon-neutral development. Before construction had started, the project won the Regeneration and Masterplanning at the 2014 Future Project Awards (World Architecture Community, 2014).

Case studies

Figure 8.19: Aerial view of the Nijmegen site after the construction of the flood relief channel.
© Baca Architects

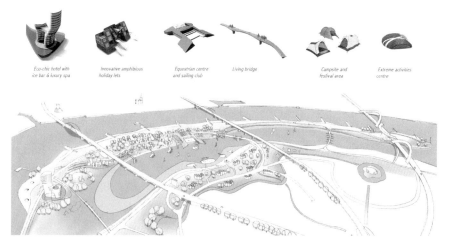

Figure 8.20: Sketch of the Nijmegen Masterplan indicating the locations of recreational facilities.
© Baca Architects

Figure 8.21: Visitors to the newly landscaped Nijmegen riverside paths. © Baca Architects

8.2.4 Tonkin Liu   *Micro practice case study*

London, United Kingdom

Practice structure

Located in Clerkenwell in central London, Tonkin Liu is a 13 strong practice led by directors Mike Tonkin and Anna Liu. The practice's research agenda builds on Tonkin's previous practice experience in Hong Kong where he employed research as a process methodology in his architectural work. This proved successful not only with clients but also with the professional bodies who presented the practice with multiple awards. The driving force behind their method is a determination to innovate; to find and create something new. As such, research forms part of the design process throughout the practice and for all members of the team and is explored through model making.

For Tonkin Liu, model making forms a critically important part of the research process that also includes multi-disciplinary methodologies and historic social, cultural and built environment precedents. Their resolve to translate their ideas into models is evident in their small studio space which accommodates conceptual, developmental and final models that have been created for all the practice's projects. Research projects form the starting point and are integral to each project whether they are exploratory, research only, or lead to a completed architectural design.

Research focus

On returning to the UK and forming Tonkin Liu, their entry in the RIBA Directory stated the practice ambition to do "something we've never done before" and this is reflected in the diversity of the design and research projects which ranges from domestic renovations and extensions to bridges, urban redevelopments and pavilions. While their sectors may be diverse, their innovation in structure as architecture is a common theme.

This is most clearly recognisable in the practice's Shell Lace structure, their single surface structural technology, that has evolved to include a cruise ship terminal in Kaohsiung, Taiwan, their proposal for the Shi Ling Bridge in the Chinese city of Yunnan, the Rain Bow Gate in Burnley and most recently its application as a medical stent, although this hasn't prevented them from building in more established materials such as timber and steel.

The benefits of research and its influence on design

The practice has identified three benefits to their research. First, the practice is certain that, reflecting on conversations with examiners and jurors, their research has played a significant role in helping them win competitions. Second, it carves out time to think and investigate new ways of reasoning, focussing the mind on a series of issues that may not be on the drawing board in the practice but can be applied to future projects if the fit is right. Finally, it has provided opportunities to work on completely different projects in different fields, fostering additional research, which has, in turn, encouraged the team to be even more open-minded to the benefits and processes of working in different ways that encourages them to approach their commissioned projects from a different perspective.

Funding and client commissions

Although the practice was a recipient of the 2013 RIBA Research Trust Fund and an Innovate UK grant for the development of their Shell Lace Stent, most of Tonkin Liu's funding, and design commissions, have come through competitions. Identifying funding for the research component of the work is not always straight forward and, like many other practices, they have yet to receive a direct client commission for research. However, as they consider research to be an integral part of the design methodology, this is not a serious concern for the practice.

Collaborations

The practice has worked regularly with structural engineers, including Arup and Jane Wernick Associates, in developing several of the Shell Lace projects. Both directors teach at the Architectural Association and the University of Bath, where Mike Tonkin is undertaking a PhD, and both are external examiners at the Bartlett School of Architecture. The practice is part of a four-way collaboration between the universities of Cambridge and Bath with Foster + Partners and Tonkin Liu as the practice partnership. Although for this project, as with most of their academic engagement, they contribute their research services to a collaborative process on a pro bono basis.

Publishing and disseminating work

The practice has participated in 28 exhibitions and their models have appeared at the Royal Academy of Arts Summer Exhibition several times including the model for Sun Rain Room, the extension to their own home and office, shown in 2016, the Tower of Light in 2018, and the Paddington Willow Pavilion and Opening Bridge to Crystal Palace Dinosaur Islands models in 2019. These most recent models were awarded the BKI Architecture and Materials Prize and the opportunity to present the work at the Royal Academy. Following their RIBA Trust Award, the Institute hosted an exhibition in 2014, The Evolution of Shell Lace Structure, which included two presentations with a self-published book following this work.

   Their first practice publication covered their story-led projects based on work in Hong Kong (Tonkin Liu, 1999). Their second details the Shell Lace structure from conception to final structure. They are considering a third that would move through the evolution of their process and beyond Shell Lace through different materials, techniques and approaches, to their cross-over into the medical world with the tracheal stent.

Tonkin Liu - Project profiles

The evolution of Shell Lace and beyond

The Shell Lace structure, for which Tonkin Liu is best known, launched their structural agenda and was first developed as their submission for a design competition for a wind shelter on the beachfront at Bexhill-on-Sea. Inspired by the structure of a shell, they developed the shelter's shape using paper models. Although the proposal did not win the commission, it established a pattern of working through ideas using hand-built models and taking inspiration for an integrated structure and form from nature.

   The practice has evolved this thinking and process through several projects, each further evolving their research and refining their designs. These include a disaster shelter that, by efficiencies in component design and cutting, produced zero waste, the 75 m Shi Ling Bridge, the perforated Corten steel Solar Lace Bridge designed to span a motorway in Lisbon offering three separate routes for walking, cycling, and running, and the Rain Bow Gate.

Figure 8.22: Elevated view of Rain Bow Gate. © Greg Storrar

Located in Burnley in the north of England outside a higher education college (see Figure 8.22), the Rain Bow Gate references the industrial heritage of the region and stands as a reminder that the city enjoys the heaviest rainfall in the UK, central to mill operations in the nineteenth century. "It's all about the rain" noted Tonkin. The piercings in the three steel arches are filled with glass prisms, projecting rainbows onto the ground when hit by sunlight.

The interaction between sunlight and the Shell Lace structure is replicated in the Solar Gate, constructed on the site in Hull, where King Charles I was denied entry to the city in 1642 (see Figure 8.23). Designed as a sundial, apertures across the ten-meter tall structure align with the sun's position

Figure 8.23: The Solar Gate showing the larger apertures which function as a sundial. © Alex Peacock

Figure 8.24: The sundial function of the Solar Gate illuminating key dates in Hull's history. © George Brown

Figure 8.25: Construction of the Solar Gate. © Tonkin Liu

on key dates in the city's history and commemorating individuals, including the date of William Wilberforce's bill calling for the abolition of slavery, the posthumous release of musician Mick Ronson's album *Heaven and Hull*, and completion of The Old Dock, creating beams of light that land on 16 metal plates on the ground (see Figure 8.24). The lace structure, pierced to reduce wind load, was fabricated by Hull-based specialist metal fabricator Pearlgreen Engineering from 4 mm thick laser-cut stainless steel sheets (see Figure 8.25) and installed in 2017 to mark Hull's status as UK City of Culture.

Completed in 2020, their 40 m tall 'Tower of Light' structure adjacent to Manchester's Piccadilly Station, again designed to the Shell Lace structure, provides a shield for the stainless steel flumes of the Vital Energi combined heat and power energy centre, providing power to the Council Building and Manchester City Council, behind. Following the initial commission, the scheme

Figure 8.26: Render of the Tower of Light. © Tonkin Liu

was expanded to include a pavilion at the base of the tower, the Wall of Energy, clad in 1,300 handmade white ceramic tiles to reflect the sky (see Figure 8.26). Their ongoing partnership with ARUP has evolved further, refining the structure with the laser-cut sheets reduced to 3–8 mm thick. The structure's lacework allows sunlight to land on internal polished reflectors that move with the wind, creating light that dances across the structure during the day and LEDs assuming this role at night.

While the stories attached to their designs have been well received particularly in competitions, convincing the jury of the structural stability of their proposals has proved a significant and persistent challenge. Despite their ongoing collaboration with ARUP on almost all structural projects, judges and external observers regularly question the structural integrity of the designs and the research that underpins their work, refusing to believe or trust that delicate structures are stable. This has led to an increase in the depth of structural components which in turn has increased material, fabrication and installation costs.

Restricting costs to provide design at as low a cost as possible is important to Mike Tonkin and Anna Liu for their Shell Lace Stent. This time adapting the Shell Lace structure with inspiration taken from the petals of the arum lily and applying elastica, Leonhard Euler's 1744 theory of the mechanics of solid materials that allows for very large scale elastic deflections of structures. The final design is c-shaped, made from silicon, and inserted into a patient's trachea in the inverted position before unfurling, much like a lily petal (see Figures 8.27 and 8.28). Expected to be used to treat collapsed airways following surgery for throat cancer or other trauma, the lace-like perforated stent should allow for a better fit without the need for future readjustments and more effective drug delivery to the affected areas. The practice has filed for patents in the United States and Europe for the stent which has been shortlisted for the RIBA London Awards (RIBAJ, 2020).

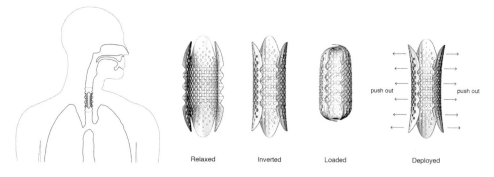

Figure 8.27: Illustration of the Shell Lace Stent. © Tonkin Liu

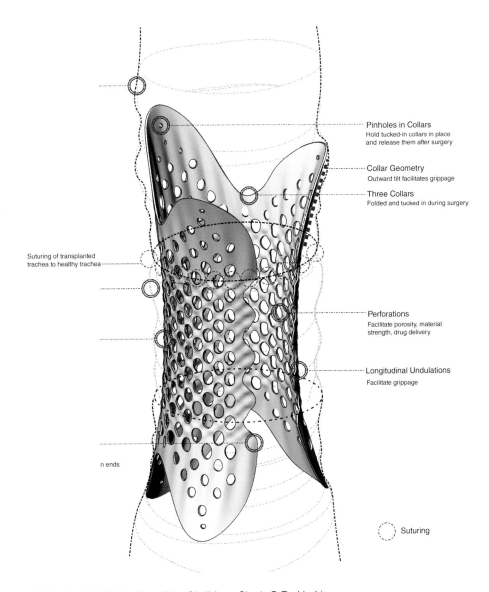

Pinholes in Collars
Hold tucked-in collars in place
and release them after surgery

Collar Geometry
Outward tilt facilitates grippage

Three Collars
Folded and tucked in during surgery

Suturing of transplanted
trachea to healthy trachea

Perforations
Facilitate porosity, material
strength, drug delivery

Longitudinal Undulations
Facilitate grippage

n ends

Suturing

Figure 8.28: Detailed illustration of the Shell Lace Stent. © Tonkin Liu

8.3 Small practice case study

8.3.1 Pomeroy Studio   *Small practice case study*

Singapore, Singapore

Practice structure

Research has been an integral part of Pomeroy Studio since it was founded in 2012 by Jason Pomeroy, with the ambition of embedding research into "the DNA of the practice". This approach followed the research focus of his academic training and previous experience in multi-disciplinary practice. Positioned alongside the architectural practice, and established at the same time, is Pomeroy Academy, a research-led education hub delivering courses focussed on environmental sustainability and the green agenda.

Of the 24 strong practice team, two are dedicated to research and are joined by colleagues depending on project requirements. Both the B House, Singapore's first carbon-negative residential property, and POD Off-Grid (POG) project, the zero-carbon, waterborne community in Venice, required five team members tasked with developing the research into a commercial project. All members of the practice have at least a Masters degree and, with a heavy focus on research, job applicants are expected to demonstrate an evidence-based approach to design and project-based research, and have obtained a research-based Masters in a specialist field with a bias towards sustainable design.

The benefits of research and its influence on design

Environmental sustainability is central to the practice and one of the six pillars to which both the research and practice respond, the other five being social, economic, spatial, cultural and technological, which are intended to redefine the conventional notions of sustainable development. Annually, the practice takes one of these pillars and conducts an in-depth engagement that forms the framework to explore other research-led design work. This has introduced a more evidence-based approach to their design process, pushing the boundaries of their design work and, through publications and engagement, industry knowledge, and government policy.

For each architecture commission, for example, the practice calculates the Green Plot Ratio (GPR). Employed as an architecture and urban design tool,

GPR is the average Leaf Area Index (LAI) that defines the single-side leaf area per unit ground area (used to monitor the ecological health of natural ecosystems, model and predict metabolic processes), and is used to assess the capacity for including of greenery in buildings and urban areas (Ong, 2003). This work is applied to all design projects to determine the potential for planting to capture dust and other particulates, reduce the air temperature around the building and retain water, meeting a wider ambition to reduce urban warming and improve air quality. In responding to the spatial pillar, this level of detailed analysis has also been applied in the assessment social space of the city around them, ensuring that it is balanced with social space provision within their buildings.

Research focus

Architectural work at the practice cuts across six sectors including residential, workplace, hospitality, retail, culture and conservation, and, with it embedded within the design process, their research reflects this. The practice has three ongoing themes that underpin their architectural projects. The first, zero energy developments, balances past cultural practices with environmental innovations in renewable energy sources to deliver environmentally responsive buildings that consume less energy. Second, greening urban habitats has seen the practice adapting the LAI to develop a quantifiable planning metric applied to developments, determining the greenery to be retained on sites in support of their environmental sustainability goals.

Finally, in vertical urban theory, the research focusses on developing alternative social spaces at high levels, including skycourts and skygardens, analysing the connectivity of spaces, their uses, and interdependencies, which replicate the street and the square that provide natural light and ventilation, challenging perceptions of urban density, and creating the opportunity to increase urban greenery (see Figures 8.29 and 8.30). The design and research of skycourts and skygardens is intended to suggest alternative social spaces, contributing to planning policy in Singapore.

The practice aims to undertake one research project per year with the expectation that it will culminate in a book, exhibition and/or a TV series, such as the publication 'Cities of Opportunities: connecting culture and innovation' (Pomeroy, 2020) was the result of work for the Abu Dhabi Department of Municipality and Transport and UN-Habitat.

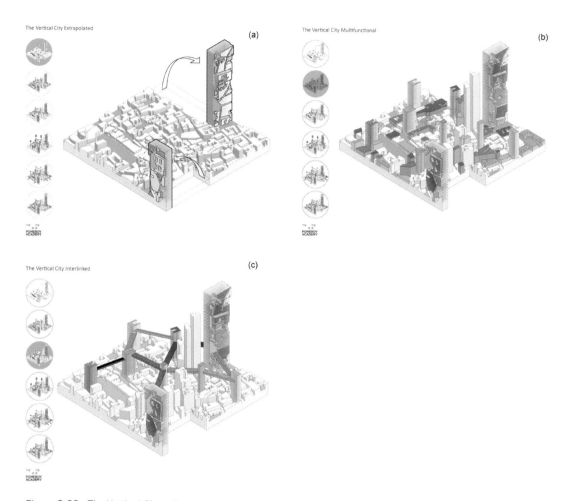

Figure 8.29: The Vertical City – Extrapolated, Multifunctional and Interlinked. © Pomeroy Studio

Funding and client commissions

Research projects at Pomeroy Studio are typically self-financed or have been undertaken as a component within a commercial project. Although clients are drawn to the practice because of the research aspect of the work, it is rarely to commission research directly as a stand-alone project. A tendering scheme is available through the Government of Singapore, as with National Research Foundation, however, the practice has found this to be a laborious process and the outcomes rarely outweighing the endeavour required.

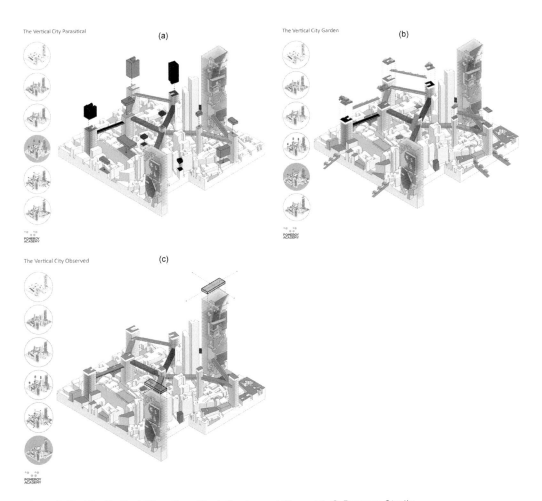

Figure 8.30: The Vertical City – Parasitical, Garden and Observed. © Pomeroy Studio

Collaborations

The practice has established relationships for teaching and research with specialist institutions to support their focus on innovative research and design for sustainable built environments. They maintain ongoing collaborations with James Cook University in North Queensland, King Saud University in Riyadh, and the University of Cambridge's Interdisciplinary Design Built Environment (IDBE) programme. The partnership with the IDBE has developed further with the establishment of the Pomeroy Academy Scholarship IDBE for graduate students from the South East Asian region.

For the POG project in Venice, the Studio worked with Universitá Iuav di Venezia whose evident expertise in waterborne cities and communities supported the technical knowledge of zero energy development and vertical urban theory, leading to a final design. The practice worked with the National Parks Board, Building Construction Authority, Urban Redevelopment Authority, and the National University of Singapore to develop a planning metric for assessing commercial, residential and industrial buildings using the green plot ratio method as a means of urban greenery enhancement.

Publishing and disseminating work

Publishing their research is critical to the studio, and their strategy, which includes producing books with major publishing houses, is intended to share their research findings with a broader audience and engage informed debate of the vital contribution of the built environment to combating climate change. This has led to invitations to lecture which have in turn led to television series, *Smart Cities 2.0, City Redesign,* and two series of *City Time Traveller,* all of which have proved to attract clients.

In a departure from most practices, Pomeroy Studios retains the intellectual property and copyright of its research. Clients are granted a licence to use the drawings and the designs to create the building. Pomeroy likens this to buying a suit from a tailor where the patterns, tools, skills and knowledge are retained by the tailor while the client owns the suit.

Pomeroy Studio - Project profiles

Lexis Hibiscus Resort

Completed in 2015, the Lexis Hibiscus Resort in Port Dickson on Malaysia's west coast is a luxury hotel complex comprising 117 suites in a tower with their commanding view of the 522 over-water villas arranged in the shape of the country's national flower, from which the resort takes its name (see Figure 8.31). The practice has applied their research in sustainable development to deliver low energy design to a sector not traditionally associated with environmental innovation. The prefabricated modular villas (see Figure 8.32) were constructed off-site using environmentally friendly and recyclable materials. Water from the

Figure 8.31: Aerial view of the Lexis Hibiscus Resort in Malaysia. © Pomeroy Studio

Figure 8.32: View of the over-water villas at Lexis Hibiscus Resort. © Pomeroy Studio

plunge pools set into the deck of each of the water villas reduces the temperature of the sea breeze, aiding passive cooling and so lessens the need for air conditioning. Energy use is mitigated further with shallow floor plates to optimise daylight penetration and window opening configurations to aid ventilation.

The Lexis Hibiscus Resort features in *POD Off-Grid* (Pomeroy, 2016) in which Pomeroy sets out his argument for waterborne living. Living on, or hovering above, water already exists around the world from London to Lagos, albeit on a much smaller scale than development on land. With acknowledged issues of land shortages, rising global population and the impacts of climate change constructing floating communities is the next logical solution, for the practice, when combined with a focus on sustainable development principles.

POD Off-Grid

A former monastery and then military base, the 22-hectare site, Venetian island Isola La Certosa, is now a holiday resort with a hotel and sailing marina. POG proposes a self-sustaining, floating development that builds on the knowledge gained in prefabricated modular development at Lexis Hibiscus to develop new prototypes that are far removed from the typical rectangular boxes of modular residential developments (see Figure 8.33). The mixed-use

Figure 8.33: Render of the view from a residential tower, part of the POG project. © Pomeroy Studio

development supports agricultural, civic and leisure facilities as well as housing (see Figure 8.34) and, as a zero-energy development, incorporates wind turbines and photovoltaic units and harnesses tidal movements to generate the power required. The scheme includes a waste treatment plant, rainwater capture, and grey water recycling mechanisms, while the towers and communal spaces are designed to maximise cross ventilation (see Figure 8.35).

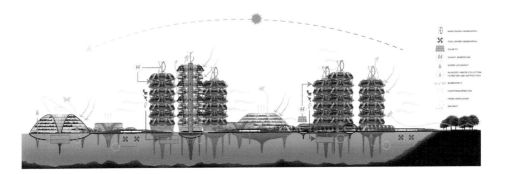

Figure 8.34: Cross section of the POG project indicating the environmental features of the proposed development. © Pomeroy Studio

Figure 8.35: Rendered view of the view into the internal shared garden at the POG project. © Pomeroy Studio

New York, United States of America

Practice structure

Located in New York, Architecture Research Office is a 30 member practice that has embedded research within the process of practice since its inception in 1993, and is led by Stephen Cassell, Kim Yao and Adam Yarinsky. Here the research work adopts an empirical methodology and is part of a larger contextual relationship with social and environmental goals, with emphasis on achieving sustainability which aims to combine beauty and form with strategy and intelligence. The research conducted is not pure research in the academic sense, but is part of applied work that feeds their architectural work. In doing so they have developed a body of work that informs design proposals and their responses to bids.

This approach is reflected in their team structure where, rather than having a permanent research only team, the practice expects that all staff are in some way involved in research. As all staff are design graduates, with no PhDs, the practice operates a mentorship model in which young architects and new recruits are placed within established and experienced teams, providing them with informal teaching and opportunities to engage at all levels including detailed briefing enquiries with clients to gather detailed information from those interviews, ensuring that the whole team is involved from the outset of the project and consistency across working practices, particularly with respect to rigour in the process.

The benefits of research and its influence on design

Research is an integrated part of the process from the outset, including at the briefing stage. However, they have found that scheduling research into live projects requires careful and experienced planning as the design process can run ahead of the research schedule, restricting the potential for research to inform the design. The process of applied design research, and the ongoing development of methodology, has generated work for the practice. They have won multiple awards including the Academy Award for Architecture from the

American Academy of Arts and Letters, the Cooper-Hewitt National Design Award for Architecture, and were the American Institute of Architects' Practice of the year in 2020.

The practice established a materials working group whose aim is to oversee the seamless integration of environmental research with the design process to provide greater control over decisions made and take greater responsibility for materials used, echoing the international movement Architect's Declare, and deliver on that manifesto.

While strategic or program research work doesn't always lead to commissioned design work, it has, in the case of the *On the Water* project and exhibition, led to further commissions for different projects. This elevated profile through the practice's research-led design agenda has also drawn large numbers of top-level job applicants.

Research focus

With a research-driven design agenda, the research conducted by the practice-driven primarily by design fields in which they are engaged although not all of the research is published alongside the architectural work. The research has a strong environmental focus with a particular interest in flood resilience and conducted a review of the economic and social value of excellence of publicly funded design, encompassing multiple directly associated and allied disciplines.

One ongoing project focusses on teaching and learning within schools of architecture, and how that is reflected in room utilisation strategic planning and strategy on working practices for several universities in North America including Harvard Graduate School of Design, University of British Columbia, Kent State Michigan, Columbia, Cornell and Princeton. This longitudinal and detailed analysis has built a body of expertise within the practice that shapes discussions with future clients and the strategic work conducted for them, challenging perceptions about the use of space based on decades old data, the working practices of schools of architecture, devising an alternative uses for studio spaces, lecture halls and classrooms reducing their low occupancy rates. A form of post occupancy evaluation, this thinking and methodology have been applied to other projects for clients in different sectors securing new work.

Publishing and disseminating work

The potential benefits of increasing knowledge capture and dissemination at the end of research projects are firmly recognised within the practice, viewed as presenting the opportunity to replicate and build upon processes or methodologies for future research and design work. As well as features on their research-led design work, their research publications produced by ARO includes their 2003 practice monograph (Cassell, Yarinsky, & Architecture Research Office, 2003) and co-authored book *On the Water: Palisade Bay* (Nordenson, Seavitt, Yarinsky, & Museum of Modern Art, 2010), which features their *Rising Currents* exhibition at the Museum of Modern Arts in New York in 2009–2010.

Funding and client commissions

While much of the research work is self-funded or part of a design project, the practice was the recipient of the AIA's 2007 Latrobe Prize in 2007, and has received several direct commissions for research, including from the Van Alen Institute, to investigate environmental defences along the Lower Mississippi River Delta, and an invitation to contribute the equity and social inclusion sections to the updated Active Design Guidelines for the Federal Design Excellence Strategy.

Following the publication of *On the Water* and corresponding exhibition at MoMA in New York, Architecture Research Office was, along with ARUP, invited by the Department of City Planning and the United States Department of Housing and Urban Design, to prepare a sustainability report following Hurricane Sandy.

Collaborations

The practice has established formal research partnerships across several fields. They have found that engineers make for beneficial collaborations as they recognise ARO's appreciation for the information generated by the work and mutual recognition of the research process and methodology development. It was their collaboration with Princeton University faculty for *On the Water, A Model for the Future: a study of New York and Jersey Upper Bay* that won them the

AIA Latrobe Prize, and the project continued through to the MoMA exhibition and following book.

More recently ARO's pre-design research collaboration with Knoll built on existing processes of texture and surface and fabrication and the experience of space, particularly the relationship with sound and noise attenuation in the workplace. This partnership resulted in a collection that Knoll developed further to create a saleable product and won the 2015 Interior Design HiP Performance Wonder award.

Architecture Research Office - Project profiles

Five principles for Greenwich South

Five principles for Greenwich South presents a flexible framework for the future of Greenwich South, a 41-acre neighbourhood at the southern tip of Manhattan, in response to a commission by the Alliance for Downtown New York. ARO led a 15 strong multi-disciplinary team, including economists, planners, engineers and landscape architects, to develop the scheme with the aim of reinvigorating an overlooked parcel directly below the World Trade Center. Rather than a traditional masterplan, the collective developed a strategic framework with an adaptable matrix of principles, objectives, and opportunities for the neighborhood and the city (see Figure 8.36).

The research team conducted an extensive assessment of the site including "programmatic, architectural, zoning, land use, and circulation studies" that "demonstrated the under-use of the area by residents, tourists, and area workers on all sides" and "nearly ten million square feet of developable air rights latent in Greenwich South" (Cassell & Barrett, 2011, p. 57). Working alongside the Downtown Alliance, ARO married these findings to establish an ongoing programme of stakeholder and community engagement including charrettes, presentations and an outdoor exhibition at Zuccotti Park (see Figure 8.37), to encourage a public dialogue debating the future of the city.

The final report identifies five principles for future development: encouraging an intense mix of uses; reconnect Greenwich Street; connecting east and west; build for density, design for people; and create a reason to come and a reason to stay (Alliance for Downtown New York, 2009). Included in this are design

Figure 8.36: Diagram showing Greenwich South, a 41-acre neighbourhood at the southern tip of Manhattan that had been overlooked for years but had seen a rise in residents and tourists.
© Architecture Research Office

proposals developed by the wider collective. ARO's design proposal for the site took the developable air rights above the multi-lane Brooklyn-Battery Tunnel as their starting point to create Market Park, connecting the neigbourhood and several key landmarks including the World Trade Center 9/11 Memorial and Battery Park. The design included a large-scale farmers market with a mixed-use tower comprising commercial and residential space, and an urban farm, a concept developed by WORKac.

Figure 8.37: An outdoor exhibition at Zuccotti Park shared the research and ideas of the Five Principles for Greenwich South. © Frank Oudeman

On the Water, a Model for the Future: A Study of New York and Jersey Upper Bay

Any projections of the future impact of rising sea levels and their impact on cities will, in all likelihood, include New York with predictions that redraws the coastline of the island and suggests that substantial parts of Manhattan under water. ARO's response, in collaboration with Guy Nordenson and Associates and Catherine Seavitt Studio (Nordenson et al., 2010).

The research process included using GIS to map the topography and bathymetry of the harbour (see Figure 8.38), allowing for a comprehensive understanding of its geological composition, tidal pattern and the potential impacts of storms and rising sea levels on Lower Manhattan, and built water tables to model storm surge damage and develop and test the design of islands to mitigate the force of storm surges and consequential flooding. Although all islands have identical footprints on the seabed, variations in the pattern of islands are created in relation to the changing

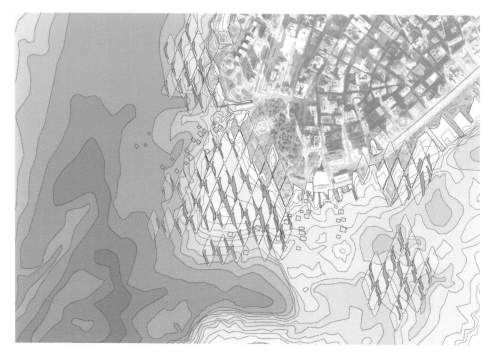

Figure 8.38: Diagram indicating the estuary bathymetry and island array pattern, with the largest cluster located near the tip of Manhattan providing the most surface area for storm surge protection and blending with the coastline. © Architecture Research Office/Guy Nordenson and Catherine Seavitt

bathymetry of the harbour. Over time, sediment would extend the size of the islands which form a framework aiding the natural processes and restoration of the estuary.

Avoiding the typical design response of rigid flood defence structures such as high walls, the project strategy includes a "soft infrastructure" scheme including an archipelago of islands accompanied by a graduated edge. With a peak higher than the current seawall elevation, geotextile tubes filled with recycled dredge material, such as Geotubes® manufactured by Tencate, are stacked to create new landforms (see Figure 8.39), designed to slow the advance of water into the built environment and provide new wetland habitats (see Figure 8.40).

Rising Currents: Projects for New York's Waterfront

Following the two-year study of Palisade Bay, ARO was invited, along with another four design teams, to contribute to the 2010 'Rising Currents: Projects for New York's Waterfront' exhibition and workshop at MoMA. Building on their earlier research and in collaboration with DLANDstudio, the partnership developed a

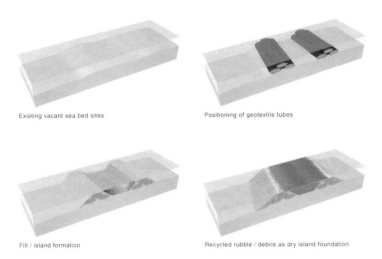

Existing vacant sea bed sites

Positioning of geotextile tubes

Fill / island formation

Recycled rubble / debris as dry island foundation

Figure 8.39: The stages of construction of the filled Geotextile tubes indicating their positioning, filling and island formation, and interstitial filing to form islands. © Architecture Research Office/Guy Nordenson and Catherine Seavitt

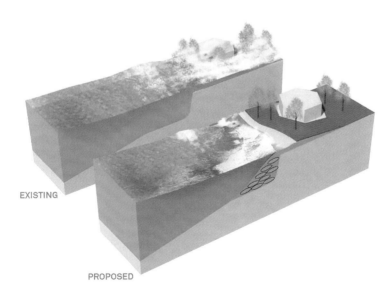

EXISTING

PROPOSED

Figure 8.40: The proposal reshapes the seawall using filled Geotextile tubes into a gentle berm higher than the current seawall elevation, gradually sloping into the river and the pedestrian promenade is reconstructed, protecting adjoining buildings. © Architecture Research Office/ Guy Nordenson and Catherine Seavitt

proposal intended not only to address flood water and mitigate against storm surge, but to also improve the overall environment and streetscape in the area, with anticipated everyday benefits for all.

The first of two parts of the scheme proposes porous green streets with absorptive surfaces, channelling storm waters out to the Harbour (see Figure 8.41) and to address surface water that contributes to new green space for an area of the city lacking a park. However, rather than a park of defined boundaries, this park extends along streets and beyond the edge of the shoreline, extended a block into the Harbour with landfill to create an esker around the peninsula (see Figure 8.42), and supported by freshwater wetlands and tidal salt marshes (see Figure 8.43).

Figure 8.41: Coenties Slip. A linear forest, with a tree canopy aligned with parkland on top of the East River esker and running along the East River to the Brooklyn Bridge, is set below street level to provide the first line of defence against storm surges. © DLANDstudio/Architecture Research Office

Figure 8.42: By 2100, Lower Manhattan's natural habitat expands out into the harbour. Dark Green areas are upland parks, medium green areas are freshwater wetlands, and light green areas are saltwater marshes. The new, continuous ecosystem encompassing the island's edge would add 2 miles of shoreline to Manhattan. © DLANDstudio/Architecture Research Office

Figure 8.43: The proposed "greening of Lower Manhattan with parks and wetlands create new ecosystems, facilitating the ecological interconnectivity of the region, improving water quality, and enhancing opportunities for habitat growth. © DLANDstudio/Architecture Research Office

8.4 Mid-size practice case study

8.4.1 Architype   *Mid-sized practice case study*

Hereford, United Kingdom

Practice structure

Architype's three UK offices accommodate around 60 people drawn from across the built environment sector and most are engaged in research. While most of those involved both in research and the environmental consultancy are permanent members of staff, the practice retains several long-standing, formal associations with experts in the field including staff sponsored through Knowledge Transfer Partnerships. The practice has won the title of AJ100 Sustainable Practice of the Year an unprecedented three times.

The interest in and commitment to research is driven from a senior management level and is, in part, reflected in the seriousness with which in-house training and CPD are approached. New recruits are introduced to the training culture and automatically enrolled on PassivHaus courses. The practice deliberately carves out time to accommodate research and staff are actively encouraged to submit research proposals to the internal Research Working Group.

Research in the practice was inspired by the late Walter Segal and the self-build typology that evolved from a temporary home he designed and built for himself using standard easily accessible components, establishing an early experimental culture and determination to approach practice differently. This was followed by work with TRADA (Timber Research and Development Association) around the year 2000 investigating English Douglas Fir as a cladding material and the potential to use fewer chemicals in the treatment of structural timber and the benefits of reducing toxicity.

The benefits of research and its influence on design

Research is the starting point for all design work, and post occupancy evaluation (POE) completes the process. Despite the potential impact on profitability, the practice considers there to be two clear benefits of high level of research engagement.

First, is a better informed and more engaged staff which follows through the practice ethos and their design work. Second, is a better informed design and delivery process and aftercare refined through ongoing POE. This has also won them repeated work, notably in the education sector where research conducted on one school building built to PassivHaus standards, identified a reduced energy consumption of 80–90%, equivalent to £30,000–£40,000 or a teacher's salary.

Research focus

Improving the environmental sustainability of buildings to meet the highest standards such as PassivHaus, has long been the focus of their research agenda. This has led to the development of software to calculate embodied energy, cost and carbon including RAPIERe (Rapid Prototyping and Analysis Tool for Environmental and Cost Performance Improvement and Emissions Reductions in Low Impact Buildings), and product and materials research. In 2019 Architype launched their in-house environmental consultancy PERFORM+, with the aim of more clearly defining their practice activity and offering a comprehensive environmental consultancy service. In the same year, the practice completed Bicester Eco Business Centre in Oxfordshire, the first certified non-domestic PassivHaus+ building in the UK for which they were again shortlisted for the AJ100 Sustainability Practice of the Year.

Future plans for the practice are being directed to develop more sophisticated studies that expand building performance to become built environment performance, and expanding to include retrofitting and adaptation of existing and heritage buildings. One project investigates the relationship between busy roads and air quality, and the influence of wind direction, speed and strength, which have the potential to influence their buildings that rely on self-regulating external air movement, and identifying solutions such as green barriers to reduce rates of childhood asthma.

Funding and client commissions

With local councils becoming more aware of environmental issues and more proactive in seeking solutions for their buildings including housing, they are among a series of clients responsible for directly commissioning research work. Although not all clients are willing to pay for POE studies, the practice has developed ongoing relationships with several local authorities, and other clients including the House of Windsor and the British Council. A key feature of the consultancy arm of the practice is its aftercare programme which includes post-occupancy studies, post occupancy training, and post-building support, and around 20% of these projects become research projects.

Their collaboration projects have been successful in continuing to attract funding from Innovate UK, including the RAPIERe project intended to optimise sustainable design, and launched at Battersea Power Station in 2015. The practice has previously received a grant from University College London, the Ashton Medal, and continues to support smaller projects proposed by staff with in-house funding.

Collaborations

Starting with a Knowledge Transfer Partnership with Oxford Brookes University in the late 2000s, the practice has fostered long-running collaborative research partnerships at Westminster University, Bath University, the University of West of England, Coventry University, and the Architectural Association that, alongside teaching, includes providing case studies for student work. The practice has also funded the PhD of a member of the Architype team at University College London's Institute for Environmental Design and Engineering to investigate the impact of external air quality on internal air quality, particularly relevant in high-density urban areas. Beyond academia, the practice has conducted collaborative research projects with three private companies, BDSP Partnership Limited, Sweett (UK) Limited, and Greenspace Live Limited on the RAPIERe project.

Publishing and disseminating work

Architype's publishing strategy is driven by a resolve to contribute to the wider understanding and advancement of environmental sustainability.

> We see publishing our work as essential. It's at the core of the way we operate. We see it not only as a benefit to our practice but we want to share this information to help improve knowledge across the industry and drive new advances.
>
> (Martindale, 2016)

In recognition of this approach, the practice has won a series of awards from the RIBA, CIBSE and UK Passivhaus Trust and has won the title of AJ100 Sustainability Practice of the Year three times with judges in 2019 remarked that "sustainability permeates the ethos of the practice" (Hartman, 2019).

Their external output includes book chapters, academic journal and conference papers, short articles and presentations. Around 15 senior members of staff regularly speak at conferences and industry events, and sharing expertise through industry panels including the RIBA, RTPI and CIBSE. The practice encourages younger staff members to participate in conferences and to take up speaking opportunities, and actively promotes options for them to do so.

Within the practice, research is shared at their annual forum and internal project presentations. Research findings, reports and presentation slides are shared through their intranet, and staff are encouraged to submit to the improvement log something that needs to be fixed or is proving problematic, and seeking solutions from colleagues.

Architype - Project profiles

Wilkinson School

Having already completed two PassivHaus schools, the UK's first, the client, Wolverhampton City Council, demanded that Wilkinson School be built to the same standard, replacing the existing school that had been destroyed by arson. The primary school accommodates a school body of 430 students and a 30-place nursery. As the surrounding community had been proactive in responding to the arson attack, helping to install and support staff and pupils temporary accommodation, the council were keen to maintain that engagement which followed through the design process and beyond with the new school offering facilities for the whole community (see Figure 8.44).

The resulting design, winner of the PassivHaus Trust Awards in 2015, employed natural, low-carbon, sustainable materials, with an emphasis on recycled and toxin-free products. Canopies on the southern side of the building were angled at 15° to reflect winter sunlight onto the internal ceiling that with high-level clerestory windows, helped to maximise natural daylight (see Figure 8.45). The practice continues to monitor thermal comfort at the school, comparing it with data from two first-generation PassivHaus schools, two

Figure 8.44: Exterior view of Wilkinson School showing the rusted steel finishes emphasising the site's links to its rich industrial heritage, important to both the client and the community. © Dennis Gilbert/ VIEW

pre-PassivHaus schools, and a school built to 1970s UK Building Regulations. This research has demonstrated a clear progression of improvement with the best overall results from Wilkinson Primary School.

University of East Anglia Enterprise Centre

The University of East Anglia Enterprise Centre (see Figure 8.46), designed to meet PassivHaus certification and BREEAM Outstanding, has won five awards including two from the RIBA (East Regional Award and Sustainable Project of The Year), two BCO National Awards, and the BREEAM Award for Best Education Project. Part of Norwich Research Park, the Centre provides accommodation primarily for new graduate startup companies and business support through the University's Low Carbon MBA and associated graduate

Figure 8.45: Natural daylight floods the school hall at Wilkinson School. © Dennis Gilbert/VIEW

programmes. Reflecting this connection to sustainability studies, and to better understand the requirements of the Centre's users, the practice conducted an extensive workshopping and consultation process that also included a range of representatives from the local planning authority and design review panel, as well as conservation officers.

Part of the research undertaken for the project included Shading Analysis to establish the optimal level of shading to improve internal comfort. Based on future UK predicted weather patterns, they concluded that the height of the shade above a window, rather than installing a shade of variable length, was most cost-effective. This analysis amended the allocation and distribution of south-facing windows to take solar gain into account. As part of their ongoing

Figure 8.46: View of the southern facade, University of East Anglia Enterprise Centre. © Darren Carter/Morgan Sindall

monitoring process, carbon monitoring systems were installed showing the impacts on energy efficiency and carbon offsetting. Architype worked with the University to generate multiple design scenarios, simulated in PassivHaus Planning Package, including a lifecycle carbon study, glazing ratios, shading and natural ventilation design.

Agar Grove

Winning two Mayor's Awards for sustainable and environmental planning, and good growth, Agar Grove in North London is the UK's largest residential PassivHaus scheme (see Figure 8.47). Originally designed by Hawkins\ Brown, Architype were responsible for the PassivHaus events of the design and project delivery. Delivering the technical aspects of the design has become one of the aspects of the practice that has continued to grow based

Figure 8.47: Street view of Agar Road residential development, built with Hawkins\Brown. © Jack Hobhouse

on their research, collaborative 'no blame' culture, and approach to sharing knowledge.

Originally built in the 1960s, the site comprised 249 social-rented homes with two construction phases adding a further 493 units, comprising family terrace housing and maisonettes each with gardens, and apartments with balconies. Most of the apartments are dual aspect with south-facing living spaces and full-width balconies (see Figure 8.48) affording views of central London. Orientation plays a significant role in PassivHaus designs and calculations which have reduced heating bills by 70–90% compared with conventional homes. Having installed temperature and humidity monitors in the apartments prior to occupation, the practice was able to confirm comfort levels in the apartments during a cold winter in 2018 and continue to collect and monitor the data.

Figure 8.48: Agar Road balcony looking over the street, built with Hawkins\Brown. © Jack Hobhouse

Duxford Paper Store, Imperial War Museums

Completed in 2019, Imperial War Museums commissioned Architype to design a storage facility to accommodate 14,000 linear meters of the Museum's paper collections and artefacts that includes artworks, photographs, letters and diaries covering the history of warfare amassed over the last 100 years, with the capacity to accommodate future articles (see Figures 8.49 and 8.50).

The Duxford archive builds on their PassivHaus expertise in other sectors, and experience completing the Herefordshire Archive and Records Centre completed in 2014 which was built to the PD5454:2012 standard. Besides the low-energy option with lower running costs, further refinements to the design guaranteed the required stable environmental conditions temperature and humidity conditions critical for archives, setting a new standard for airtightness result at 0.03 ach.

Figure 8.49: Exterior view of the new Cor-Ten steel structure, with panels that signify each year of archived collections from 1914, and existing brick facade of the Imperial War Museum Paper Store. © Richard Ash/Imperial War Museum

Figure 8.50: View of the interior of the Imperial War Museum Paper Store with light filtering through perforations in the Cor-Ten steel facade that represent the collection, with heavy perforations identifying significant years. © Richard Ash/Imperial War Museum

Copenhagen, Denmark

Practice structure

Architecture and urbanism led practice Gehl Architects was founded in 2000 in Copenhagen by Jan Gehl and Helle Søholt following Gehl's retirement from the Royal Danish Academy of Fine Arts in Copenhagen. While teaching at the School of Architecture, part of the Academy, Gehl developed a community engagement research methodology. Based on the concept that a city should work for all of its citizens, his analysis of the city was conducted at different times of the day, on different days and times of the year, to better understand how people used places and their relationship with the urban environment rather than traffic movement that had previously dominated urban analysis. Building on this Gehl founded the Centre for Public Space Research at the School of Architecture that employed a team of 5–7 people including Birgitte Bundesen Svarre, now a Director at Gehl.

In 2014 the practice opened studios in San Francisco and New York and now employs approximately 70 staff across the three studios supported by a bank of international associates who are experts in their respective fields. The early years of the practice were spent developing knowledge of the political mechanisms and the citizen engagement strategies for which the practice is well known. Currently, the practice conducts fewer pure research projects, in part because the relatively small practice spot between three studios can make it difficult to manage, instead choosing to focus on making research part of the design process.

The benefits of research and its influence on design

Rather than an independent research arm attached to the practice, the ethos and research methodology are embedded within the project development and design processes of the practice, driving the design and engagement with clients. Their longitudinal approach to data collection feeds an incremental development of knowledge, expertise and competencies across the practice team.

As Birgitte Bundesen Svarre noted, research embedded "within the DNA of the practice" provides a solid base for engaging with and influencing policy makers and planners. This approach also instils confidence in their clients of the process and potential outcomes and has proved attractive to job applicants, attracted to the practice's value-based design approach.

Research focus

The unremitting focus of the practice, since Jan Gehl's first observational work in the mid-1960s, has been to understand and create better urban spaces summed up by Svarre as "What type of city do we want? Who is it for? Who is it not for?" Using Copenhagen as their primary, and ongoing, case study and urban laboratory, the practice has a reputation for its community engagement-focussed work with an international client base that stretches from New Zealand and Australia, through China, the United States, the United Kingdom, Germany and across Scandinavia.

More recently the practice has been working with different age groups including young children, around six years of age, to capture their perceptions of the city with the aim of developing new knowledge and tools for designers, planners and policy makers. Another project explored foodscapes in the city, engaging teenagers to better understand their time spent in fast-food restaurants, such as MacDonald's, which provide safe locations for teenagers to meet and socialise, indicating the lack of suitable alternatives in other urban locations.

The development of future research projects is inspired by existing projects, as Svarre declared, "there is so much more to be explored!" One such potential project uses a qualitative approach to examine the health dimensions of microclimates, the implications for city design, social equity and social patterns. To facilitate this, the practice is designing a new platform for collecting data.

Funding and client commissions

Other than securing a grant in 2003 from Danish philanthropists the Realdania Foundation, for research that led to the production of *How to Study Public Life* (2013) and other grants around this period, the practice has received no direct funding for research projects as the focus is on research-driven design projects. Neither have they sought funding, including from centralised EU sources, as it feel it is time-consuming and rarely yields results.

Around half of all projects are conducted in northern Europe and Scandinavia, with the other half in Australia, New Zealand, India, China. By developing and focusing on ongoing relationships, particularly with the community reasoning that the experts in any location are its citizens, they are better able to understand the culture, deepen practice knowledge and provide qualified advice. Reflecting this the City of Wellington invited the practice back to the city to perform a follow-up study and reassessment of their 2004 work. Using their approach to facilitate the conversation, they have been nicknamed the Scandinavian Icebreakers for their capacity to initiate dialogue.

Collaborations

The focus for Gehl's collaborations lies in academia with the aim of supporting student learning, and have developed multiple academic collaborations with several staff members teaching at local Copenhagen universities. The practice has, for example, partnered with the University of Utrecht to conduct a study examining the links between air quality and health, looking at micro-particles, employing Google data, and applying the same techniques used in the Copenhagen surveys.

Publishing and disseminating work

Jan Gehl sees both his and the practice's publication as the legacy of their work and that this role is very important. To date, the practice has published more than ten significant reports and toolkits, and seven books including *Life between buildings: using public space* (Gehl, 2011) and *Cities for people* (Gehl, 2010) both of which have been translated into more than 30 languages, and *How to study public life* (Gehl & Svarre, 2013). Their documentary, *The Human Scale* (Dalsgaard, 2012) was nominated for several awards at the Copenhagen International Documentary Festival, and the Hamburg and Zurich film festivals.

While there are several established speakers in the practice, they are increasingly mindful about where and to who they deliver talks, aiming to both focus on projects based work and reduce the environmental impact of travelling. This has meant delivering fewer talks to specific markets that align with the practice's work and future direction potentially generating greater impact. They deliver masterclasses in Copenhagen and their American studios, and host in-house training and talks for invited guests.

Gehl Architects - Project profiles

Mapping foodscapes

The role that food plays in Copenhagen's ambition to become climate neutral by 2025, was recognised with the city's signatory to the Good Food Cities Declaration (C40Cities, 2019), through the city's own policies and response to the UN Sustainable Development Goals which outlined a series of initiatives and targets to improve the health of its residents and address the impact food transport, consumption and waste has on the environment (City of Copenhagen, 2018). Funded by Climate KIC, Shifting Urban Diets is a 3-year collaboration between Gehl, the EAT Foundation, City of Copenhagen, City University London, Potsdam Institute for Climate Impact Research, and World Resources Institute. Having already identified in earlier work that teenagers (between 13 and 17) are the most likely age group to change their habits, Gehl's role in the project focussed on mapping foodscapes, where public space, public life and food places converge, from their perspective. The team conducted workshops and led walking tours of two Copenhagen neighbourhoods, Nørrebro and Vesterbro, with 20 young people, observing the group's dynamics and individual behaviours, their routes through these areas, and their food choices (see Figures 8.51 and 8.52).

Figure 8.51: One of the Copenhagen workshops with teenagers, mapping their food choices. © Gehl Architects

Figure 8.52: The Foodscapes walking tour conducted in two Copenhagen neighbourhoods. © Gehl Architects

The research, aimed at identifying how the built environment influences food choices, presented three findings. First, that food is a catalyst to socialise, and as cost is a consideration, supermarkets and fast food outlets were the most common outlets selected by the group (see Figure 8.53). Second, the design quality of the school's outdoor and play areas, and their maintenance, influenced eating habits. Students at schools without engaging areas to sit, play or shelter, left the school premises each break time, while those with better facilities stayed at school. Third, the design of the public realm lacked the sociable

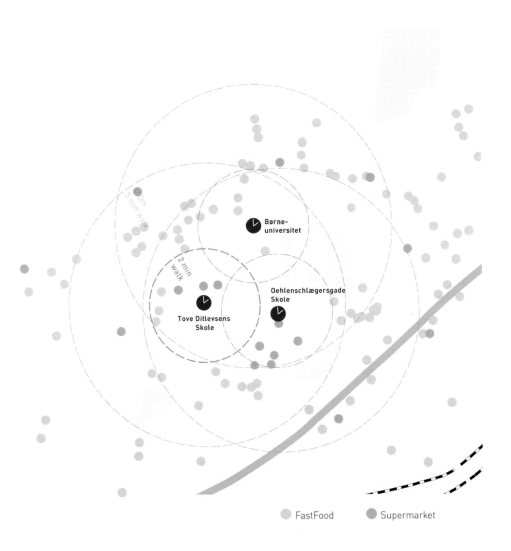

Børne-
universitet

5 min walk

2 min
walk

Oehlenschlægersgade
Skole

Tove Ditlevsens
Skole

● FastFood   ● Supermarket

Figure 8.53: Map of the proximity of fast food outlets and supermarkets to three schools in Copenhagen. © Gehl Architects

seating options and bright and creative furniture they sought, in locations that don't make them feel as though they are constantly being surveilled. The team identified the Superkilen park in Nørrebro as being a good example of a well-designed, engaging space for young people. Interventions were trialled in Nørrebro and Vesterbro in August and September 2020, with the outcomes and responses part of the ongoing project.

This research project was later replicated in the South London districts of Camberwell and Peckham which, at 52% and 32% respectively, experience some of the highest childhood obesity rates in the UK for children aged 10–11 years old. Conducted for Guy's and St Thomas' Charity, the practice worked with community researchers from The Social Innovation Partnership to conduct an observational analysis of the sites including walking tours, 400 on-site inter-views with residents aged 6–16 and adults, and host workshops with 25 young people (see Figure 8.54).

In contrast to their Danish peers, young people in Camberwell and Peckham rarely use public parks and squares, preferring to spend time in fast food outlets and around bus stops. Their London project presented two key findings, the first, that bus stops were the main location for young people eating with their friends (see Figure 8.55). The research discovered that the strength of the connection between fast food outlets and public transport stops is such that food outlets are prepared to pay very high rents for these locations, enabling them to supply cheap, speedily cooked food to commuters and young people (see Figure 8.56). Their second conclusion found that government funding cuts had left young people with few amenities or locations to socialise. Fast food outlets have evolved, therefore, into the main socialising spaces for this age group, notably

Figure 8.54: Conducting on-street interviews with teenagers about their food choices in a London hot spot between fast-food restaurants to bus stops. © Gehl Architects

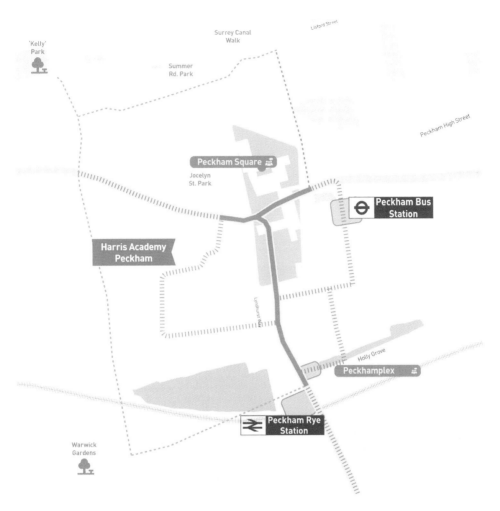

Figure 8.55: London Foodscapes concept solution for Peckham, indicating alternative routes for children to lessen their exposure to fast food. © Gehl Architects

for their ability to spend long periods of time there without being moved on or being required to spend much money.

Gehl's recommendations include redesigning transit stops including reducing fast food outlets in close proximity, and improving streetscapes with young people in mind that provides them with safe, inviting spaces in which to socialise and travel through (see Figure 8.57).

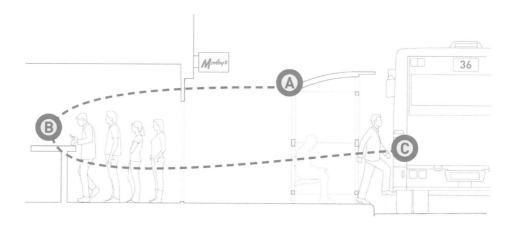

Figure 8.56: The public transit and fast food triangle identified on London's high streets. © Gehl Architects

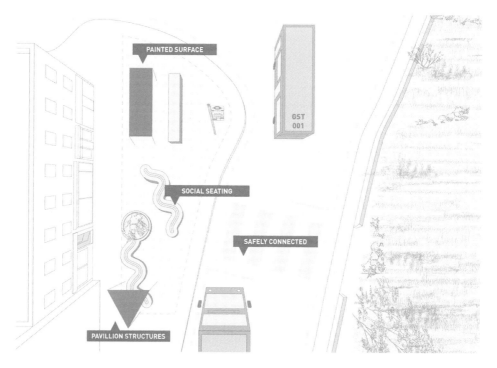

Figure 8.57: An alternative bus stop design solution for the London Foodscapes project, including seating and shelter options. © Gehl Architects

8.5 Large practice case study

Sydney, Australia

Practice structure

Hayball Architecture employs around 160 people working across three studios in the eastern half of Australia. The practice was established in the early 1980s with research conducted on an informal basis from the outset. The practice underwent a rebranding and regeneration in 2008 that included a formalised research agenda aimed at providing a structure to support this activity, better integrating research into the design process with an evidence-based response, and disseminating knowledge across the practice. As director Fiona Young explained, "evidence-based design, and design-led research, are a part of our design ethos. There is a greater need to be accountable, to explain design propositions and, in this way, open the process to wider evaluation and participation."

The research team is led by one full-time staff member dedicated to research, with around three colleagues, two with formal research training, working between architecture project and research. A research committee was established to oversee and evaluate research opportunities for interested staff. Committee members, made up of a diverse group of leaders from the practice covering a broad range of project typologies, act as mentors, providing feedback on research proposals and offering ongoing guidance, and connecting the applicant with professional contacts.

The benefits of research and its influence on design

Improving operations, optimising building performance, and enhancing the end-user experience are cited as the main benefits of research to Hayball. Applying an evidence-based approach to design that examines the intersection between business and behaviour supports their clients to actively manage future challenges. The practice believe that research significantly de-risks their project from the initial design phases through to project delivery, allowing for innovation and it helps to depoliticise decision-making. Within the practice, research has proved influential in improving practice culture, staff retention, and development.

Research focus

Hayball applies an evidence-based design and design-led research approach to all design sectors in which they currently operate including education, workplace, design technology, affordable housing, urban design, child-friendly cities, native ecologies, and the regeneration of cities, and designing with Indigenous communities.

Their first formal research project was 'Smart Green Schools', a collaboration with the University of Melbourne and funded by the Australian Research Council (ARC), to investigate the influence of innovative and sustainable school building designs on middle years education in Victoria. This sector, from kindergarten to universities, continues to be a key research and design interest for the practice.

This draws on workplace research the practice has been conducting looking at alternative methods of working and occupying, using space wellbeing, mobility and flexibility as markers of an effective and desirable environment. For example, Students at Monash University completed a post-evaluation report on Holman and Campbell halls of residence designed by Hayball aimed at assessing the extent to which the design intentions had been met. Mapping research captured data through both researcher observation with behavioural mapping and participant recollection with cognitive maps.

Developing new methods of delivering affordable and alternative housing models is a field the practice intends to develop further, building on their work on multi-residential projects with Nightingale Housing and Assemble Communities. Researching the quantitative and quantitative outcomes through post-occupancy evaluation studies interviewing to follow on from and respond to the knowledge gained from both projects in the briefing and design stages.

Going forward their research process and methods are expanding to include virtual and augmented reality with a view to building data analytics solutions for internal efficiencies and data-driven design. Their longer-term ambition lies with an in-house laboratory to develop innovative materials, fabrication techniques and design robotics.

Funding and client commissions

In addition to ARC funding for four projects in partnership with Learning Environments Applied Research Network (LEaRN) at the University of

Melbourne, Hayball staff have received research funding from Winston Churchill Memorial Trust (Churchill Fellowship), NSW Government (Byera Hadley Travelling Scholarship), and the Australian Institute of Architects (David Lindner prize). The practice has also undertaken several studies commissioned by the Department of Planning and Community Development.

Collaborations

Aside from the partnership with the University of Melbourne, the practice has several established and formal research collaborations including the robotics research program at Swinburne University of Technology. Starting with the development of materials (3D printed concrete), this project is expected to become a longer-term collaboration aimed at developing novel design and robotic fabrication techniques to improve structural performance and offer a sustainable alternative to regular concrete.

Working with the University of Technology Sydney, Hayball has installed environmental sensors in their Melbourne and Sydney studios and a school to assess the correlation between occupant perceptions on the influence of space and its impact on their wellbeing and creativity. Continuing with the school work, the practice was engaged by NSW Government Architects Office, through their Sydney studio to compile the Sustainable Schools Guide and contribute to the Good Design for Schools Guide.

Publishing and disseminating work

Several members of the practice have delivered presentations and keynotes at conferences held in Adelaide, Melbourne, Sydney, Singapore, Shanghai, Chicago, and Stanford University, and published papers in the conference proceedings as well as academic journals, industry and business publications. Senior staff hold posts on several committees and advisory panels to Government departments and industry associations, and teach design studios at several Australian universities including Swinburne University of Technology, RMIT University and the University of Melbourne.

Young notes that "sharing information is one of the biggest challenges for a big practice" and to that end, Hayball has developed a series of knowledge sharing and communication fora available via video conferencing systems to encourage interstate collaboration and regular knowledge sharing. The Tech Symposium is a bi-monthly series with presentations, discussions or workshops focusing on novel technologies and innovative design and production method-ologies delivered by a mix of internal and external presenters. While CONNECT is a monthly professional development series that hosts external and internal speakers delivering formal presentations and Q&A sessions. Access to both Tech Symposium and CONNECT are restricted to Hayball staff but their monthly GLEAM forums are open to our clients and collaborators, with external speakers and an interdisciplinary audience debate themes of community, culture and learning.

Hayball - Project profiles

Domremy College

Also known as 'Solais Sandpit', Domremy College in the Sydney suburb of Five Dock, is a radical refurbishment of an existing school building for pupils in years seven and eight, the first part of a 20-year masterplan with a new two-storey collaborative learning hub, library, gallery, theatre and senior study area to follow in later stages. The first phase has already won two awards from the Learning Environments Australasia. The Solais Sandpit was developed as a prototype to establish an Innovative Learning Environment that supports diverse teaching practices from direct instruction to more collaborative and independent learning activities for the school's current student body of over 570, expected to grow to 810 pupils (see Figures 8.58 and 8.59).

The design response followed six months of extensive research that included the development of an Education Brief developed in collaboration with Dr. Ben Cleveland from the University of Melbourne School of Design, the clients, and Hayball. The brief identified the need to develop a collaborative, entrepreneurial and interdisciplinary education. This experimental process reflects existing research conducted within the practice (Young and Martin, 2020) and the role that ongoing qualitative and quantitative engagement processes with the staff and students play in informing future design decisions and Hayball's research agenda.

Figure 8.58: Students in a boardroom setting at Domremy College. © Henry Lam

Figure 8.59: Moving away from traditional teaching sets arrangements to more collaborative working spaces at Domremy College. © Henry Lam

South Melbourne Primary School

As available land becomes increasingly scarce and progressively more expensive, for new or expanding schools in urban locations, building up is increasingly seen as the best option. South Melbourne Primary School accommodates 525 pupils on 5,000 m² set across six storeys (see Figure 8.60). The school is located in the Fishermans Bend Urban Renewal Area, a high-density suburb in need of social infrastructure and with a population that has increased by 3,000 residents per year. The design team developed a scheme that provides an early learning centre, maternal and child health centre, multi-purpose community rooms, and indoor and outdoor multi-purpose sports courts, in addition to the primary school. To continue the building's wider role within the community, the project includes the design of pedestrian, cyclist and public transport infrastructure with the aim of improving accessibility and connectivity with the suburb as it develops.

Figure 8.60: Exterior view of South Melbourne Primary School, part of the Fishermans Bend Urban Renewal Area. © Henry Lam

Figure 8.61: Younger children from South Melbourne Primary School play in the school's roof level sand pit. © Dianna Snape

Challenging the default for primary schools in which play spaces for small children are always located at ground level, Hayball's design places both play facilities for younger children and a sports court on the school's roof (see Figures 8.61 and 8.62). This both makes use of a traditionally underused space for schools and advances the understanding and design options for schools. These innovations have won the practice a total of eight awards from Learning Environments Australasia, World Architecture Festival, Association for Learning Environments, Victorian School Building Authority, and the Urban Developer, for design excellence and inclusive design.

Richmond High School

Advancing further the concept of shared facilities, Richmond High School, located in one of Melbourne's densest suburbs, was a new build school designed for 650 students from years 7 to 12. Research conducted specifically for this architectural project identified the need not only for shared community facilities

Figure 8.62: The basketball court at South Melbourne Primary School with views over central Melbourne. © Dianna Snape

but also the potential educational facilities shared with neighbouring schools. Beyond the obvious financial advantages of shared facilities, this offered the opportunity for cross-cultural learning opportunities. Out of hours, the wider community has access to the performing arts space and cafe, and pupils share the food technology facility at the adjacent Lynall Hall Community School and swimming pool and gym at the neighbouring community sports centre.

The design response proposed a masterplan with two precincts, one academic and the other sports focussed, an amphitheatre and a 'town square', was awarded the title of Best Secondary School in the 2019 Victorian School Design Awards. The sports precinct building (see Figure 8.63) opens onto competition standard netball courts while overlooking the oval and space of Citizens Park. The triangular four-storey academic building includes an outdoor horticulture deck, two large courtyard areas connecting with a ground floor library, and a kitchen garden at one end. Beyond a teaching space, the entrance opens out into an atrium with a flexible seating area allowing students to meet and sit with friends without causing congestion seen in most school corridors and entranceways (see Figure 8.64).

Figure 8.63: Street view of the sports percent building at Richmond High School © Emily Bartlett

Figure 8.64: The atrium and meeting space at Richmond High School. © Dianna Snape

8.5.2 PLP Architecture   *Large practice case study*

London, United Kingdom

Practice structure

Lars Hesselgren joined PLP Architecture at its inception in 2009 with the objective of continuing the digital and parametric work he'd spent much of his career developing, and has been the driving force behind the research agenda at the practice since. Research within the practice, conducted as part of design projects, often involved new technology to optimise performance to the benefit of the building, its occupants and the wider built environment.

With the intention of capitalising on this research and development already underway, and influenced by a shift in staff skill sets which is increasingly digital, the practice established PLP Labs in 2019. PLP Labs is divided into three groups, People Labs, Place Labs and Systems Lab, with staff linked to their areas of expertise; strategy and forecasting, advanced systems and technologies, and digital technologies research and development. With the exception of Hesselgren who is dedicated to research, those involved in Labs are all senior staff members and operate across the practice rather than in a stand-alone research team, ensuring that research is integrated across the practice in a more structured manner.

The benefits of research and its influence on design

PLP's website announces that "Technology is fast. Buildings are slow. We are changing this, creating and advocating radical change to our cities and the systems that build them" and their response to the challenges faced by contemporary practice was the establishment of PLP Labs. The greater focus and innovative thinking that requires, presents the practice with the opportunity to expand their research. Ultimately, their aspiration is that the research conducted will benefit positively their design process, the buildings realised, the city, and the wider community, as well as their clients directly.

The work they have conducted to date has demonstrated the potential of this ambition, attracting new clients and broadening the conversations in which they are invited to engage. This follows on from higher-profile propositional work, such as SuperTall Timber and IUMO, almost regardless of the potential to realise those projects or the relation to the needs of a new client, offering an insight into the way that the practice thinks.

Within the practice, and aside from the project linked research and published propositions, the practice encourages colleagues to develop 'passion projects'. Working on research projects that are unrelated to architectural projects fosters intellectual curiosity which, in turn, benefits practice projects, develops and demonstrates the expertise and skills sets of the architects in the practice, and facilitates interesting conversations with clients and the wider profession.

Research focus

Having formally structured research activity within the practice into three sectors, the practice has detailed further the focus within each Lab. People Lab focusses on reimagining the spaces and places occupied by people and their needs through pre and post occupancy studies, and includes developing new approaches to workplace design, the search for new models and forms of housing, knowledge and innovation institutes. Place Lab considers the urban fabric at a larger scale and incorporates large-scale master planning, urban regeneration and ecosystems down to smaller-scale sites, environmental and community impacts. While Tech Lab focusses on the development and application of digital design tools and the conceptual, multi-scale urban mobility projects including IUMO and Hyperloop, alongside research of materials including heavy timber and robotics, engineering of mechanical systems and structure, geometry and generative components.

Funding and client commissions

To date, research has been funded through four routes. First, as many of the architectural projects adopt a research approach those costs are absorbed into the project costs. Second, is through internal funding, which includes writing off time spent on propositional work and small passion projects by team members. Third is directly through collaborative partners and, finally, where collaborations have been conducted with academic partners, research grants have been secured by the universities involved.

Collaborations

The practice has a long history of academic collaborations including an ongoing engagement with the University of Cambridge's School of Architecture, the University of Bath, London School of Economics and Political Science, Westminster University, Imperial College London, Harvard (University) Health, University of Oregon, the University of California at Berkeley and the University of Delft. This involvement also includes providing access to buildings and architectural projects to students as case studies for their own research, later submitted to the practice (such as Williams, 2019; Ye, 2019).

Beyond academia, PLP has worked with the World Economic Forum, Tyrens Engineering in Sweden, logistics organisation Bouygues and Sweden's Ministry of Trade and Industry, Smith and Wallwork Engineers and continue to develop other international collaborations. In addition, PLP also has researchers in residence working with Autodesk and their tools. Most of these research partnerships involve Lars Hesselgren and Ron Bakker but draw on the wider team in a bid to develop collaborative ideas and foster a more collaborative atmosphere.

Publishing and disseminating work

Most of PLP's research is shared through academic lectures, international industry talks, or on their website. Several partners and Labs leaders sit on international panels for sustainability, real estate and technology. For print publications, where the project has been collaborative, the project and results are often promoted and published through their partners, for example, the ongoing collaboration with the University of Cambridge and Smith and Wallwork Engineers (Ramage et al., 2017) and the Urban Land Institute (Jarvis, 2019).

PLP Architecture - Project profiles

People Lab – Krea University Campus

In 2018 PLP Architecture won the competition to design the 200-hectare campus masterplan for Krea University, to be located in Sri City, a special economic zone 50 km north of Chennai. Although the campus aims to be carbon neutral, use 100% renewable energy, be self-sufficient in water consumption, send zero waste to landfill, and enhance biodiversity on the site, these sustainability aspects were not the focus of the practice's research for the project. As a new academic institution that, when completed, will be part of a Smart Integrated Business City, the university offers an interwoven education that dispenses with traditional faculty and school structures and the research commissioned as part of the masterplan development reviewed the organisational principles and relationship between different components of academia.

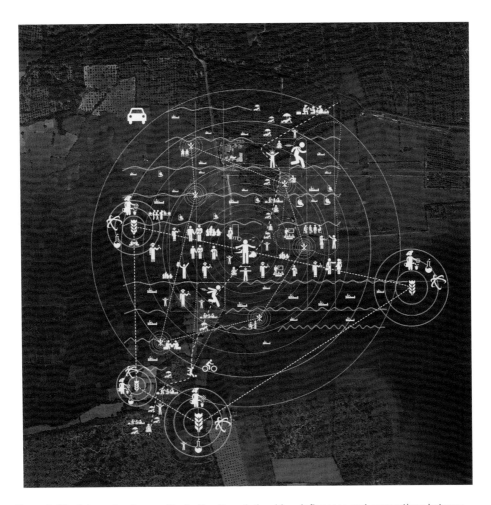

Figure 8.65: Schematic diagram illustrating the relationships, influences and connections between different elements of the Krea University. © PLP Architecture

Figure 8.66: Sketch indicating the permeability of buildings for the new campus at Krea University. © PLP Architecture

Working from an existing knowledge base developing innovative ideas for education with spatial typologies for learning, the research team engaged the university leadership and academics to discuss the dynamics of the campus, the future of education, campus environments, workplaces and contemporary urban living, following their own analysis of the organisation of the university (see Figure 8.65). With no faculties or departments, the living lab campus with integrated learning opportunities from the campus from interactions with people, machines and the environment. This fluid structure, with professors and educational specialists drawn from around the world operating across the university, is reflected in the masterplan with open buildings offering spaces for collaborative learning and engagement (see Figure 8.66). The campus includes a working farm both for educational purposes and to provide food for the academic community, a business centre, performance centre, and a library, which is open to the wider community.

Place Lab - Tall timber

The practice embarked on a collaborative research project with the Department of Architecture at the University of Cambridge and Smith and Wallwork

Engineers in 2015 to establish the challenges of using engineered timber materials including glued-laminated timber (glulam), cross laminated timber (CLT), laminated veneer lumber and structural bamboo in tall buildings. With the established understanding of the detrimental environmental impacts of concrete and steel, recently there has been significant interest in structural timber, with benefits including the potential of prefabrication and carbon sequestration, and its applications. However, with the tallest timber building only reaching 14 storeys, PLP designed a 300 m tall tower, set among the brutalist towers of the Barbican in central London, to test the limits of this relatively new material (see Figure 8.67).

Known as the Oakwood Timber Tower I, the project employed both physical testing and modelling, with an analysis of design codes, precedents and the role of creative thinking in improving the design and adoption of high-rise timber. By

Figure 8.67: View north across the River Thames to the proposed SuperTall Oakwood Timber Tower. © PLP Architecture

verifying conceptual failures, the team could identify weaknesses in the design and the properties required of the timber structure, comparing different combinations of materials. The research found that while timber could cope with the lateral wind loads tall buildings are subjected to, a considered design response. The project won the Design and Technical category of the 2016 RIBA President's Award for Research and was a finalist in the 2016 Structural Timber Awards and 2017 Architect's Journal – AJ 100 Architectural Collaboration of the Year.

Working with the collaboration with the same research team, PLP has continued this stream of research, although not to the same heights, through several buildings including The Lodge. Designed for Dutch developer Provast, The Lodge is a 25,000 m², 130 m tall, mixed-use development with residential at the higher levels, situated alongside a river in one of The Netherlands' major cities (see Figures 8.68 and 8.69). The proposal was presented as an exercise in engagement and debate with City authorities various technical departments, on the feasibility of such a tower and the evolving process has been reflected in changes to the original oval footprint and location. Consistent throughout the design, and continuing the same structural premise as the Oakwood Timber Tower, is a buttressed mega-truss. Structural calculations revealed that additional loading was required on the top ten floors to increase inertia in case

Figure 8.68: Rendered sunset view of The Lodge. © PLP Architecture

Figure 8.69: Testing perceptions of timber in buildings for aesthetics and structure at The Lodge
© PLP Architecture

of high winds as the low weight of the structure exposed a vulnerability under dynamic loading. Part of the ongoing research conducted by the practice will address the lack of evidenced evaluations of the aesthetic preferences towards timber, while graduate students at the University have contributed to the research, examining the structural dynamics (Ye, 2019) and assumptions of the environmental benefits of tall timber structures (Williams, 2019).

Systems Lab – New mobility

IUMO is PLP's propositional response to inefficiencies in the built environment with an integrated urban, on-demand, point-to-point, looped mobility system operating in both the vertical and horizontal planes that would take users from their homes to connected locations within the city. The vertical travel element, previously referred to as SkyPod, relocates movement in tall buildings to their exterior away from the building's core, freeing up the floor plate to be inhabited in different ways, and facilitating alternative design options (see Figure 8.70). Pods are propelled by a linear induction motor system, and it employs the same dynamic digital stabilisation systems used in high-speed trains that, like a gyroscope, ensures that the floor is always horizontal.

Figure 8.70: Nighttime render of the IUMO proposal that locates vertical movement on the building's exterior, freeing up floor space inside. © PLP Architecture

At street level, IUMO connects automated electric cars and mass transit on existing roads with some routes for exclusive use by IUMO, and a network of small-bore tunnels across a fluid, integrated network transforming the streetscape and encouraging public realm and development that is designed around people rather than vehicles (see Figure 8.71). Previously known as CarTube, the autonomous cars would be controlled by a dynamic platoon protocol that allows for a continuous flow at high speed, exceeding the current capacity of privately owned cars and public transport. Calculations conducted by the team suggests that urban travel time could be reduced by 75% using existing technology to schedule travel (CarTube Global, 2020).

For both facets of IUMO, the practice developed software in-house, used to test the concepts involved, to model and refine the building's geometry, pods, their speeds and their routes, the optimal density, routes and platoon protocol for the automated cars, and model traffic behaviour notably at junctions as traffic in tunnels does not stop. It was important that the software was straight-forward enough for use by everyone in the practice, supporting a collaborative and inclusive approach to the project's development.

Figure 8.71: Moving vehicular travel to small-bore tunnels provides the opportunity for alternative use of the public realm. © PLP Architecture

Göteborg, Sweden

Practice structure

Established as a practice in 1951, White Arkitekter's interest and engagement in research, although informal, was in place from the outset. Two decades ago a trust, allied but external to the practice, was established to focus and develop research activity in the practice in a more organised way. As the Trust is open to external applications, much of the research remained external to the practice. In response to this, the Trust's remit was expanded to better disseminate this work across the practice of now over 800 staff in 13 studios across Scandinavia and the UK, facilitated by the formation of 16 research networks in 2000. Many of the staff have research qualifications or training, although the practice has found that those with the strongest research leanings are those from allied fields such as engineers and anthropologists, rather than architects.

Formal research activity within the practice is overseen by White Research Lab (WRL) which is led by Research and Development Director, Anna-Johanna Klasander with four managers, all of whom spent 30–60% of their time dedicated to WRL. Research is a bottom-up movement and operates within 16 flexible competency networks led by a head of development specialising in the field. Eleven of these reflect business areas with the remaining five address particular cross-disciplinary fields of development including Dsearch (computational design), Tectonics, Wood and Light, and Transformation and Circularity.

The benefits of research and its influence on design

For Klasander, one of the most significant benefits of their research strategy is its capacity to bring "some oxygen into the office," stimulating fresh thinking across design projects and teams, has proved hugely beneficial. It has further aided the development of competencies and knowledge across the practice, leading to an increase in the "absorptive capacity" of the practice, making them open to new knowledge and its application in the practice, while engaging with a wider group of professionals and the community, and developing new projects within the practice. This multi-disciplinary approach has brought job applicants and new clients to the practice. The research conducted informs architectural designs and allows the team to take responsibility for the whole project rather than hiving off segments to specialists such as engineers.

Research focus

Every three years, research themes and priorities are identified and published in a strategy document on the practice website. The themes identified are deliberately broad to encourage as broad a participation from across the practice as possible. The most recent strategy, covering 2020 to 2023, builds on the previous three streams of equitable architecture, resource efficiency, and informed design in greater detail, with the themes of Circular Architecture, Healthy Living Environments, and Collaboration, relating to environments as well as health and wellbeing issues for humans (White Arkitekter, 2020a).

Of these, Circular Architecture includes an ongoing project looking at the opportunities for reusing the interior fittings, fixtures and materials from commercial fit-outs including furniture
working with clients to minimise waste from refurbishments. Completed in 2019, the Selma Lagerlöf Centre, Gothenburg, exemplifies White's commitment to sustainable design. Their own research determined that the project reused 92% of existing furniture and materials for the 6,300 m² site, saving the client, the City of Gothenburg, Kr8.7 million (White Arkitekter, 2020b) has led to the publication of a handbook (White Arkitekter, 2018).

Funding and client commissions

Much of the research activity at White Arkitekter is internally funded. As a reflection of the practice's established dedication to research, the practice reserves 10% of their annual turnover to fund research and development activity. This includes co-funding PhDs, research network activities, digitalisation and BIM as well as a 'budget' of 2000 hours of staff time and expenses associated with approved research projects. Open calls for internal projects are issued fortnightly and all staff are able to apply. Applicants are asked to submit a short, one-sided proposal that states the research topic, methodology, motivation for the work, and its broader applicability with resource allocation a reflection of an individuals' enthusiasm for a topic and strategic interest for the company. In 2019 WRL received 64 applications, most from teams of two or more, of which 40 received funding for between 8 and 140 hours.

Research projects for clients rarely start out as directly commissioned research projects. Conversations at the briefing stage and, reflecting White's integrated approach to research and design, leads to further development of the brief with research forming part of the overall project. Offsetting research costs through tax relief schemes, another form of 'funding' research in practice, has not always benefitted White. Although some of their external projects have been eligible for available lower tax schemes, they have not been able to claim tax benefits for their staff as none are full time researchers. External funding for research conducted with academic collaborations has been secured through those partners, although few grants have covered all of the research costs within the practice.

Collaborations

Around 60% of their research is through collaborations conducted with academic and research institutes, government authorities at the local, regional and national level, developers, contractors, real estate owners, competitors and colleagues in business, and civil society organisations. These have included 'Be-Smart', an innovative building envelope for mass production, funded by Horizon2020, with manufacturers, researchers, public authorities from nine countries. Another project with the International Energy Agency used a residential development in Uppsala to consider energy efficiencies in existing dwellings. The practice has also conducted a study with manufacturers of timber buildings over 20 storeys and their research into the circular economy of furniture and building materials has led to several long-term partnerships.

Their reputation for research attracts invitations from universities to participate in research projects, particularly in the healthcare sector and computational design, and they have collaborated with all of the Swedish schools of architecture while their London studio has links with the Bartlett School of Architecture at University College London.

Publishing and disseminating work

Within the practice, the 16 subject networks, active in all of the studios, organise the dissemination of research projects including holding lunchtime events and seminar presentations, allowing researchers to present more substantial work. However, with 13 studios in three countries sharing research findings across the practice takes substantial effort. In support of this Klasander, delivers summaries of research work conducted across the practice when visiting other studios.

Recent and selected reports appear on the website and White's Communications Unit have lead the initiative to publish more research work including annual reports that extend to include a short synopsis of key research projects (White Arkitekter, 2020c). They continue to expand their publications, written either by themselves or through project partners, increasingly bilingual published in English and Swedish.

White Arkitekter - Project profiles

Flickrum – Places for girls

The Flickrum project started as a conversation about how young women and girls feel excluded in the built environment, reflecting on a growing body of research that examines the inequalities between boys and girls and how they use public space (see Figure 8.72).

> Statistics shows that from [the age of eight,] 80 percent of the users are boys, while girls feel ten times more insecure in public places... If young boys make up 80% of the users of shared spaces, how do we design more equitable places that cater to all?
>
> (White Arkitekter, 2017)

Figure 8.72: One of Stockholm's urban spaces that the teenage girls found uninviting. © Jonas Jörneberg/White Arkitekter

White invited teenage girls from the Stockholm municipality of Skarpnäck, local government learning facilitators and local theatre company UngaTur, to a workshop at their Stockholm studio (see Figure 8.73). Using a site familiar to them but that they did not use (see Figure 8.74), the girls redesigned the sites presenting their work in models (see Figure 8.75). Through the workshop identified several design characteristics that were important including place character expressed through colour and form, seating options that allowed them to sit face to face, shelter from inclement weather, spaces that allowed them to view without being constantly surveilled and offered a sense of enclosure, and "to be able to leave an imprint on their city" (White Arkitekter, 2017).

The findings from the project were developed as a play performed by the young women and girls involved in the research (Zinn, 2020). Local political leaders and key stakeholders were invited and reported that they had a far better understanding of the challenges the girls faced than would have been

Figure 8.73: A workshop with the girls as part of the Flikrum engagement process. © White Arkitekter

Figure 8.74: Photographs indicating the site selected for a streetscape analysis and design intervention. © White Arkitekter

Figure 8.75: One of the models made by the girls in the workshop with their proposed design. Labels in English added later. © White Arkitekter

conveyed in a report or academic paper. The project concluded that the lack of knowledge about how to design for the requirements and preferences of the built environment for young girls and teenagers, due to their absence from urban planning processes. Flickrum has developed into a series of projects, including a replication of the research in London, and has established new strategies and protocols for working with young people and girls within the practice, and a new design strategy that is applied to projects and won the practice the Årets Arkitekt(hen) Architect of the Year award in 2018.

NCC Headquarters

Completed in 2019, Swedish contractor NCC's headquarters Solna north of Stockholm. With their ambition to deliver buildings that are close to zero-carbon impact in terms of energy, materials and construction, the NCC building is part of a series of projects including the 19 storey high Sara Culture Centre in Skellefteå,

Figure 8.76: View of the main atrium at NCC's headquarters in Solna. © Anders Bobert/White Arkitekter

an Observation Tower in Varberg, and Sweden's largest wooden office building, Magasin X in Uppsala, that develop this agenda. The drive for sustainability for the NCC building includes an exterior clad in blue and grey integrated solar cells developed with ISSOL, recycling the concrete frame from the company's previous office, and extensive use of eco-labelled timber throughout the building contributing to its BREEAM Excellent certification.

Above the publicly accessible ground floor restaurant and fitness facility are two atria and views of the structural timber components (see Figure 8.76). Solid timber stairways and walkways connect living and active rooms where the office's 800 employees and guests can meet or work taking one of several routes through the building. The flexible layout is designed with a healthy lifestyle in mind that encourages movement and spontaneous encounters between colleagues (see Figure 8.77) and contributes to a warmer and more human environment. As acoustics play a significant role in building comfort, walkways, bridge floors and strings have been clad inside with dark blue carpet, leaving the timber components, CLT using FSC-certified Austrian spruce, exposed (see Figure 8.78).

Figure 8.77: The stairways and footbridges through the main atrium space, designed to encourage accidental meetings between colleagues. © Anders Bobert/White Arkitekter

Figure 8.78: Dark-blue carpet clads the atrium stairways and footbridges offering acoustic and safety benefits. © Anders Bobert/White Arkitekter

San Francisco, United States of America

Practice structure

Perkins&Will was established in Chicago in 1935 by Lawrence B. Perkins and Philip Will Jr. Following an aggressive expansion programme that commenced in the mid-1990s that involved buying architecture studios with a similar outlook, approach and value set, and the practice now has more than 25 studios across four continents. Growing the practice into new geographic locations through acquisition rather than organic growth provided the firm with a diversified portfolio and established connections and relationships with clients and suppliers. This federalist structure remains in the practice with studios retaining much of their original ethos, and some offering a stronger research presence than others.

In 2004, Perkins&Will merged with Canadian practice Busby and Associates, led by Principal Peter Busby. Their Vancouver studio had an established research agenda that focussed on social justice, resilience and sustainability with the ambition of driving innovation through their work. David Green led the research agenda and their publication AREA Research from 2010 until John Haymaker took over in 2014, reducing the research labs to seven enabling a more manageable structure, and providing a greater focus and clarity to the work.

The full-time research team comprises the Director of Research, a Research Knowledge Manager, 20 Lab leaders who work on research on a part-time basis, around 20 PhDs, and 40 additional staff members with masters degrees, often in sustainability, engineering or other technical fields, working on projects across the practice. To foster internal collaboration, Lab leaders identify opportunities across the practice, projects and studios and potential for cross-over of work from themes across sectors. Five of the Lab leaders spend around 50% of their time on research work, supported by corporate designated funds, and the remainder of their time on design projects, while the remaining 15 leaders typically work on architectural projects and spend a day to a day and a half each week on research projects. This structure is intended to embed research thinking, process and findings within design thinking, process and outcomes. A ten-member research board, including the CEO, COO (to ensure continued funding for the project's agenda), and CIO (to ensure that the research agenda and outputs are integrated across the firm) and meets quarterly to oversee research activity across the practice.

The Innovation Incubator offers a year-long leadership development scheme. In 2010, this was expanded to offer micro-grants available to all staff on a biannual basis, offering a week away from work and research expenses. Since its launch, the scheme has received over 700 applications and now averages 200 per year, with around 10–15 approved for funding in each round that are collaborative applications as well as single author proposals. Proposals are reviewed by a committee of eight including Incubator alumni who review the submissions and match successful applicants with mentors to develop skills. The scheme offers a research guide for those applicants with no previous research experience. The grant awardees are convened at the start of the program to form a research community, ensuring awareness of other projects, fostering collaboration on these or future research projects, providing peer support, and developing long-term research and alumni communities.

The benefits of research and its influence on design

There has been a positive response from clients and the practice feels it has improved the briefing process and delivers buildings that are more sustainable and perform better for their occupants. CEO Phil Harrison believes that research makes their projects better, smarter, more efficient and more resilient. Research is a resource for the firm with findings feeding directly into design work and influencing software including Rhino and Grasshopper.

Lab leaders are the experts in the practice and the Lab structure is intended, with time split between design and research, to embed research thinking in design projects and is an effective method for engaging across the practice. As a reflection of the extent to which research is integral to design, Haymaker commented that 'it is difficult to quantify the value of research within a project versus what's happening anyway". Being known as a practice with a strong research presence has proved an incredible recruitment tool particularly with graduating architects and the practice sees a flurry of interest and applications following practice presentations in schools of architecture. It also supports staff retention, as the opportunity to engage in projects and apply for time out to pursue a short-term project is seen as a staff perk.

Research focus

The breadth of the practice's architectural work is reflected in the scope of their research interests. The seven labs, whose direction is influenced by their leaders, are not fixed and will evolve with the practice and to reflect the needs of clients and is always under review. However, there is a reluctance to grow the number of labs beyond their current number as this risks losing focus and makes their management more challenging. The seven Labs are: Building Technology; Design Process which includes parametric work acoustics and sound attenuation; Energy, which has delivered a new software package SPEED; Human Experience highlighting pre and post-occupancy evaluation; Material Performance which focusses on embodied carbon and making healthy buildings; Mobility which covers building lobbies and what happens at the end of the working day to larger-scale logistics and individual travel; and Resilience that intends to develop a LEED equivalent for resilience.

Future areas for development include a focus on their AREA Research publication, an expansion of work on sustainable communities, which is currently under the remit of the Resilience Lab, modular and prefabrication which would be accommodated within the Building Technology Lab, housing affordability which would come under Resilience Lab, and cultural insights, currently part of the work conducted by futurists and trend spotters the Portland Design team, part of the practice and based in the London studio.

Funding and client commissions

There has been an increase in pre and post occupancy evaluation commissions directly from clients and early engagement with some clients, led by entrepreneurial design team leaders has created opportunities for further work. Perkins&Will launched the Research Journal in 2009 and, being a peer-reviewed journal, lends the credibility required to access grant funding from the National Science Foundation which supports the PhDs on staff. Other funding has been secured from American Institute of Architects (Upjohn Grant), local government, clients, direct commissions, and private donors.

Collaborations

Perkins&Will has long-established academic collaborations with Georgia Tech, Harvard, Texas A&M and the University of Washington. Many of these collaborations evolved from teaching appointments and developed into research collaborations leading to students conducting research at Perkins&Will with the practice providing access to projects and data, and acting as supervisor. Additionally, the practice is working with the University of Cambridge to develop

'Rely', a LEED equivalent for resilience and the outcome has been donated to the US Green Building Council. The Material Performance Lab continues to work with Harvard University on a healthy buildings research project, while the Mobility Lab is collaborating with Susan Shaheen from the University of California at Berkeley, the University of Oregon and Terra Curtis of Nelson Nygaard.

The practice established collaborations with industrial experts and specialist engineering consultancies to work on heavy timber and robotics in their Building Technology Lab, and a Researcher-in-Residence at Autodesk working with their software tools. Specialist software engineers have worked with the practice, helping to test and refine the SPEED software developed in the Perkins&Will Energy Lab following rigorous testing by the practice IT team to ensure that the program can cope with project demands.

Publishing and disseminating work

External engagement comes predominately through speaking opportunities and presentations at industry events, academic conferences and universities and through publications, which have included chapters for a book edited by Susan Shaheen at the University of California at Berkeley, publishing research articles on an open-access basis on the website, and the *Perkins&Will Research Journal*. Most of the articles published in the Journal are authored by practice staff with occasional papers from collaborations with academic institutions and other partners.

Internal dissemination includes a yearly report and quarterly newsletter that contains a synopsis of research projects and contact details for the project leaders. Each of the 26 studios accommodates a knowledge manager in each studio who is responsible for identifying relevant articles in external literature and publications, sharing internally conducted research work, and coordinating the research agenda in their studio.

Perkins&Will - Project profiles

The design of behavioural health rooms for emergency departments

A visit to the emergency department can be challenging, even traumatic, experience for vulnerable patients with behavioural health (BH) issues, typically understood to include mental illness and substance abuse disorders. This project aimed to identify architectural interventions to support both staff and patients that were sufficiently flexible as to accommodate the "medical emergency patients of differing severities... creat[ing] a healing environment that promotes patient well-being and sensitivity in patient care by staff" (Jayachandran, Ramsey, & Roehl, 2017, p. 32), reflecting the understanding of the positive impacts offered by an integrated approach to healthcare.

The multi-disciplinary collaborative team assessed existing design guidelines, and conducted observational analysis of similar facilities at several institutions, and interviews with key staff within emergency departments to understand staff challenges and patient experiences. The research found that a lack of suitable facilities including too few and inadequate specialist treatment rooms. The team established guidelines that "address safety, dignity, flexibility, acuity adaptable, efficient, positive distraction, acoustics, lighting control, therapeutic interventions" (Jayachandran et al., 2017, p. 39) materials, lighting and furniture. The design proposal divides facilities in the room into three zones, two alcoves and a headwall with panels that rotate all concealing different medical equipment not all of which is required at all times. The design proposed moveable panels opening in differing combinations depending on the patient's requirements, in line with the Emergency Severity Index (Figure 8.79), ranging from prescription refill to cardiac arrest, accommodating the specific needs of BH patients (Figure 8.80).

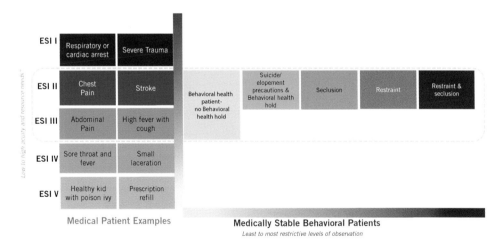

Figure 8.79: The Emergency Severity Index (ESI) categorises levels of physical and behavioural health. © Perkins&Will

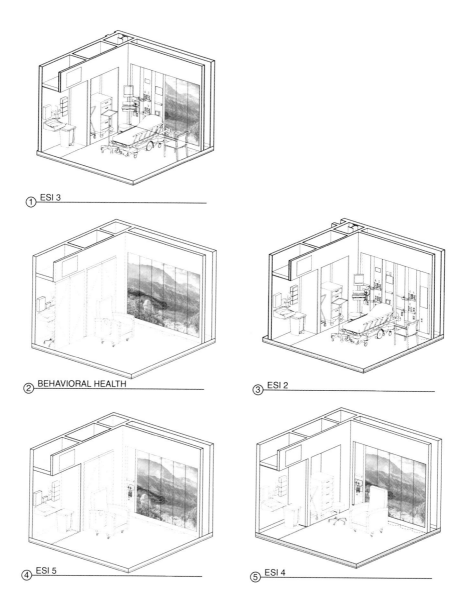

[1] ESI level 1- Medication refill or low-risk behavioural health
[2] ESI level 2- Low acuity patient (fever)
[3] ESI level 3- Medium acuity patient (abdominal pain)
[4] ESI level 4- High acuity patient (chest pain or stroke)
[5] ESI level 5- High risk behavioural health

Figure 8.80: The treatment room has been designed to transform incrementally in response to patient requirements using the ESI scale. © Perkins&Will

The future net-zero energy office building

With a Washington, DC based environmental stewardship association as the client, the ambition for the project to design an "office building that revolutionized sustainability" (Knutson, 2019a, p. 8), eclipsing existing green building standards for offices including guidelines set out in the DC Climate Adaptation Plan from the city's Department of Energy and Environment.

Applying Passivhaus principles to the design reduced energy consumption by 60% with the required energy, an estimated 1,542,000 kWh/year (Knutson, 2019a), provided by integrated photovoltaic panels on the facade and at rooftop level and a wastewater heat recovery system, delivering a net-positive energy building (Knutson, 2019b). In addition, there is a complete rainwater capture and grey-water recycling systems, and seven floors of the 11-storey building to

Figure 8.81: West elevation of the case study building. © Perkins&Will

be CLT, sitting above three floors of a concrete and timber hybrid structure. The technologies adopted were finalised after an analysis of a range of options. The assessment dismissed those, such as wind generation for energy production, considered to be ineffective in a commercial building or in the location selected.

The urban form of Washington, DC has been heavily influenced by the 1910 Height of Buildings Act which stipulates that no structure in the city should exceed the height of the US Capitol building. So, when the research team compared two sites for the building, they opted for the site that offered increased solar potential and limited neighbourhood shading. This is reflected in the building's envelope and design (Figure 8.81) where "the use of self-shading facades reduces solar heat gain and, thus, overall heating and cooling energy consumption" (Knutson, 2019a, p. 8) and the integrated PV solar shades (Figure 8.82) "enhanced the energy potential and reduced solar glare". The proposal won the 2019 AIA Northern Virginia Award of Excellence for Conceptual/Unbuilt Architecture (AIA Northern Virginia, 2020).

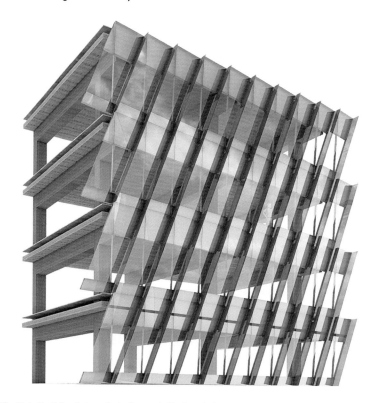

Figure 8.82: Detail of the integrated diagonal Photovoltaic solar shades. © Perkins&Will

A National Ordinance and the Kuwait National Master Plan 2040

Kuwait's first master plan, delivered in 1952, saw the demolition of part of the old town to make way for wider roads and more housing. Eighteen years later, a second masterplan sought to develop its housing stock to accommodate the increase in international workers, creating new urban centres distant from the old town, while the 1997 and third masterplan, proposed 17 satellite cities to accommodate growth outside the Kuwait Municipal Area (Perkins&Will, 2020b and 2020c). The 2040 National Master Plan builds on these schemes while referencing the structure and character of the original town. This is evident in the design intention that reinterprets the concentric walls of the historic pattern of Kuwait City through urban green infrastructure (Figure 8.83).

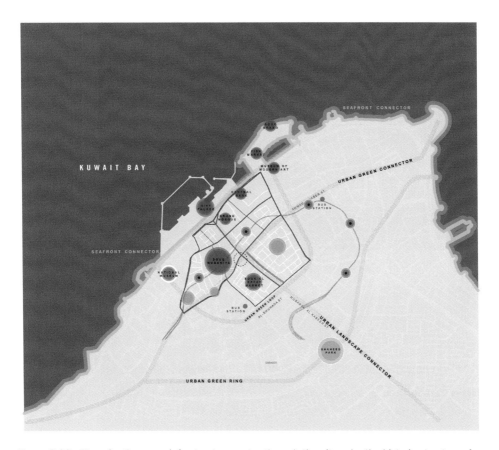

Figure 8.83: Plans for the green infrastructure routes through the city echo the historic structure of the old town of Kuwait. © Perkins&Will

The Plan's ambition lies in delivering a liveable city which for "Kuwait is fundamental and the challenge is to move away from a lifestyle that has become internalized and embrace the external spaces between the buildings" (Green, Al Rashad, Knight, & Cammelli, 2019, p. 510). To this end, there is a detailed exploration of existing and further development of cycling and pedestrian networks with pedestrian routes connecting parks, plazas, civic spaces, the Fabric Market and Souk (Figure 8.84). The design proposals are supported by "a programme of measures aimed at making walking and cycling safer, providing pedestrian and cyclist priority

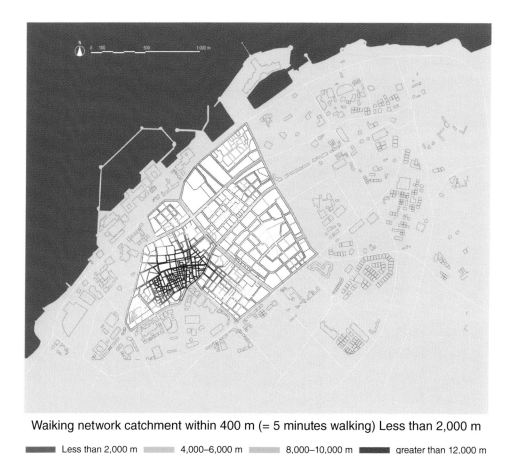

Waiking network catchment within 400 m (= 5 minutes walking) Less than 2,000 m

▰▰▰ Less than 2,000 m	▰▰▰ 4,000–6,000 m	▰▰▰ 8,000–10,000 m	▰▰▰ greater than 12,000 m
▰▰▰ 2,000–4,000 m	6,000–8,000 m	▰▰▰ 10,000–12,000 m	

Figure 8.84: Analysis of the pedestrian network and its connectivity, with the density of red lines around the Souk indicating a high degree of connectivity. © Perkins&Will

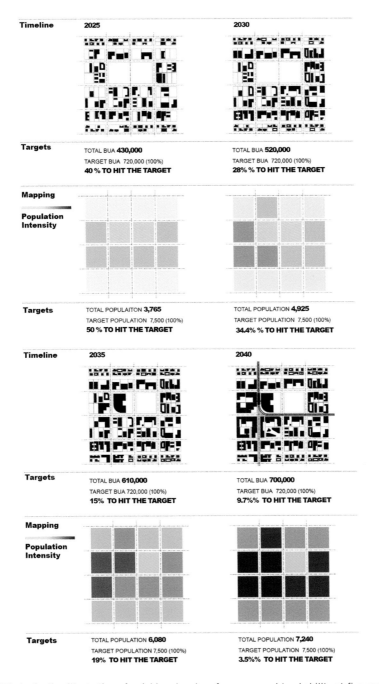

Timeline	2025	2030
Targets	TOTAL BUA **430,000** TARGET BUA 720,000 (100%) **40 % TO HIT THE TARGET**	TOTAL BUA **520,000** TARGET BUA 720,000 (100%) **28% % TO HIT THE TARGET**
Mapping **Population Intensity**		
Targets	TOTAL POPULAITON **3,765** TARGET POPULATION 7,500 (100%) **50 % TO HIT THE TARGET**	TOTAL POPULATION **4,925** TARGET POPULATION 7,500 (100%) **34.4% % TO HIT THE TARGET**
Timeline	2035	2040
Targets	TOTAL BUA **610,000** TARGET BUA 720,000 (100%) **15% TO HIT THE TARGET**	TOTAL BUA **700,000** TARGET BUA 720,000 (100%) **9.7%% TO HIT THE TARGET**
Mapping **Population Intensity**		
Targets	TOTAL POPULATION **6,080** TARGET POPULATION 7,500 (100%) **19% TO HIT THE TARGET**	TOTAL POPULATION **7,240** TARGET POPULATION 7,500 (100%) **3.5%% TO HIT THE TARGET**

Figure 8.85: Indicative illustration of neighbourhood performance and trackability at five years interval targets. © Perkins&Will

Figure 8.86: Neighbourhood performance and trackability of data across the city employing 150 m² block scale. © Perkins&Will

at junctions and promoting urban design and building designs that increase shade and provide a high-quality walking environment" (Perkins&Will, 2020b, p. 147). The Masterplan proposes planting trees along primary routes, improvements to pedestrian areas and pavements, new recreational spaces, and locating community facilities, and increasing development density around new metro stops.

Underpinning the demographic and best practice urban design principles is the National Ordinance, "a way of organizing the patterns of settlement and development in a growing and changing city, town or other inhabitation" (Green et al., 2019, p. 493), inspired by Thomas Jefferson's 1785 Land Ordinance that sought to measure, divide and sell land across much of the United States (Geib, 1985). Following the spatial construct that measures and subdivides Kuwait, the analytical construct of the Ordinance focusses on the analysis and management of the data generated by future development that operates at national level using a GIS-based grid set on a 6 km² pattern, down to a single neighbourhood block at 150 m² to "objectively evaluate characteristics and indicators across various scales (Green et al., 2019, p. 514). Figures 8.85 and 8.86 illustrate the potential for rigorous analysis of future development both in terms of building development and population changes, measured in five-year intervals.

8.6 Conclusions

These case studies share common features; first among them, the challenges of funding their research. Across the board, direct client commissions specifically for research-only projects are rare. Those practices that have been more successful at securing research funds from clients have done so by including research as part of an architectural project rather than being a stand-alone project. In all cases, it is a matter of building credibility and a profile for conducting rigorous research that has led to further client commissions and attracted future colleagues and collaborations all made possible by sharing their work.

Those who publish their research work on an open-access basis have been more successful at both of these aspects. This is in no small part due to evidencing their knowledge and expertise. This expertise was reflected in positions on panels, boards and committees for industry bodies, speaking opportunities at industry and mainstream events, invitations to write for industry publications which, in turn, led to either write or be interviewed for articles in more mainstreams publications. Internally all practices are aware of the challenges of research dissemination with studio presentations considered the most effective method of addressing this.

One of the key features shared across all case studies is the significance of senior leadership in driving facilitating research within practice. Where the directors or principals are not researchers themselves, appointing a research leader and supporting their work is critical for its delivery. For all of the small practices in this chapter, the determination to lead a research-driven practice was significant and often part of the practice's process from their founding. This is distinct from most large, long-established practices whose research teams are more recent additions to the practice.

Chapter Nine

Conclusions

As practice becomes increasingly aware of the numerous benefits of research to their work, colleagues and clients, this is reflected in the number of practices expanding their work to include research. Regardless of size, all practices face challenges when conducting research. For small practice, it is often an issue of resources, both people with the necessary skills and their time, and internal funds in addition to the challenge of identifying external funding that is accessible. While large practice may have dedicated, specialist staff and a ring-fenced fund to draw on for research related activities, the scale of their practice means that this is not always sufficient, and their greatest challenge is typically knowledge management and dissemination, which becomes progressively more demanding the larger the practice, with a greater number and geographic distribution of studios.

Dissemination of research to an external audience is limited through traditional architecture media although architects are adept at presenting the breadth of their work, showcasing it through a range of mediums that extend beyond the established output options for academic research, formally documenting this work should be an aspect of the process to be developed. The methods and data sources introduced in Chapter Five are another aspect of research to which architects can, with sufficient rigour, apply creative thinking, evolving established norms and processes and adapting them for use on projects and advance the understanding and scope of architectural research, its methods and application.

This book set out to demonstrate that research is within the grasp of any practice regardless of size, geographical location, sector expertise or research experience. The recent shift in understanding the scale of the impact that the industry has had and continues to have on the environment, is one of several factors that has encouraged practice to expand their process to include some aspect of research, either through recruitment or upskilling. Through case studies drawn from around the world with research reflecting the remarkable breadth of architectural practice, a guide to ethics, methods, funding and process, this book hopes to contribute to that.

References

Abrantes, P., Rocha, J., Marques da Costa, E., Gomes, E., Morgado, P., & Costa, N. (2019). Modelling urban form: A multidimensional typology of urban occupation for spatial analysis. *Environment and Planning B: Urban Analytics and City Science, 46*(1), 47–65. https://doi.org/10.1177/2399808317700140

ACNC. (2020). Governance Toolkit: Safeguarding vulnerable people. Australian Charities and Not-for-profits Commission. Retrieved 30 January 2020, from https://www.acnc.gov.au/for-charities/manage-your-charity/governance-hub/governance-toolkit/governance-toolkit-safeguarding

AIA Office of General Counsel. (2020). 2020 *code of ethics and professional conduct*. Washington, DC: American Institute of Architects. http://content.aia.org/sites/default/files/2020-08/2020_Code_of_Ethics.pdf

AIA Northern Virginia. (2020). AIA Northern Virginia: 2019 design awards. Retrieved 23 November 2020, from https://aianova.org/DA19/701.php

AL_A. (2020). *Pitch/Pitch - AL_A*. Retrieved 1 March 2020, from https://www.ala.uk.com/projects/pitch-pitch/

Allen, M. (Ed.). (2017). *The SAGE encyclopedia of communication research methods*. Thousand Oaks, CA: Sage.

Alliance for Downtown New York. (2009). *Five principles for Greenwich South: A model for Lower Manhattan*. New York: Alliance for Downtown New York. https://www.downtownny.com/sites/default/files/Five%20Principles%20%28smaller%29.pdf

Allies and Morrison. (2016). *Historic England: London's local character and density*. London, Historic England. Retrieved 1 March 2020, from https://historicengland.org.uk/content/docs/get-involved/allies-morrison-london-local-character-density-final-report-pdf/

American Psychological Association. (2019). *Publication manual of the American Psychological Association*. Washington, DC: Author.

Appelt, S., Galindo-Rueda, F., & González Cabral, A. C. (2019). *Measuring R&D tax support. Findings from the new OECD R&D tax incentives database*. Paris: Organisation for Economic Co-operation and Development. https://doi.org/10.1787/d16e6072-en. https://ideas.repec.org/p/oec/stiaaa/2019-06-en.html

Arthur, E., McLaughlin, N., & Manolopoulou, Y. (2017). Losing myself: Spatial perception and architectural design. In K. A. Martindale (Ed.), *Shortlist 2017* (pp. 149–171). London: Royal Institute of British Architects.

Australian Government. (2017). Eligible activities. Retrieved 1 March 2020, from https://www.ato.gov.au/Business/Research-and-development-tax-incentive/Eligibility/Eligible-activities/?anchor=core&anchor=core#core

Baca Architects. (2009). *The LiFE project: Long-term initiatives for flood-risk environments*. London: IHS BRE Press.

Ballesty, S., Leifer, D. Henriksen, J., Martindale, K. A., et al. (2007). *Facilities management as a business enabler: Solutions for managing the built environment*. Sydney: Cooperative Research Centre for Construction Innovation.

Barker, R., & Coutts, R. (2016). *Aquatecture: Buildings and cities designed to live and work with water*. London: RIBA Publishing.

Barker, R., & Coutts, R. (2015). Flood aware design. In P. Buxton (Ed.), *Metric handbook: Planning and design data* (pp. 12-1–12-14). Oxford: Routledge.

Barlex, M. J. (2006). *Guide to post occupancy evaluation*. London: HEFCE/AUDE. http://www.smg.ac.uk/documents/POEBrochureFinal06.pdf

Bornat, D. (2020). Towards a child-friendly city. In Greater London Authority (Ed.), *Making London child-friendly – Designing places and streets for children and young people*. London: Greater London Authority. https://www.london.gov.uk/sites/default/files/ggbd_making_london_child-friendly.pdf

Bornat, D., & Shaw, B. (2019). *Neighbourhood design: Working with children towards a child friendly city*. London: ZCD Architects. https://issuu.com/zcdarchitects/docs/neighbourhood_design_cfc

Braidwood, E. (2016). PLP proposes 'CarTube' concept to move traffic underground. 5th December. Retrieved 1 March 2020, from https://www.architectsjournal.co.uk/news/plp-proposes-cartube-concept-to-move-traffic-underground/10015450.article

British Copyright Council. (2019). Information: Copyright basics. Retrieved 1 March 2020, from https://www.britishcopyright.org/information/information-copyright-basics-a5-guide/

C40Cities. (2019). 14 cities commit to sustainable food policies that will address the global climate emergency. Retrieved 4 May 2020, from https://www.c40. org/press_releases/good-food-cities

Calabuig, D., Gomez, R., & Ramos, A. (2013). The strategies of mat-building. *Architectural Review*. 13th August. Retrieved 1 March 2020, from https://www. architectural-review.com/essays/the-strategies-of-mat-building/8651102.article

Candido, C., Kim, J., de Dear, R., & Thomas, L. (2016). BOSSA: A multidimensional post-occupancy evaluation tool. *Building Research & Information*, 44(2), 214–228. https://doi.org/10.1080/09613218.2015.1072298

Carthey, J. (2006). Post occupancy evaluation: Development of a standardised methodology for Australian health projects. *The International Journal of Construction Management*, 6(1), 57–75. https://doi.org/10.1080/15623599.20 06.10773082

CarTube Global. (2020). CarTube | How it works. Retrieved 8 April 2020, from https://www.cartube.global/how-it-works.html

Cassell, S., & Barrett, A. (2011). Five principles for Greenwich South: A strategic framework for Lower Manhattan. *Projections 10: MIT Journal of Planning: Designing for Growth and Change*, 10, 53–71. http://cityform.mit.edu/projects/ projections-10-designing-for-growth-and-change#articles

Cassell, S., Yarinsky, A., & Architecture Research Office. (2003). *ARO: Architecture Research Office*. New York: Princeton Architectural Press.

Castleberry, A., & Nolen, A. (2018). Thematic analysis of qualitative research data: Is it as easy as it sounds? *Currents in Pharmacy Teaching and Learning*, 10(6), 807–815. https://doi.org/10.1016/j.cptl.2018.03.019

Chen, C., Marshall, T., & Imam, M. (2020). Resilient future – A design energy simulation of the future. *Perkins&Will Research*. Retrieved 1 March 2020, from http://research.perkinswill.com/wp-content/uploads/2020/02/20190207_ ResilientFuture_compressed.pdf

Cheng, J., & Masser, I. (2003). Modelling urban growth patterns: A multiscale perspective. *Environment and Planning A*, 35(4), 679–704. https://www. researchgate.net/profile/Ian_Masser/publication/23539289_Modelling_urban_ growth_patterns_A_multiscale_perspective/links/0d1c84f6c5da63322c000000/ Modelling-urban-growth-patterns-A-multiscale-perspective.pdf

City of Copenhagen. (2018). *The capital of sustainable development: The city of Copenhagen's action plan for the sustainable development goals*. Copenhagen: City of Copenhagen Department of Finance. https://international.kk.dk/ sites/international.kk.dk/files/the_capital_of_sustainable_development_ sustainable_development_goals_2018.pdf

Croft, C., & Macdonald, S. (Eds.). (2019). *Concrete: Case studies in conservation practice* (Vol. 1). Los Angeles, CA: Getty Publications.

Dalsgaard, A. (2012). *The human scale* [Film]. Denmark: Final Cut for Real.

Denison, E., Teklemariam, M., & Abraha, D. (2017). Asmara: Africa's Modernist City (UNESCO World Heritage Nomination). *The Journal of Architecture, 22*(1), 11–53. https://doi.org/10.1080/13602365.2016.1276093

Dollard, T. (2019). *Designed to perform: An illustrated guide to providing energy efficient homes*. London: RIBA Publishing.

Eggertson, L. (2010). Lancet retracts 12-year-old article linking autism to MMR vaccines. *CMAJ: Canadian Medical Association Journal = journal de l'Association medicale canadienne, 182*(4), E199–E200. https://doi.org/10.1503/cmaj.109-3179

Enright, S. (2002). Post-occupancy evaluation of UK library building projects. *Liber Quarterly, 12*, 26–45. http://doi.org/10.18352/lq.7665

ESRC. (2020). *Research with potentially vulnerable people – Economic and Social Research Council*. Retrieved 1 March 2020, from https://esrc.ukri.org/funding/guidance-for-applicants/research-ethics/frequently-raised-topics/research-with-potentially-vulnerable-people/

European Commission Directorate General for Research and Innovation. (2011). *Towards a European framework for research careers*. Retrieved 1 March 2020, from https://cdn5.euraxess.org/sites/default/files/policy_library/towards_a_european_framework_for_research_careers_final.pdf

Fielden Clegg Bradley Studios. (2020). FCBSCarbon. Retrieved 20 November 2020, from https://fcbstudios.com/fcbscarbon

Fielden Clegg Bradley Studios. (2019a). Eleven practical steps to tackle climate change. *RIBA Journal*. 18th September. Retrieved 1 March 2020, from https://www.ribaj.com/intelligence/adapt-your-practice-for-climate-emergency-feilden-clegg-bradley

Fielden Clegg Bradley Studios. (2019b). *Carbon Counts*. Retrieved 1 March 2020, from https://www.fcbstudios.com/work/view/carbon-counts

FLOW Architecture. (2018). *HeartBit Walks*. Retrieved 1 March 2020, from https://www.flowarchitecture.co.uk/heartbit-walks

Foster + Partners. (2016). Foster + Partners. In K. A. Martindale (Ed.), *Knowledge and research in practice* (pp. 22–23). London: Royal Institute of British Architects. https://www.architecture.com/-/media/gathercontent/knowledge-and-research-in-practice/additional-documents/knowledgeandresearchinpracticepdf.pdf

Foster + Partners. (2015). *Cathedral cities in peril.* London: Foster + Partners. http://chichestersociety.org.uk/wp-content/uploads/2016/07/Cathedral-Cities-in-Peril-59pp-FosterPtners-Mar2015-17Mb.pdf

Gehl, J. (2011). *Life between buildings: Using public space.* Washington, DC: Island Press.

Gehl, J. (2010). *Cities for people.* Washington, DC: Island Press.

Gehl, J., & Svarre, B. (2013). *How to study public life.* Washington, DC: Island Press.

Geib, G. W. (1985). The land ordinance of 1785: A bicentennial review. *The Indiana Magazine of History, 81*(1), 1–13.

Gensler. (2020). U.S. Workplace Survey 2020 | Research & Insight. Retrieved 1 March 2020, from https://www.gensler.com/research-insight/workplace-surveys/us/2020

Gensler. (2017). *Gensler research catalogue Volume 2.* San Francisco, CA: ORO Editions.

Gensler. (2012). WPI Analytics | Gensler Research Institute | Research & Insight | Gensler. Retrieved 1 March 2020, from https://www.gensler.com/research-insight/gensler-research-institute/wpi-analytics

Goldreich, A. (2020). Connect more. *Architecture Today,* (306), p. 12. https://edition.pagesuite-professional.co.uk/html5/reader/production/default.aspx?pubname=&edid=7171093f-06ba-4af7-a69d-9858642f9b27&pnum=1

Government of Canada. (2015). Eligibility of work for SR&ED investment tax credits policy. Retrieved 1 March 2020, from https://www.canada.ca/en/revenue-agency/services/scientific-research-experimental-development-tax-incentive-program/eligibility-work-investment-tax-credits.html

Grant, H. (2019a). Too poor to play: Children in social housing blocked from communal playground. Retrieved 1 March 2020, from https://www.theguardian.com/cities/2019/mar/25/too-poor-to-play-children-in-social-housing-blocked-from-communal-playground#maincontent

Grant, H. (2019b). London officials ban segregated play areas in future housing developments. Retrieved 1 March 2020, from https://www.theguardian.com/cities/2019/jul/19/london-officials-ban-segregated-play-areas-in-future-housing-developments

Greater London Authority. (2020). *Making London child-friendly – Designing places and streets for children and young people.* London: Greater London Authority. https://www.london.gov.uk/sites/default/files/ggbd_making_london_child-friendly.pdf

Green, D., Al Rashad, S., Knight, P., & Cammelli, N. (2019). A 21st century national ordinance. Planning the physical disposition and use distribution of a Nation. *Proceedings of the 55th ISOCARP World Planning Congress* (pp. 491–521), Jakarta-Bogor, Indonesia. https://dryfta-assets.s3.eu-central-1. amazonaws.com/assets/isocarp2019/eventdocs/1576665851ISOCARP_55th-Congress_Proceedings2.pdf

Halej, J. (2017). Ethics in primary research (focus groups, interviews and surveys). Retrieved 28 February 2020, from https://warwick.ac.uk/fac/cross_ fac/ias/schemes/wirl/info/ecu_research_ethics.pdf

Hampton, G. (2009). Narrative policy analysis and the integration of public involvement in decision making. *Policy Sciences*, 42(3), 227–242. https://doi. org/10.1007/s11077-009-9087-1.

Hart, C. (2018). *Doing a literature review: Releasing the research imagination.* London: Sage.

Hartman, H. (2019). Architype crowned AJ100 sustainable practice of the year 2019. 19th June. Retrieved 11 March 2020, from https://www.architectsjournal.co.uk/ news/architype-crowned-aj100-sustainable-practice-of-the-year-2019/10043196. article

Hawkins\Brown (2018). *Industrial rehab \ A new space of opportunity.* London: Hawkins\Brown. https://www.hawkinsbrown.com/research/projects/ industrial-rehab

Hay, R., Bradbury, S., Martindale, K. A., Samuel, F., & Tait, A. (2017). *Pathways to post-occupancy evaluation.* London: Royal Institute of British Architects. https://www.architecture.com/-/media/gathercontent/post-occupancy-evaluation/additional-documents/buildingknowledgepathwaystopoepdf. pdf

Hillier, B., & Hanson, J. (1989). *The social logic of space.* Cambridge: Cambridge University Press. https://d1wqtxts1xzle7.cloudfront.net/30374693/Hiller___ Hansen.pdf?1356565448=&response-content-disposition=inline%3B+fi lename%3DThe_Social_Logic_of_Space_B_Hillier_and.pdf&Expires=1 603750415&Signature=MGDoueuEgqr43jbVuEW7Jv-oRE6mxPDmB2vG 5JEim4qAx909djlPJI~s8Yy-egRYGG2TRhzAOOhBfeRY4980uMi4bi3R~ 267Zs6-sDuV81UroOe9tnd9HLzvPvSXqnx-SUXxuJrB8W8amruOy3KfAkkkVf-gpDtMFIepiflfpvlhs-M8aUDswRa6OY4DPUXQlrRMH5n-UBZmKqkoEUNbH-6d8qLi2bionkhZDS6HsZAn7EJ8N2cVogNCKxGVqG602OMRuk~H1G3VIFiLm PaBT8EqRPMh~U4Ygwqi462ks7CO9j3wrYZIq5Sv6r1MjeOS2uHJ88w~WoTpS DlrXohhOxHg__&Key-Pair-Id=APKAJLOHF5GGSLRBV4ZA

HM Government. (2006). Safeguarding Vulnerable Groups Act 2006. https://www.legislation.gov.uk/ukpga/2006/47/contents

Holtzman, Y. (2017). U.S. Research and Development Tax Credit. Retrieved 1 March 2020, from https://www.cpajournal.com/2017/10/30/u-s-research-development-tax-credit/

Hughes, C. (2016). *Made you look. Made you stare: Inspiration from a museum road trip*. London: Feilden Clegg Bradley Studios. https://www.wcmt.org.uk/sites/default/files/report-documents/Hughes%20C%20Report%202016%20Final.pdf

Hutton, D. (2016). ZAMAZAMA4LIFE. 10th May. Retrieved 11 April 2020, https://web.archive.org/web/20160510015012/, originally located at http:/www.2point8.co.za/video/zamazama4life/

Imperial College London. (2020). Why you must apply for ethical approval. Retrieved 1 March 2020, from https://www.imperial.ac.uk/research-ethics-committee/what-is-ethics-/why-you-must-apply-for-ethical-approval/

Invest in Canada. (2020). Do your research and development in Canada: It pays off! Retrieved 1 March 2020, from https://www.international.gc.ca/investors-investisseurs/assets/pdfs/download/factsheet-rd.pdf

Iphofen, R. (2016). *Ethical decision making in social research: A practical guide*. New York: Springer.

Israel, M., & Hay, I. (2006). *Research ethics for social scientists*. Thousand Oaks, CA: Sage.

Jalaladdini, S., & Oktay, D. (2012). Urban public spaces and vitality: A socio-spatial analysis in the streets of Cypriot towns. *Procedia-Social and Behavioral Sciences, 35*, 664–674. https://www.sciencedirect.com/science/article/pii/S1877042812004478

Jarvis, S. (2019). *Including culture in development: A step-by-step guide*. London: Urban Land Institute. https://issuu.com/urbanlandmagazine/docs/uli_including_culture_in_development_guide

Jayachandran, C., Ramsey, R., & Roehl, A. (2017) A protectED ROOM: Design of responsive and acuity adaptable behavioral health room for emergency departments. *Perkins&Will Research Journal, 09*(01), 31–47. https://issuu.com/perkinswill/docs/issue_17_pwrj_vol0901

Jayalath, A., Navaratnam, S., Ngo, T., Mendis, P., Hewson, N., & Aye, L. (2020). Life cycle performance of Cross Laminated Timber mid-rise residential buildings in Australia. *Energy and Buildings, 223*, 110091. https://doi.org/10.1016/j.enbuild.2020.110091

Jha, A. K., Bloch, R., & Lamond, J. (2012). *Cities and flooding. A guide to integrated urban flood risk management for the 21st century.* Washington, DC: The World Bank. https://openknowledge.worldbank.org/handle/10986/2241?CID=WAT_TT_Water_EN_EXT&locale-attribute=en

Johnson, B. J., & Gore, N. (2016). What do the professions 'profess'? Comparing architecture and planning codes of ethics. *Architectural Science Review, 59*(6), 449–464. https://doi.org/10.1080/00038628.2016.1194255

Jurkiewicz, C. L. (2018). Big data, big concerns: Ethics in the digital age. *Public Integrity, 20*(Suppl 1), S46–S59. https://doi.org/10.1080/10999922.2018.1448218. https://www.researchgate.net/profile/Carole_Jurkiewicz2/publi-cation/324368146_Big_Data_Big_Concerns_Ethics_in_the_Digital_Age/links/5eac571e299bf18b958d2799/Big-Data-Big-Concerns-Ethics-in-the-Digital-Age.pdf

Kayaçetin, N., & Tanyer, A. (2009). Exploring knowledge management in the practice of architecture: A pilot study in the Turkish capital. *Middle East Technical University Journal of the Faculty of Architecture, 26.* http://jfa.arch.metu.edu.tr/archive/0258-5316/2009/cilt26/sayi_2/279-308.pdf. https://doi.org/10.4305/METU.JFA.2009.2.14

Kishimoto, T., & Taguchi, M. (2014). Spatial configuration of Japanese elementary schools: Analyses by the space syntax and evaluation by school teachers. *Journal of Asian Architecture and Building Engineering, 13*(2), 373–380. https://www.tandfonline.com/doi/abs/10.3130/jaabe.13.373

Knutson, C. (2019a). Revolutionizing the Office Paradigm: The Future Net-Zero Energy Office Building. *Perkins&Will Research Journal, 11*(02), 7–19. https://webcontent.perkinswill.com/research/journal/issue_22_vol1102/issue_22_pwrj_vol1102_1_revolutionizing_the_office_paradigm.pdf

Knutson, C. (2019b). *Revolution: Changing the Office Paradigm.* Presentation, 50 Forward | 50 Back: The Recent History and Essential Future of Sustainable Cities. 10th CTBUH World Congress, Chicago.

Lackney, J. A., & Zajfen, P. (2005). Post-occupancy evaluation of public libraries: Lessons learned from three case studies. *Library Administration and Management, 19*(1). https://journals.tdl.org/llm/index.php/llm/article/viewFile/1506/786

Lange, A. (2014). Opinion: Alexandra Lange on how architects should use social media. 7 January. Retrieved 1 March 2020, from https://www.dezeen.com/2014/01/07/opinion-alexandra-lange-on-how-architects-should-use-social-media/

Lendlease. (2018). First timber arrives for the world's largest and tallest engineered timber office building. Retrieved 1 March 2020, from https://www.lendlease.com/-/media/llcom/investor-relations/media-releases/2018/feb/20180215-first-timber-arrives-for-the-worlds-largest-and-tallest-engineered-timber-office-building.pdf

Lipscomb, M., & Stewart, A. (2020). Analysis of therapeutic gardens for children with autism spectrum disorders. *Perkins&Will Research Journal*, 06(02), 42–56. Retrieved from https://perkinswill.com/research-journal-vol-06-02/

LOLA Architects. (2013). Stadsrandenatlas van de Zuidvleugel. Retrieved 1 March 2020, from https://issuu.com/lola-landscape-architects/docs/asz_atlas_150411_ebook

Maina, J. J. (2014). Housing, architectural theory and practice: Exploring the unique adequacy approach in housing research for communities in Nigeria. In *Proceedings of the 40th IAHS World Congress on Housing* (p. 263). https://www.researchgate.net/profile/Joy_Maina2/publication/316881985_Housing_architectural_theory_and_practice_Exploring_the_unique_adequacy_approach_in_housing_research_for_communities_in_Nigeria/links/5bdcba9892851c6b27a2971d/Housing-architectural-theory-and-practice-Exploring-the-unique-adequacy-approach-in-housing-research-for-communities-in-Nigeria.pdf

Mairs, J. (2016). PLP proposes London's first wooden skyscraper at Barbican. 5th April. Retrieved 1 March 2020, from https://www.dezeen.com/2016/04/08/plp-architecture-cambridge-university-london-first-wooden-skyscraper-barbican/

Major, M. D. (2018). *The syntax of city space: American urban grids*. Routledge.

Manning, J., Rifkin, A., Noble, G., Garofalakis, G., & Elsea, D. (2018). London's local character and density. *The Journal of Architecture*, 23(1), 42–77. https://doi.org/10.1080/13602365.2018.1427377

Mark, E. L. (1881). *Maturation, fecundation, and segmentation of Limax campestris, Binney* (Vol. 6, No. 12). Museum.

Martindale, K. (2020). Industry driven innovation in healthy housing delivery: The case for Cross Laminated Timber. *Cities & Health*, 1–7. https://doi.org/10.1080/23748834.2020.1735157

Martindale, K. A. (Ed.). (2017). *Knowledge and research in practice*. London: Royal Institute of British Architects. https://www.architecture.com/-/media/gathercontent/knowledge-and-research-in-practice/additional-documents/knowledgeandresearchinpracticepdf.pdf

Martindale, K. (2016). Living the dream. Retrieved 24 March 2020, from https://www.ribaj.com/intelligence/research-in-practice 11th October

Martindale, K. A., & Dixon, D. (Eds.). (2017). *The President's awards for research 2017: Book of abstracts.* London: Royal Institute of British Architects.

Martindale, K. A., & Tait, A. (Eds.). (2016). *The President's awards for research 2016: Book of abstracts.* London: Royal Institute of British Architects.

Minnesota Legislature. (2019). 2019 Minnesota Statutes 609.232 crimes against vulnerable adults: Definitions. https://www.revisor.mn.gov/statutes/cite/609.232.

Morphogenesis. (2020). Sustainable smart city. Retrieved 1 March 2020, from https://www.morphogenesis.org/media/sustainble-smart-city/

Naccarella, L., Redley, B., Sheahan, M., & Morgan, K. (2017). Emergency talks: Designing for team communication in hospital emergency departments. In K. A. Martindale (Ed.), *Shortlist 2017.* London: Royal Institute of British Architects.

National Science Foundation. (2020). About the National Science Foundation – Overview. Retrieved 1 March 2020, from https://www.nsf.gov/about/

Níall McLaughlin Architects. (2016). Losing myself, Venice Biennale Architettura 2016. Retrieved 1 March 2020, from http://www.niallmclaughlin.com/projects/losing-myself/

Nordenson, G., Seavitt, C., Yarinsky, A., & Museum of Modern Art. (2010) *On the water: Palisade Bay.* New York: Hatje Cantz.

NSPCC. (2020). Research with children: Ethics, safety and avoiding harm | NSPCC Learning. Retrieved 1 March 2020, from https://learning.nspcc.org.uk/research-resources/briefings/research-with-children-ethics-safety-avoiding-harm/

OECD. (2019). *Compendium of R&D tax incentive schemes: OECD countries and selected economies, 2018.* March. Paris: Organisation for Economic Co-operation and Development. https://www.oecd.org/sti/rd-tax-stats-compendium.pdf

OECD. (2015). *Frascati manual 2015: Guidelines for collecting and reporting data on research and experimental development.* The Measurement of Scientific, Technological and Innovation Activities. Paris: OECD Publishing. https://doi.org/10.1787/24132764

OECD Publications. (2002). Frascati manual: Proposed standard practice for surveys on research and experimental development. OECD. https://doi.org/10.1787/9789264199040-en

Office of Revenue Commissioners. (2019). *Tax and duty manual – Research and development (R&D). Tax Credit Part 29-02-03.* Dublin: Office of Revenue Commissioners. Retrieved 1 March 2020, from https://www.revenue.ie/

en/tax-professionals/tdm/income-tax-capital-gains-tax-corporation-tax/part-29/29-02-03.pdf

Ong, B. L. (2003). Green plot ratio: An ecological measure for architecture and urban planning. *Landscape and Urban Planning, 63*(4): 197–211. https://doi.org/10.1016/S0169-2046(02)00191-3

Park, A., Ziegler, F., & Wigglesworth, S. (2016). *Designing with downsizers: The next generation of 'downsizer homes' for an active third age.* The University of Sheffield, UK. http://www.housinglin.org.uk/_assets/DWELL_DesigningWithDownsizers.pdf

Patton, C. V., Sawicki, D. S., & Clark, J. J. (2013). *Basic methods of policy analysis and planning.* Oxford: Routledge. http://surjonopwkub.lecture.ub.ac.id/files/2019/01/Basic_Methods_of_Policy_Analysis_and_Planing.pdf

Perkins&Will. (2020a). Game changer: "SPEEDing" up energy modeling for energy efficient buildings – Perkins&Will. Retrieved 12 September 2020, from https://perkinswill.com/news/game-changer-speeding-up-energy-modeling-for-energy-efficient-buildings/

Perkins&Will. (2020b). *4th Kuwait Masterplan: 2040/towards a smart state – Spatial strategy.* Chicago, IL: Perkins&Will.

Perkins&Will. (2020c). *4th Kuwait Master Plan 2040 – Towards a smart state. Stage 2.3 Development of Strategic Capital and Implementation Plan. Action Area 5 Kuwait City Centre.* Chicago, IL: Perkins&Will.

Perry, F. (2016). A tube for cars? Proposal to bury London's traffic says it's 'next best thing to teleportation'. 2nd December. Retrieved 1 March 2020, from https://www.theguardian.com/cities/2016/dec/02/cartube-tube-underground-cars-proposal-bury-traffic-next-best-thing-to-teleportation

Peter Barber Architects. (2019). Hundred Mile City. Retrieved 1 March 2020, from http://www.peterbarberarchitects.com/hundred-mile-city-1

PLP Architecture. (2020). *IUMO (formerly known as CarTube).* Retrieved 1 March 2020, from http://www.plparchitecture.com/iumo-(formerly-known-as-cartube).html

Pomeroy, J. (Ed.). (2020). *Cities of opportunities: Connecting culture and innovation.* Oxford: Routledge.

Pomeroy, J. (2016). *POG: Pod Off-Grid: Explorations into low energy waterborne communities.* San Francisco, CA: ORO Editions.

Powell, M., Taylor, N., Fitzgerald, R., Graham, A., & Anderson, D. (2013). *Ethical research involving children.* Florence: Innocenti Publications. UNICEF Office of Research – Innocenti. Retrieved from https://www.unicef-irc.org/publications/706-ethical-research-involving-children.html

Purcell. (2020). Durham Cathedral. Retrieved 25 February 2020, from https://www.purcelluk.com/projects/open-treasure-at-durham-new-access-to-the-cathedrals-hidden-architecture-and-artefacts

Ramage, M., Foster, R., Smith, S., Flanagan, K., & Bakker, R. (2017). Super Tall Timber: Design research for the next generation of natural structure. *The Journal of Architecture, 22*(1), 104–122. https://doi.org/10.1080/13602365.2016.1276094. https://www.tandfonline.com/doi/full/10.1080/13602365.2016.1276094

Ramos, M., & Burrows, K. (2015). The zero carbon compendium: The future of low energy cities and communities. *PRP Innovate*. London: PRP. https://media.prp-co.uk/web/brochures/AA5118_Zero_Carbon_Compendium_March_2015_.pdf

Rendell, J., & Padan, Y. (2019). Ethical practice: Hotspots and touchstones. In Knowledge in Action for Urban Equality (Ed.), *In the KNOW #2* (pp. 6–11). London: University College London. Retrieved from https://www.ucl.ac.uk/bartlett/development/sites/bartlett/files/intheknow_iss2-vf_share.pdf

Research, Innovation and Enterprise Secretariat. (2016). Research innovation enterprise 2020 plan: Winning the future through science and technology. Retrieved 1 March 2020, from https://www.mti.gov.sg/-/media/MTI/Resources/Publications/Research-Innovation-and-Enterprise-RIE-2020/RIE2020.pdf

RIBA. (2020). RIBA plan of work. Retrieved 1 March 2020, from https://www.architecture.com/knowledge-and-resources/resources-landing-page/riba-plan-of-work

RIBA. (2019). *Ethics in architectural practice.* London: Royal Institute of British Architects.

RIBA. (2013). RIBA plan of work 2013. Retrieved 1 March 2020, from https://www.pedr.co.uk/Content/downloads/RIBA_POW_2013_Template.pdf

RIBAJ. (2020). Shell Lace Stent, London. Retrieved 30 June 2020, from https://www.ribaj.com/buildings/regional-awards-shortlist-2020-london-west-tonkin-liu-medical-device-shell-lace-stent-london

Roe, E. (1994). *Narrative policy analysis: Theory and practice.* Durham, NC: Duke University Press.

Sailer, K., Pomeroy, R., & Haslem, R. (2015). Data-driven design—Using data on human behaviour and spatial configuration to inform better workplace design. *Corporate Real Estate Journal, 4*(3), 249–262. https://discovery.ucl.ac.uk/id/eprint/1465065/1/Sailer_etal205_DataDrivenDesign_CREJ.PDF

Sailer, K., & Thomas, M. (2019). Correspondence and non-correspondence: Using office accommodation to calculate an organisation's propensity for new ideas. https://eprints.lancs.ac.uk/id/eprint/136569/1/166_submission_final.pdf

Scott Brownrigg. (2020). *Articles & publications*. Retrieved 1 March 2020, from https://www.scottbrownrigg.com/design-research-unit/articles-publications/

Serra, M., & Pinho, P. (2013). Tackling the structure of very large spatial systems-Space syntax and the analysis of metropolitan form. *The Journal of Space Syntax,* 4(2), 179–196. https://www.researchgate.net/profile/Miguel_Serra5/publication/312197806_Tackling_the_Structure_of_Very_Large_Spatial_Systems_-_space_syntax_and_the_analysis_of_metropolitan_form/links/5876039708ae6eb871ce5b6e/Tackling-the-Structure-of-Very-Large-Spatial-Systems-space-syntax-and-the-analysis-of-metropolitan-form.pdf

Shanahan, E. A., Jones, M. D., & McBeth, M. K. (2018). How to conduct a narrative policy framework study. *The Social Science Journal,* 55(3), 332–345. https://static1.squarespace.com/static/5b103b4d50a54fb7298b571e/t/5cddd880ee2d9a00017882ed/1558042754535/SOCSCI_1439_Revised+proof_small+corrections+02.02.18.pdf

Sheahan, M. (2016). What if academics interacted as much as students? Retrieved 1 March 2020, from https://www.hassellstudio.com/research/what-if-academics-interacted-as-much-as-students

Skånfors, L. (2009). Ethics in child research : Children's agency and researchers' 'ethical radar'. *Childhoods Today,* 3(1). Retrieved from http://urn.kb.se/resolve?urn=urn:nbn:se:kau:diva-11326

Space Syntax Network. (2020a). Space Syntax Network. Retrieved 12 January 2020, from https://www.spacesyntax.net

Space Syntax Network. (2020b). Space Syntax Network. Retrieved 12 January 2020, from https://www.spacesyntax.net

Sputnik Architects. (2020). Good affordable housing. Retrieved 1 March 2020, from http://www.studiosputnik.nl/good-affordable-housing/

Stoss. (2015). Working vacancy. Retrieved 1 March 2020, from https://static1.squarespace.com/static/5ae4926236099b34d8f79912/t/5c82ed7ee4966b5f3f2f4cef/1552084352251/STOSS+Working+Vacancy+Presentation.pdf

Summers, S., & Corti, L. (2020). Storing and moving data. In L. Corti, V. Eynden, L. Bishop, M. Woollard, M. Haaker, & S. Summers (Eds.), *Managing and sharing research data: A guide to good practice* (2nd ed., –). Thousand Oaks, CA: Sage.

The Ethics Centre. (2019). *Ethics in procurement report: The ethics alliance*. Sydney: The Ethics Centre. Retrieved from https://ethics.org.au/ethics-in-procurement/

Tonkin, M., Liu, A., & Clark, E. (2013). *The evolution of Shell Lace*. London: Tonkin Liu.

Tonkin Liu. (1999). *Asking looking playing making*. Hong Kong: Tonkin Liu.

Transport for London. (2016). *Review of the TfL WiFi pilot. Our findings*. London: Transport for London. Retrieved 19 February 2020, from http://content.tfl.gov.uk/review-tfl-wifi-pilot.pdf

UCL. (2020a). *Guidance for external researchers*. Retrieved 1 March 2020, from https://www.ucl.ac.uk/research/integrity/ethics/guidance-external-researchers

UCL. (2020b). Journal of Space Syntax. Retrieved 26 January 2020, from http://joss.bartlett.ucl.ac.uk/index.php/joss/UNICEF. (1999). *United Nations convention on the rights of the child, 1989*. Geneva, Switzerland: Author. https://www.unicef.org.uk/wp-content/uploads/2010/05/UNCRC_united_nations_convention_on_the_rights_of_the_child.pdf

United Nations General Assembly. (2015). *Transforming our world: The 2030 agenda for sustainable development*. New York: United Nations. https://sustainabledevelopment.un.org/post2015/transformingourworld

University of Chicago Press. (2017). *Chicago manual of style* (17th ed.). https://www.chicagomanualofstyle.org/book/ed17/frontmatter/toc.html

University of Oxford. (2020). *Plagiarism*. Retrieved 1 March 2020, from https://www.ox.ac.uk/students/academic/guidance/skills/plagiarism?wssl=1

University of Queensland. (2020). *ARC research hub for advanced solutions to transform tall timber buildings*. Retrieved 19 February 2020, from https://futuretimberhub.org

University of Sheffield. (2016). DWELL | Designing for well-being in environments for later life. Retrieved 26 January 2020, from http://dwell.group.shef.ac.uk

U.S. Copyright Office. (2020). Chapter 3: Circular 92 | U.S. Copyright Office. Retrieved 1 March 2020, from https://www.copyright.gov/title17/92chap3.html

V&A. (2020). A history of the V&A on Exhibition Road. Retrieved 1 March 2020, from https://www.vam.ac.uk/articles/a-history-of-the-va-on-exhibition-road

Vally, S. (2019). Golden Plateaus. *Conditions – E-Flux, 7*. Retrieved 12 March 2020, from https://www.e-flux.com/architecture/conditions/296274/golden-plateaus/

Van Nes, A., & López, M. J. (2007). Micro scale spatial relationships in urban studies: The relationship between private and public space and its impact on street life. In *Proceedings of the 6th Space Syntax Symposium (6SSS)*, Istanbul,

Turkiye, June 12–15, 2007. http://www.spacesyntaxistanbul.itu.edu.tr/papers/longpapers/023%20-%20VanNes%20Lopez.pdf

Vening, S. (2016). Amphibious flood proof house in Buckinghamshire. *Grand Designs Magazine*. Retrieved 31 March 2020, from https://www.granddesignsmagazine.com/grand-designs-houses/160-amphibious-flood-proof-house-in-buckinghamshire

Vischer, J. (2001). Post-occupancy evaluation: A multifaceted tool for building improvement. In *Learning from our buildings: A state-of-the-practice summary of post-occupancy evaluation* (pp. 23–34). Washington, DC: National Academy Press. https://www.researchgate.net/publication/236144016_Post-Occupancy_Evaluation_A_Multifaceted_Tool_for_Building_Improvement

Waite, R. (2017). *New practice Richard John Andrews: '40% of my work comes from Instagram'.* 26 September. Retrieved 1 March 2020, from https://www.architectsjournal.co.uk/10035323.article?sm=10035323

Walter, A. (2020). *France requires new public buildings to contain at least 50% wood.* 10th February. Retrieved 1 March 2020, from https://archinect.com/news/article/150183480/france-requires-new-public-buildings-to-contain-at-least-50-wood

Wasserman, B., Sullivan, P. J., & Palermo, G. (2000). *Ethics and the practice of architecture.* New York: John Wiley & Sons.

Webster-Mannison, M. (2013). Rethinking practice: Architecture, ecology and ethics. In E. Felton, O. Zelenko, & S. Vaughan (Eds.), *Design and ethics* (pp. 175–191). Oxford: Routledge.

Wener, R. E. (1994). *Post occupancy evaluation procedure: Instruments & instructions for use.* Washington, DC: Orange County Corrections Division and National Institute of Correction Jail Centre.

White Arkitekter. (2020a). *R&D programme 2020–2023 – Informed design.* Göteborg: White Arkitekter. https://whitearkitekter.com/wp-content/uploads/2020/06/FoU-program-2020-2023-webb-utskriftsversion.pdf

White Arkitekter. (2020b). Circular architecture is a winning concept. Retrieved 19 February 2020, from https://whitearkitekter.com/news/circular-architecture-is-a-winning-concept/

White Arkitekter. (2020c). *Annual and sustainability report 2019: Architecture for a sustainable way of life.* Göteborg: White Arkitekter. https://whitearkitekter.com/wp-content/uploads/2020/05/White_rapport2019_ENG_low_res_desktop_view.pdf

White Arkitekter. (2019). *Make sense: Architecture by white.* London: Laurence King Publishing.

White Arkitekter. (2018). *Arkitektens återbruksmetodik. En rapport från White Research Lab White Arkitekter AB*. Göteborg: Author.

White Arkitekter. (2017). Flickrum—Room for girls. Retrieved 6 February 2020, from https://whitearkitekter.com/project/places-for-girls/

Whyte, W. F. (2012). *Street corner society: The social structure of an Italian slum*. Chicago, IL: University of Chicago Press.

Whyte, W. H. (1980). *The social life of small urban spaces*. Washington, DC: Project for Public Spaces.

Williams, E. (2019). *Supertall timber the lodge: An environmental study* (Masters). University of Cambridge.

Wilson, R. (2019). *Child's play*. Retrieved 1 March 2020, from https://architectus.com.au/insight/childs-play/

World Architecture Community. (2014). The MIPIM architectural review future project award winners 2014. Retrieved 28 February 2020, from https://worldarchitecture.org/architecture-news/pmhvf/the-mipim-architectural-review-future-project-award-winners-2014.html

Ye, J. (2019). *Dynamics of tall timber buildings* (Masters). University of Cambridge.

Yoon, H., & Srinivasan, S. (2015). Are they well situated? Spatial analysis of privately owned public space, Manhattan, New York City. *Urban Affairs Review, 51*(3), 358–380. https://doi.org/10.1177%2F1078087414552457

Young, F., Cleveland, B., & Imms, W. (2020). The affordances of innovative learning environments for deep learning: Educators' and architects' perceptions. *The Australian Educational Researcher, 47*, 693–720. https://doi.org/10.1007/s13384-019-00354-y

Young, F., & Martin, D. (2020). Learning environments: Designing space for every body. *Architecture Australia, 109*(5), 23. https://architectureau.com/magazines/architecture-australia/2020/architecture-australia-sep-oct-2020-5-1/

ZCD Architects. (2016). *Housing design for community. Researching how residents use external spaces in new developments*. London: ZCD Architects. https://static1.squarespace.com/static/58aaff9b17bffc6029da965f/t/5b8fe14e4d7a9c8dcd2003b8/1536156027366/HD%26CL_report_screen+ZCD_WEB.pdf

Zinn, M. (2020). Girls' room in public place – Planning for equity with a girl's perspective. In M. Besters, R. Marrades, & J. Kahne (Eds.), *Our city? Countering exclusion in public space* (pp. 167–172). Rotterdam: STIPO Publishing. https://issuu.com/stipoteam/docs/our_city_e-book

Index